Colección Támesis

SERIE A: MONOGRAFÍAS, 288

# FEDERICO GARCÍA LORCA
# THE POETICS OF SELF-CONSCIOUSNESS

This volume is one of few surveys in English of the whole of Lorca's poetry and the first to concentrate entirely on self-consciousness, a subject which it sees as central to our understanding of the work of a poet writing in the most self-conscious of literary periods: the Modernist era.

Focusing on poems which have the poet, art and creativity as their subject, or which draw attention at a formal level to issues of practice or style, it shows how these poems speak for or against contemporary aesthetic doctrine, thereby revealing the extent of the poet's allegiance to it and the positions he takes up in the process of making his own mark in the literary field. In so doing it charts the development of a poet whose self-conscious engagement with his art offers an explanation as to why his work, in the space of little more than a decade and a half, should have been so singular and diverse.

FEDERICO BONADDIO lectures in Modern Spanish Studies at King's College London.

FEDERICO BONADDIO

# FEDERICO GARCÍA LORCA
## THE POETICS OF SELF-CONSCIOUSNESS

TAMESIS

First published 2010 by Tamesis, Woodbridge

ISBN 978 1 85566 221 6

Tamesis is an imprint of Boydell & Brewer Ltd
PO Box 9, Woodbridge, Suffolk IP12 3DF, UK
and of Boydell & Brewer Inc.
668 Mt Hope Avenue, Rochester, NY 14620, USA
website: www.boydellandbrewer.com

A CIP catalogue record for this book is available
from the British Library

The publisher has no responsibility for the continued existence or accuracy of
URLs for external or third-party internet websites referred to in this book,
and does not guarantee that any content on such websites is,
or will remain, accurate or appropriate

This publication is printed on acid-free paper

Printed in the United States of America by
Edwards Brothers, Inc, Lillington NC

# CONTENTS

For Luigi, Maria and Matteo

# ACKNOWLEDGEMENTS

I would like to extend my thanks to Manuel Fernández-Montesinos García and the *Herederos de Federico García Lorca* for permission to reproduce Lorca's texts and to William Peter Kosmas for his help and advice in this matter. Thanks also to Stephen Hart of Tamesis and Elspeth Ferguson and the editorial team at Boydell & Brewer, as well as the Department of Spanish and Spanish American Studies, King's College London, for its assistance with the publication. I am grateful also to all those who have shown me support over the years and who have in one way or another informed and shaped this book. Thanks in particular to Derek Harris, Xon de Ros and Gareth Walters; thanks also to my brother and to my parents; and finally, a very special thanks to Patricia McDermott, without whom I would not have come to Lorca in the first place.

# INTRODUCTION
## SELF-CONSCIOUSLY LORCA

Federico je n'ai vu qu'une fois ton visage
Dans un journal à trente centimes d'avant la guerre
De celui-là je ne me souviens guère
Mais ta face éternelle est partout chez moi
(René Guy Cadou, 'Bonjour Federico')

My first profound experience of Lorca – my first real contact – occurred as I leafed through a copy of *Romancero gitano* on a bench on Bristol's Brandon Hill, the Cabot Tower looking down at me from above as the tower of the church upon the Sacramonte rose towards me from the pages of the poem 'San Miguel (Granada)'.[1] The first two stanzas, in particular, were revelatory:

Se ven desde las barandas,
por el monte, monte, monte,
mulos y sombras de mulos
cargados de girasoles.

Sus ojos en las umbrías
se empañan de inmensa noche.
en los recodos del aire,
cruje la aurora salobre. (*OC*, I, p. 410)

I had no idea that the poem was an 'encoded description of the festivities on September 29th, when the people of Granada would go in pilgrimage to the church of St Michael that stands on top of the [...] hill that rises above

---

[1] Federico García Lorca, *Obras completas*, I, ed. Arturo del Hoyo, 3 vols, 22nd edn (Madrid: Aguilar, 1986), 410–11. Abbreviated henceforth to *OC*. A version of this introduction was published under the title 'Lorca, Self-Consciousness (and Myself)' and appears in Catherine Boyle (ed.), *Exploración y proceso: investigando la cultura hispánica* (Valencia: Biblioteca Valenciana, 2007), 277–91.

the old Moorish quarter of the Albaicín.'[2] Nor that these 'opening lines are
a description and evocation of this ascent, which was quite commonly made
by mule'; nor still, that 'sunflowers are, by local custom, particularly linked
to the celebration of the saint's day' (Harris 1991, p. 42). But I was overjoyed
at my realization of the image – so simple and ingenious (neogongorine, no
doubt) – and at my sudden transportation to another, penumbral, location
where the distant yellow of sunflowers on the barely perceptible dark backs
of climbing mules was at once the earliest haze of the yellowy hues of dawn
competing with the dominion of the night.

It is not easy to separate the simplicity from the ingenuity, although I
might try by pointing to the contrast between the unremarkable lexis and the
remarkable implications of its combined effect. And it is not easy either to
distinguish in my response between the emotions and the intellect, although
what I can say is that I still associate the moment of that reading with a
moment of innocence – an innocence from which I inevitably fell. The fall, to
begin with, was quick but not very far, as I continued my way down through
the poem:

> Un cielo de mulos blancos
> cierra sus ojos de azogue
> dando a la quieta penumbra
> un final de corazones.
> Y el agua se pone fría
> para que nadie la toque.
> Agua loca y descubierta
> por el monte, monte, monte.   (*OC*, I, p. 410)

In the half-light of my reading of the previous stanzas, the logic of reason
now staked its claim, the sky of white mules becoming clouds or the whiter
hues of dawn; the closing of its mercurial eyes, those clouds or that whiteness blocking out the stars. The insidious temptation to not let things be
– to continue to uncover meanings – perversely aided and abetted by the
increasing elusiveness of the language and the spectre of polysemy, required
that I made sense of the calm penumbra as a 'resting place for hearts' or
sweethearts, or as some kind of emotional finale, whilst the reference to the
water as 'wild' or 'mad', the allusion to an intention on its part to turn cold
'so no one will touch it', acquired the function of additional devices in the

---

2   Derek Harris, 'Introduction', in Federico García Lorca, *Romancero gitano*, ed. Derek
Harris, Grant and Cutler Spanish Texts (London: Grant & Cutler, 1991), 7–87 (p. 42).

poem's initial rendition of a mysterious, magical, animate landscape.[3] For the rest of the poem, for its ambivalent, eroticized description of the saint housed in the church on the hill, set in ironic contrast with the pilgrims making the ascent – with Granadan society which could never share the poet's effeminate portrayal of the image of St Michael – I gladly looked for guidance and support in expert criticism, in commentaries, in context (see Harris 1991, pp. 44–5).[4] Yet however much I marvelled at the processes that could lift the lid of the box and let out all that a poem could impossibly condense, I could never rid myself of the nostalgia of that first revelation on the hill.

And so I fell more slowly but much further, 'por el monte, monte, monte', into language, into criticism, into academia. I travelled back through literary history, listened to Romantics, symbolists, decadents, *modernistas*, and the new avant-garde; I traced symbolic and mythological patterns, meeting the ancients, the primitives, Jung, Freud; I scoured biographies, thought Lorca elitist,[5] then biography irrelevant; decided in favour of the reader, against interpretation, against intention; moved between deconstruction, psycholinguistics, socio-cultural systems and back to biography.

'I'm not intelligent, it's true!' Lorca apparently once confessed. 'But I'm a poet.'[6] It seems ironic that the work of someone who shied away from intellectual discussion, who emphasized the instinctual, the magical, the popular, who through his many recitals of his poetry professed the importance of the immediacy of the spoken word, should be the cause of so much intellectual enquiry, some of which rests, I admit, on the hierarchical view that the intellect is superior to emotion or instinct and that it is merely reductive to think of the latter as representing Lorca best. This is not to argue against the profundity of Lorca's work, for if it has given rise to so much intellectual reflection it is precisely because it has the inherent potential to do so. It is, however, with my nostalgia firmly in mind, to lament my very need to have plunged those depths on the weight of secondary material.

That descent, however, my fall, is irreversible – to this fact I am almost reconciled, as I am to the rules and restrictions of academic practice, to the

---

[3]  For a translation of the poem, see Federico García Lorca, *Collected Poems*, revised bilingual edition, ed. Christopher Maurer (New York: Farrar, Straus & Giroux, 2002), 567, 569 and 571.

[4]  See also, Herbert Ramsden, *Lorca's 'Romancero gitano'. Eighteen Commentaries* (Manchester: Manchester University Press, 1988), 50–6.

[5]  See Federico Bonaddio, 'Lorca and the Spanish Avant-Garde: Autonomous and Elitist Art', in Derek Harris (ed.), *Changing Times in Hispanic Culture* (Aberdeen: Centre for the Study of the Hispanic Avant-Garde, 1996), 97–109.

[6]  See Leslie Stainton, *Lorca: A Dream of Life* (London: Bloomsbury, 1998), 148.

politics and culture of the academic field. This is not to look for a scapegoat in academia, to blame it for my fall, for I went there willingly, joyfully, not once, as I remember, enticed by its sirens towards the rocks. My original sin is embedded in that moment of innocence, and it is only by realizing this that I can begin to make my own way through Lorca. And so I look again to those stanzas, to that simplicity and ingenuity, and what I find there is my own motivation for reading on and for reading in the way that I did and still do. In that verse on and about the hill I was mesmerized by how something so simple could say so much, by how saying one thing could also mean saying something else, and all the while part of me was conscious of language – my language – as representing sheer difficulty, disability, inability; language not so much as a means of communication, but as an obstacle to it; and thus, I imagined, it must have been for the writer of that verse whose ingenuity was to have confronted and surmounted the limitations of language, to have seemingly effaced them, but without effacing the truth of their vital, dynamic role in the creative task.

It is therefore no accident, but destiny, that I should have been drawn to the verse of a writer writing in the most self-conscious of eras. Which is why, in what follows, the Lorca I will invoke is one who will speak of the creative process, of the paths and obstacles to creativity, to becoming a poet, to being able to say 'what I want' and say it 'as I wish'.

The young Lorca was not meant to be a poet, but a musician. Yet he turned from the piano to the pen (although he never gave up his piano-playing), and in that turning, perhaps, lay the first seeds of his self-consciousness, a natural consequence of his measure of two related but distinct forms. So much of his poetry, for a time, seemed to want to approximate itself to music, evidence of which we may find not only in the musical references of titles of collections or individual poems, but in the increasingly anti-discursive character it assumed, a result also of the poet's contact with the artistic trends of the day. Thus his movement from music to poetry was a propitious one, well-placed as he was, between the two forms, to appreciate contemporary artistic issues. And yet this was also his fall – his fall from music into language – his poetry often marked by the nostalgia for that freedom beyond and before words.

His first step, however, was to begin to assume his new role, as much a question of the mind as it was a matter of consigning words to paper. Becoming a poet implied knowing what a poet was before ever imagining what else it could be. Thus Lorca looked to an existing model by which to affirm his own poetic credentials, to the figure of the Romantic, his choice defined perhaps by his prior reading, his personal circumstances or his adolescent mood, although it is impossible to tell from his pronouncements in letters or from the texts of his poems the extent to which he really embodied its principles, speaking, as he already was, in the language he had adopted. Its accoutrements are melancholy – above all, melancholy – heightened sensibilities, acute sensitivity, estrangement, lyrical longing and a total devotion to art, not all of which pertains exclusively, of course, to historical Romanticism but which have since then contributed to the image of the modern poet and its various mythic constructions – martyr, priest, seer, decadent or dandy – through to the *fin de siècle* and into the early twentieth century.

A glance at two letters Lorca wrote in 1918 provides evidence of his romantic affiliation and of the poet in construction. The first is addressed to María del Reposo Urquía, a young pianist, whom Lorca, then a student at the University of Granada, befriended during a study trip to Baeza in 1917. In it he asks whether she would mind him dedicating to her a chapter of his forthcoming publication, *Impresiones y paisajes* (1918), a prose work (his first published volume) inspired by visits to Castile and Galicia, as well as by excursions in Andalusia. Evident in his letter is his youthful, romantic alignment with sensibilities marked by estrangement, spiritual thirst and a deeply rooted sadness. 'En la época actual,' he writes, 'nosotros, los románticos, tenemos que hundirnos en las sombras de una sociedad que sólo existe en nosotros mismos.'[7] 'Usted,' he adds, 'es una, quizá, romántica como yo, que sueña, sueña en algo muy espiritual que no puede encontrar. [...] Siempre tenemos una amargura que no logramos arrancarnos' (*EC*, p. 46). Ever the poet, he communicates his affection for María with an idealized vision of femininity: 'Fue usted una de esas mujeres que pasan por el camino de nuestra vida dejando una estela de tranquilidad, de simpatía, de quietud espiritual. Algo así como el perfume de una flor escondida en las lejanías' (*EC*, p. 47). And just for a moment he doubts his own capacities – perhaps the rhetoric of affected modesty, but perhaps also another sign of the stirrings of the writer's self-consciousness: 'Qué mal escribo, ¿verdad? Perdón.'

The second letter (*EC*, pp. 47–51) is addressed to Adriano del Valle, a young Andalusian poet who asked to be put in contact with Lorca after reading his prose work. The letter is well known for what seems to be an early allusion by Lorca to his homosexuality.[8] It has also been noted for the *modernista* style in which it is couched (see Gibson 1989, p. 73). Here Lorca's recourse to poetic language, in this early stage of his becoming a poet, is another example of how the poetic persona spills out from pages devoted specifi-

---

[7] Federico García Lorca, *Epistolario Completo*, ed. Andrew A. Anderson and Christopher Maurer (Madrid: Cátedra, 1997), 46–7. Abbreviated henceforth to *EC*.

[8] See Ian Gibson, *Federico García Lorca: A Life* (London: Faber & Faber, 1989), 73–4.

cally to creative expression into the arguably more functional scenario of his correspondence. Aware of the poetic aspirations shared by the addressee, he takes the opportunity to present himself equally as a poet. 'Yo me presento a su vista nada más que como compañero,' he writes, thus entering into the company of poets, '(un compañero lleno de tristeza) que ha leído algunas de sus preciosas poesías'. 'Soy un pobre muchacho apasionado y silencioso,' he adds, 'que, casi casi como el maravilloso Verlaine, tiene dentro una azucena imposible de regar' (*EC*, p. 47). He emphasizes his melancholy, his devotion to lyricism, and implicit in his vision of poetry is his ability to see beyond the confines of the material world, to enter 'el reino donde vive esa virgen blanca y azul que se llama Melancolía ..., o sea, el reino de la Poesía' (*EC*, p. 48). Modestly, he declares his book of prose 'muy malo', a book in which 'sólo hay una gran emoción que siempre mana de mi tristeza y el dolor que siento ante la naturaleza' (*EC*, p. 50), and, notably, he insists on his sincerity, a sincerity that any true and honest poet cannot fail to perceive:

> No sé si adivinará V. cómo soy yo de sincero, de apasionado y de humilde corazón. Me basta saber que es su espíritu el de un poeta. Y si esta escasa luz de mi alma que pongo en esta carta no la supiera V. ver o se riera, sólo me quedaría la amargura íntima de haberle enseñado algo de mi relicario interior a un alma que cerró los ojos y sonrió escéptica. (*EC*, p. 50)

He reminds his addressee of their common obligations, that theirs is a vocation to 'amar a la luna sobre el lago de nuestra alma y hacer nuestras meditaciones religiosas sobre el abismo magnífico de los crepúsculos abiertos', and he concludes by reaffirming what must be patently true, that when all is said and done he is a poet: 'Lea V. esta carta triste, medítela, y después estoy seguro que dirá "... pero ¡pobre muchacho !, ¡tan joven ...!, al fin, poeta"' (*EC*, p. 51).

On his study trips to Baeza in the summers of 1916 and 1917 Lorca had met the poet Antonio Machado (see Gibson 1989, pp. 47–8, 62; Stainton, pp. 34, 42), himself a master of melancholy and solitude. Lorca was enthralled by their first encounter, so it is perhaps no coincidence that he began writing poetry in earnest that very winter. At the first opportunity, he borrowed a copy of the new, 1917 edition of Machado's *Poesías completas* (see Stainton, p. 35) and on its first pages pencilled in violet a poem entitled 'Sobre un libro de versos', a response, it would seem, to his reading of the work.[9] Like his

---

[9]   The poem is dated 9 August 1918 and may be found in Federico García Lorca, *Poesía inédita de juventud*, ed. Christian de Paepe, Letras Hispánicas 374, 2nd edn (Madrid: Cátedra, 1996), 449–52, abbreviated henceforth to *PJ*. See also Antonio Gallego Morell's reference

letter to Del Valle, this poem demonstrates the young writer's inclination to reflect upon the poetic task and also his desire to align himself with the all-important figure of the poet.

The poem begins with an evocation of what is nothing less than the poet's communion with the book he has read and provides what may be interpreted as a passionate summary of its contents and effects. Machado's work is cast as the reader's companion on his travels through the landscapes which the book depicts and the precious hours devoted to the sacred task of reading:

> Dejaría en el libro
> Este toda mi alma.
>
> Este libro que ha visto
> Conmigo los paisajes
> Y vivido horas santas.
>
> ¡Qué pena de los libros
> Que nos llenan las manos
> De rosas y de estrellas
> Que se esfuman y pasan!
> ¡Qué tristeza tan honda
> Es mirar los retablos
> De dolores y penas
> Que un corazón levanta!
>
> Ver pasar los espectros
> De vidas que se borran,
> Ver al hombre desnudo
> En Pegaso sin alas,
> Ver la vida y la Muerte,
> La síntesis del mundo,
> Que en espacio profundo
> Se miran y se abrazan.    (*PJ*, pp. 449–50)

In these laudatory stanzas, suffused with the melancholy that he associates with the poetic art, Lorca is under the spell of his model, the lyrical poet: singer of sorrows, captor of meanings beyond the confines of material limits, interpreter of the grandeur of life's most essential dramas. In the stanzas that follow, the representation of the poet and his art are equally familiar. Lines of verse lie like fallen leaves across autumnal pages; the poet is a tree of sad

---

to the poem (which he dates 7 August 1918) in his article 'El primer poema publicado por Federico García Lorca', *Bulletin Hispanique*, 69 (1967), nos 3–4, 487–92 (p. 487). The book Lorca borrowed belonged to Gallego's father.

fruit and withered leaves; he is Nature's medium, able to comprehend the
incomprehensible, embrace what others detest; his poems are the product
of his afflictions, bitterness transformed into the divine sweetness of honey;
they make possible the impossible, heavenly bodies bringing sound to the
silent void of the sky:

Un libro de poesías
Es el Otoño muerto.
Los versos son las hojas
Negras en tierras blancas,
Y la voz que lo lee
Es el soplo del viento
Que los hunde en los pechos
—Entrañables distancias—.

El poeta es un árbol
Con frutos de tristeza
Y con hojas marchitas
De llorar lo que ama.
El poeta es el médium
De la Naturaleza
Que explica su grandeza
Por medio de palabras.

El poeta comprende
Todo lo incomprensible
Y a cosas que se odian
Él hermanas las llama.
Sabe que los senderos
Son todos imposibles
Y por eso en lo obscuro
Va por ellos con calma.

En los libros de versos,
Entre rosas de sangre,
Van desfilando tristes
Y eternas caravanas
Que hirieron al poeta
Que lloraba en la tarde,
Rodeado y ceñido
Por sus propios fantasmas.

Poesía es Amargura,
Miel celeste que mana
De un panal invisible
Que fabrican las almas.

Poesía es lo imposible
Hecho posible. Arpa
Que tiene en vez de cuerdas
Corazones y llamas.

Poesía es la vida
Que cruzamos con ansia
Esperando al que lleve
Sin rumbo nuestra barca.
Libros dulces de versos
Son los astros que pasan
Por el silencio mudo
Al reino de la Nada
Escribiendo en el cielo
Sus estrofas de plata.

¡Oh, qué penas tan hondas
Y nunca remediadas,
Las voces dolorosas
Que los poetas cantan!    (*PJ*, pp. 450–2)

Clearly the poem lacks the wherewithal or confidence to discard romantic cliché, Symbolist assumptions, *modernista* echoes. Yet it is possible to detect amongst its stanzas a voice yearning for, or even claiming and assuming, independence. It can be heard in the rather swift movement from initial considerations of the particular and the use of the demonstrative 'this', as in 'this book', in the first five lines, to considerations of the general, the plural, and the use of definite and indefinite articles, as in 'books', 'a book', 'the poet', 'poetry' or 'poets'. Even if the first five stanzas may be read specifically as an evocation of Machado's work, that direct link is not as clear in subsequent stanzas: 'Un libro de poesías', 'Los versos', 'El poeta', 'los libros de versos', 'Poesía', 'los poetas'. In the final stanza, the poem does return, it seems, to the subject of Machado's book, with its echo of the opening lines:

Como en el horizonte
Descanso las miradas.
Dejaría en el libro
Este, ¡toda mi alma! (*PJ*, p. 152)

However, the preceding digressions have now shifted the emphasis from the text read to the reader himself, who is also a poet. The first person dominates ('Descanso', 'Dejaría', 'mi alma'), whilst the simile 'Como en el horizonte' brings to the fore the reading poet's own artifice and subordinates the sentiments evoked by, or in, the book to his gaze, to his need for rest. After all, it is his soul that has tired, not only in his reading of the book, but also in the construction of his verse. The force of the final, exclamatory '¡toda mi alma!' may be read as much as an affirmation of the writing self as an indicator of the intensity of the reading experience. In acknowledging what has inspired him the poet has also made his own voice heard. However derivative his imagery and style may be, the poet, in taking his violet pencil to his borrowed book, has succeeded in writing on, or even over, Machado.[10]

In 'Sobre un libro de versos', then, we can detect the first signs of the poet's resistance to his dependence on, and his indebtedness to, his fore-bears, even though, paradoxically, he has not found a language of his own in which to couch that resistance. The poem is an example of Lorca's self-consciousness in as much as it refers to the very subject of poetry, but also because, in the context of his apprenticeship, it bears traces of that self-awareness implicit in the effort of becoming a poet. This self-consciousness would eventually acquire other dimensions, the question 'What is poetry?' no longer finding a sufficient response in the poet's early enthusiasm for the lyric subject or for earnest self-disclosure; an enthusiasm which characterizes his juvenilia and, to a certain extent, his first book of poems, *Libro de poemas* (1921), whose themes have generally been noted as being the 'Nostalgia for the innocence of childhood, the disenchantment of the world, the confused awakenings of adolescent desire'.[11] Instead, the question becomes entangled with other, fundamental questions about language, its origins, its scope and perfectibility, and with questions about the self and the unity of the origi-nating subject.

The context for this shift is provided, of course, by the aesthetics of the avant-garde and its own fall into language, occasioned by the impact of rela-tivism, subjectivism, perspectivism and later, psychoanalysis, all of which meant redefining the very purpose of art and, indeed, the figure of the poet himself. Increasing metaphysical doubt had all but done away with the tran-scendental possibilities of poetry and the visionary poet, where these rested upon the Platonic view of 'the outer world of apparent realities [...] as a

---

[10] For a description of the points of contact between the early Lorca and Machado, as well as a concise discussion of the derivative character of Lorca's juvenilia, see D. Gareth Walters, *'Canciones' and the Early Poetry of Lorca* (Cardiff: University of Wales Press, 2002), 43–61.

[11] Michael Iarocci, 'Romanticism, Transcendence, and Modernity in Lorca's *Libro de poemas*, or the Adventures of a Snail', in *Lorca, Buñuel, Dalí: Art and Theory*, ed. Manuel Delgado Morales and Alice J. Poust (London and Toronto: Associated University Presses, 2001), 120–35 (p. 120).

veil that masks the inner world of eternal truths',[12] where poetry was thus a means of penetrating that reality in order to glimpse a mysterious world of infinite harmony, the Symbolists' *azure*. And if, as Schopenhauer had argued, 'the world is my idea', if human beings could never get beyond their idea of the world and its objects, never know the *thing-in-itself*,[13] then poets were as cut off from the world around them, and consequently from their fellow human beings, as they were from any ideal place beyond terrestrial limits. The knell had been rung, or so it seemed, for mimesis, anecdote and discursiveness, and writers could not be sure either that their readers would ever get beyond their own idea of the work they had read. If the world was idea, then ideas would become the world of poets, the objects of the external world lifted from their conventional frame of reference to acquire a more personal significance. And if there was any knowledge to be had, then the starting point was self-knowledge: 'we must learn,' wrote Schopenhauer (III, p. 405), 'to understand nature from ourselves, not conversely ourselves from nature'. The path left open to writers led directly back to their texts, to their selves, to self-consciousness. 'The articulation of self-consciousness', explains Julia Kristeva, 'begins when it loses the object – the other – with respect to which it was posited; this object is [...] the foundation of sense-certainty. Self-consciousness denies the object in order to return to itself.'[14] Poems now asserted their independence from the world, became objects in their own right, subsisting on their own logic, self-referential, universes apart, formed (or deformed) by the poet's own perception,[15] word-games drawing attention away from external reality towards their own artifice, or, in the shadow of Freud, the products of alternative realities signalled as lying deep within unconscious realms. Metaphor would come into its own, allowing poets to maintain an emotional distance from their subjects and lending poems a degree of immediacy and independence, a consequence of the pictorial quality of the image and of its apparent release from bonds tying it to its sources.

---

[12] Richard A. Cardwell, *Juan Ramón Jiménez. The Modernist Apprenticeship 1895–1900* (Berlin: Colloquium Verlag, 1977), 172.

[13] See Arthur Schopenhauer, *The World as Will and Idea*, 3 vols (London: Kegan Paul, Trench, Trübner, & Co., 1981), vol. II, 404: 'our knowledge, because it consists of subjective forms, affords us always mere *phenomena*, not the true being of things'.

[14] Julia Kristeva, *Revolution in Poetic Language* (New York: Columbia University Press, 1984), 133.

[15] See, for example, the description of the aesthetics of *creacionismo* and *ultraísmo* in Anthony Leo Geist, *La poética de la generación del 27 y las revistas literarias: de la vanguardia al compromiso (1918–1936)* (Barcelona: Labor, 1980).

If in his introductory words to *Libro de poemas* Lorca could claim to be offering his readers 'la imagen exacta de mis días de adolescencia y juventud', 'el reflejo fiel de mi corazón y de mi espíritu' and 'esta obra que tan enlazada está a mi propia vida' (*OC*, I, p. 5), no such claim could be valid, or desirable, in respect of subsequent works. However personal his poetry would be and despite the fact that the self would still be a subject of exploration, his verse could no longer be associated with lyrical outpouring, with self-disclosure, with the idea that a poem could somehow faithfully translate for others the details of an author's personal life. As José Ortega y Gasset famously observed of poetry in the early 1920s, 'Vida es una cosa, poesía es otra […]. El poeta empieza donde el hombre acaba.'[16] Yet his term 'dehumanization', coined to describe the literary and artistic scene he was observing, seems strangely inappropriate when applied to Lorca's own case.

Some of Lorca's poems – for example, a number of his Suites – do appear to be almost totally closed in on themselves, having language, the word, as their sole subject. However, Lorca was never drawn to the kind of highly self-conscious experimentation that set about redefining the typographical limits, the very layout or visual patterns, of poems. Nor did his poetry ever quite lose sight of humanity. At most, the lyric subject was displaced, disembodied, like the voices of popular songs, ballads and lullabies upon which Lorca drew, forms that dwell in the public domain, ready to be embodied by singers and speakers, though never exclusively or forever. To speak no longer directly of himself was not tantamount to effacing human emotion, ever present in the tenderness of poems inspired by childhood ('¿Dónde estará / la miel? // Está en la flor azul, / Isabel. / En la flor, / del romero aquel' ['Cancioncilla sevillana', *OC*, I, p. 299]), or in his evocation of the sorrow expressed in the cries of flamenco song ('Dejadme en este campo / llorando' ['¡Ay!', *OC*, I, p. 171]), or in the lyrical commentaries suffusing the dramas of his ballads ('¡Oh pena de cauce oculto / y madrugada remota!' ['Romance de la pena negra', *OC*, I, p. 409]). Here was yet another instance of resistance. Lorca moved towards the aesthetics of the avant-garde, but never quite at the expense of what he most cherished.

When in 1928 Lorca wrote in a letter to the art critic Sebastià Gasch that his poetry was flying in a new direction – 'otro vuelo más agudo todavía', 'un vuelo personal' (*EC*, p. 585) – he seemed to be anticipating his New York poetry, in which the voice would return once more to the very body of the

---

[16] 'La deshumanización del arte', in José Ortega y Gasset, *Obras completas*, III (1917–1928), 5th edn (Madrid: Revista de Occidente, 1962), 353–86 (p. 371).

poet: the poet in New York; a voice self-consciously aware of its indebtedness, and strained resistance, to the pressures of context. Here, in New York,
something of the visionary poet would resurface, albeit to protest the sky's
emptiness, its godlessness, the very absence of an *azure*. Yet even before New
York the visionary poet had not totally disappeared. If in *Libro de poemas*
he flounders under a process of self-scrutiny characteristic of verse indebted
to the old but increasingly aware of the new, he eventually comes to accept
the restrictions of new limits and simply works within them, turning his gaze
inwards, divining the mystery of intimate spaces, setting his hand to conjuring
up the magic of his locality ('por el monte, monte, monte'), becoming a
spinner of myths, a master of ritual – as is the case in *Poema de cante jondo*,
where the invocation of deep song is at once, self-consciously, the religious
experience of poetic re-creation. In the poem 'Conjuro' (*OC*, I, p. 207), the
spell that the poet casts transforms appearances, animates objects, removes
the line dividing presence and absence:

> La mano crispada
> como una medusa
> ciega el ojo doliente
> del candil.
>
>    As de bastos.
> Tijeras en cruz.
>
>    Sobre el humo blanco
> del incienso, tiene
> algo de topo y
> mariposa indecisa.
>
>    As de bastos.
> Tijeras en cruz.
>
>    Aprieta un corazón
> invisible, ¿la veis?
> Un corazón
> reflejado en el viento.
>
>    As de bastos.
> Tijeras en cruz.

And so, here, the poet is also a medium, a leader of séances, and it is I, the
reader, who am called to his table, called from my side of the dividing line
into his, a witness to how the dead matter of print can be resurrected into a
life of appearances beyond the restrictions of the referential aspect of words,
somewhere beyond the page to which those words, materially, are confined.

'Do you see it? Do you see that heart?' Yes, I do, however invisible it may be amidst the fingers – the fingers of the poet – that clasp it.

*Poema del cante jondo* seeks to evoke the mystery, the emotion, the images, but also the stages, the rhythm, the very music, of the performance of flamenco deep song, and the (impossible) challenge it sets itself is precisely to do all these things without ever succumbing to the earthly pull of words and of a referential logic that works against mystery, against magic. It is poetry about song, that very combination of music and words, but it is also poetry that is song (as evident and elusive as the intangible presence of singing), as are too *Canciones* and the Suites. Similarly, the poems of *Romancero gitano* are about, as well as being, ballads, and the poems of *Poeta en Nueva York* are about, but also the embodiment of, poetic creation in the most difficult of unpoetic circumstances. This is the self-consciousness into which Lorca's early, uncertain, impetuous self-consciousness evolved, although it would always be with the image – the self-image – of the poet in mind, and always in the context of that dynamic tension between, on the one hand, self-affirmation and belief, and on the other, the measure of his alliance to the dominant, contemporary aesthetic – to the pronouncements and credos of the avant-garde. To become a poet is to enter the world of poets, to become subject to the desires that cohabit there, though not always comfortably: the desires for creativity, for self-integrity and authenticity, for recognition and affiliation, for originality and self-differentiation.

Equally, to become a critic is to enter the world of critics. So what should I make of, how should I defend, my own self-consciousness here, a self-consciousness that many might consider out of place, in a book that is not about me, but about Lorca? Well, it is not about me, but by me, and in this sense it is always a question of my faith and a test of my honesty. 'The articulation of self-consciousness', explained Julia Kristeva, 'begins when it loses the object ...' I inherited this loss, unable ever to be absolutely certain why Lorca spoke, why he wrote, as he did, the object I lost being that very 'foundation of sense-certainty'. If I deny this certainty in order to return to myself it is because, as Schopenhauer suggested, the starting point for our access to the knowledge of the world is our selves. 'Do we perhaps understand the rolling of a ball when it receives an impulse,' asked Schopenhauer (III, p. 405), 'more thoroughly than our movement when we feel a motive?' In his mind, we do not. Thus my movement towards Lorca, 'por el monte, monte, monte', began with a moment of self-conscious intuition in face of the only object I could be sure of: the printed words on the page. That self-conscious encounter precipitated my fall, and I fell into Lorca, but also with Lorca, into the world of his texts, the world of self-reference, and, it goes without saying, into language itself. To point to the humanity in Lorca's self-consciousness – an antidote to art-for-art's sake, to texts closed in on themselves – is to recover something of my own humanity also, my initial innocence (and guilt), up there on that bench on the hill. 'Para entrar en el gris / me pinté de gris. / ¡Y cómo relumbraba / en el gris!' ('Canción cantada', *OC*, I, p. 302).

# 1

# *Libro de poemas*: The Sincere Poet

all bad poetry springs from genuine feeling ...
(Oscar Wilde, *The Critic as Artist*)

Sincerity is not a virtue of modern poets, at least not where it implies total surrender to the lyrical impulse, to the need, the desire, to speak earnestly of oneself, to speak genuinely and directly of one's unique, personal experience, albeit in a language that is necessarily not unique to one's person but belongs equally to other poets. Over the course of the nineteenth century and into the Twentieth, the movement of poets was increasingly away from speaking as men to other men.[1] 'Poetry,' Eliot concluded, 'is not a turning loose of emotion, but an escape from emotion; it is not the expression of personality, but an escape from personality,' although he added that, 'of course, only those who have personality and emotion know what it means to want to escape from these things'.[2] Irrespective of people's natural curiosity about the lives of others, including, of course, the lives of writers, sincerity in art came to be considered artless, and we have come to feel as uncomfortable around the emotional outpourings of the lyric subject as we are around the unprompted personal revelations of a complete stranger. For if poets moved away from speaking to men as men, they turned instead to speaking as artists to other artists, to the initiated, the able, which is why the discomfort in face of such utter sincerity is shared in great part by those who are privy to the secrets of artful art, which no longer inhabits, as they see it, that most earnest of places. 'There are many people', wrote Eliot (1986, p. 59), 'who appreciate the expression of sincere emotion in verse, and there is a smaller number of people who can appreciate technical excellence. But very few know when there is expression of *significant* emotion which has its life in the poem and not in the history of the poet. The emotion of art is impersonal.'

---

[1]  See Lionel Trilling, *Sincerity and Authenticity* (London: Oxford University Press, 1972), 7.
[2]  T. S. Eliot, 'Tradition and the Individual Talent', *The Sacred Wood. Essays on Poetry and Criticism* (London and New York: Methuen, 1986), 47–59 (p. 58).

The sincerity with which Lorca associates himself in his first letter to Adriano del Valle and which is apparent in his introductory words to *Libro de poemas* is precisely the element that he needed to expurgate en route to his becoming a poet of the day. But this was no easy task, particularly for a young man who needed to speak of himself, a young man in the midst of introspection who might be forgiven the desire for the self-revelation that self-discovery excites. For this reason *Libro de poemas* is an inconsistent volume but equally the work of competing voices; a work in which sincere emotion and impersonality vie for space. Michael Iarocci, for example, in his reading of the poem 'Los encuentros de un caracol aventurero' (*OC*, I, pp. 9–14), argues that 'Lorca's engagement with the neoromantic – indeed a rewriting of the romantic – can be understood metapoetically as an exploration of the limits of that particular cultural legacy' (Iarocci, p. 133). For him, the poem 'enacts a familiar neoromantic metaphysical crisis, but [...] simultaneously registers the crisis of the poetic discourse in which such anxiety has traditionally been expressed'. He concludes that 'the lyric subject's search throughout the *Libro de poemas* is, amongst other things, a search for new expressive modes, a search to which Lorca's subsequent poetic evolution would bear witness'. Whereas some criticism has dwelt upon *Libro de poemas*' imitative aspect or on its sentiments, having in mind always that most elusive of notions, namely the poet's 'true' or 'singular' voice, Iarocci has hit upon the very dynamic of Lorca's early, self-conscious exploration of the poetic domain: one that is the product of the tension between the poet's adoption of a romantic rhetoric and his increasing awareness of new modes of expression; between his attraction to the sincere expression of lyric verse and his movement towards more impersonal modes – a move necessary for him to be counted amongst his contemporaries.

Something of the same tension is noted by D. Gareth Walters, who sees in *Libro de poemas* evidence of both a learning process and a poetic crisis (Walters 2002, pp. 64, 78). Inscribed in the book's mixture of the old and the new, in its pull between the past and the future, are moments of poetic discovery and achievement but also a sense of failure and limitation. These mixed feelings accompanying the learning process are telling indeed. They point not to the unqualified acceptance of new poetic norms, but rather to a degree of doubt and uncertainty about future directions and the poet's own creative capacities. They suggest, moreover, certain anxieties about letting go, or perhaps even the disquiet of a poet who has no fixed alliances. 'For the awareness of the new', writes Walters (2002, p. 84), 'involves simultaneously the realization that the old has disappeared. But there is a liminal point somewhere between the two that breeds the anxiety of the void.' The ambivalence residing in *Libro de poemas* is well illustrated in Walters' reading of the poem 'Sueño' (*OC*, I, pp. 130–1), which he compares with Rubén Darío's sonnet 'Pegaso' (see Walters, pp. 72–5). On the one hand, Lorca's appropriations of *modernista* style and rhetoric testify to his continuing fascination with the essence and spirit of *modernismo*. Yet his ironic twist on the theme of poetic flight – Darío's Apollonian winged-horse replaced by the Dionysian billy goat – marks also his disengagement with its aesthetic, but at a price: the self-assured triumphalism and clear direction of Darío's poetic vision have now given way to the most unpredictable of journeys: 'Alumbran el camino / los ojos luminosos y azulados / de mi macho cabrío.'

We should bear in mind, however, that by the time Lorca was writing these lines of verse (the poem is dated May 1919), *modernismo* had already had its heyday, and it is not unreasonable to suppose that at least some of its exponents had long undertaken the self-conscious revision that he was now engaged in. A point in case is Juan Ramón Jiménez, one of the many probable influences on Lorca's early poetry cited by critics (see Walters 2002, p. 63).[3] His elegy 'Una a una, las hojas secas van cayendo', for example – one of those in the collection *Elejías intermedias* (published in 1909) – appears at one level to lament the loss of creative fertility:[4]

> Una a una, las hojas secas van cayendo
> de mi corazón mustio, doliente y amarillo.
> El agua que otro tiempo salía de él, riendo,
> está parada, negra, sin cielo ni estribillo.
>     ¿Fue un sueño mi árbol verde, mi copa de frescura,
> mi fuente entre las rosas, de sol y de canciones?
> ¿La primavera fue una triste locura?
> ¿Viento aquella florida bandada de ilusiones?
>     Será mi seco tronco, con su nido desierto;
> y el ruiseñor que se miraba en la laguna,
> callará, espectro frío, entre el ramaje yerto
> hecho ceniza por la vejez de la luna.[5]

---

[3]   For Lorca's early *modernista* influences, see José Hierro, 'El primer Lorca', *Cuadernos Hispanoamericanos*, 224–5 (August–September 1968), 437–62, and Carlos Edmundo de Ory, 'Salvador Rueda y García Lorca', *Cuadernos Hispanoamericanos*, 255 (March 1971), 417–44.

[4]   For a reading of the poem from this perspective, see Federico Bonaddio, 'Grammar and Poetic Form: Limits and Transcendence in Juan Ramón Jiménez's 'Una a una, las hojas secas van cayendo', *Words in Action: Essays in Honour of John Butt*, ed. Xon de Ros and Federico Bonaddio, *Bulletin of Spanish Studies*, 83.1 (January 2006), 149–60.

[5]   Juan Ramón Jiménez, *Segunda antolojía poética (1898–1918)* (Madrid: Espasa Calpe, 1976 [1st edn 1975]), 79.

Yet the autumnal melancholy of the tree-poet acquires a certain ambivalence when read in light of the epigraph heading the poem, a fragment of
Albert Samain's poem 'Automne' from his collection *Au Jardin de l'Infante*
(1893): 'Et chaque feuille d'or tombe, l'heure venue / Ainsi qu'un souvenir,
lente, sur le gazon.' A major exponent of the Symbolist-Decadence, the
melancholy Samain was undoubtedly an influence on Jiménez and on this
particular poem, as the association of falling leaves and memories within the
epigraph seems to suggest (see Bonaddio 2006, p. 151). And yet the fading
creativity that Jiménez evokes in 'Una a una' also points to disengagement
with that influence, one that is reinforced in the final quatrain of the poem
by the certainty in the use of the future tense, which constitutes a temporal
break with the preceding lines of verse. Whether we take 'corazón' or 'florida
bandada de ilusiones' to be the subject of 'Será', what is clear is that the
creativity of yesteryear, of which Samain is representative, will now take the
form of a 'seco tronco', 'nido desierto', 'ramaje yerto' – in other words, a
poetry stripped bare of the lyricism of which the nightingale is an emblem,
this song-bird reduced to ash in the final line by that other aging, romantic
motif, the moon ('O graziosa luna,' wrote Leopardi, 'io mi rammento / Che,
or volge l'anno, sovra questo colle / Io venia pien d'angoscia a rimirarti'[6]).
Once again, this transformation is not taken lightly, perhaps because it is
inevitably the heart – the direct, personal, human element – that will agonize
on the altar of a new aesthetic, as Jiménez increasingly looks for inspiration
not from within but in the poetry of objects and things themselves.

The evidence of mixed feelings in Jiménez's poem, written some ten years
or so before the poems of *Libro de poemas*, thus raises the possibility that
the very ambivalence in Lorca's book is no less imitative than the overtly
*modernista* style and tone of some of his early poetry. As a point of reference,
'Una a una' is interesting also because of its use of the tree-motif.

Walters has noted the poetic themes of two poems in *Libro de poemas*
which take up the tree-motif – 'Encina' (*OC*, I, pp. 133–4) and 'Invocación
al laurel' (*OC*, I, pp. 135–7), both dated 1919 – concluding that the crucial
point, arising in both, about the nature of poetic creation 'is that the starting-
point is not the raw material of experience but the stimulus and example of
art' (Walters 2002, p. 82). No less significant, perhaps, is the fact that, unlike
the tree-poets in Jiménez's poem and, indeed, in a later poem of Lorca's own,
'Canción del naranjo seco' (*OC*, I, p. 389) – from the collection *Canciones*
– the poet in 'Encina' and 'Invocación del laurel' has not undergone the

---

[6]  Giacomo Leopardi, 'Alla luna', *Canti*, ed. Giorgio Ficara (Milan: Mondadori, 1987),
116–17 (p. 116).

process of tree-metamorphosis and thus his view is an external one on the members of that sacred wood into which he has walked. The sense of being on the outside contributes in *Libro de poemas* to the melancholy that has been related to the need to let go of the old in order to embrace the new. In fact, since both the old and an awareness of the new converged at an early point in his poetic apprenticeship, Lorca's approach to either was necessarily that of an outsider, despite his own conviction that he did belong in that wood. 'Me siento lleno de poesía,' wrote Lorca in another letter to Del Valle in 1918, 'poesía fuerte, llana, fantástica, religiosa, mala, honda, canalla, mística. ¡Todo, todo! ¡Quiero ser todas las cosas! Bien sé que la aurora tiene llave escondida en bosques raros, pero yo la sabré encontrar ...' (*EC*, p. 52). And as late as 1921, writing from Asquerosa around the time of the publication of his book of poems, he confided in a letter to his friend Melchor Fernández Almagro that he believed that his place was 'entre estos chopos musicales y estos ríos líricos' (*EC*, p. 119), a comment which he made in the context of that most romantic of contrasts between the hustle and bustle of town life and countryside tranquillity.

'La presencia de símbolos vegetales en la obra de García Lorca', writes Javier Salazar Rincón, 'es tan variada y abundante [...] que, sin miedo a exagerar, podemos calificar a Federico de poeta de la vida vegetal, o poeta agrario, como a él mismo le gustaba definirse.'[7] Indeed, we cannot fail to notice the presence of nature and its elements in much of the poet's work, including *Libro de poemas*, although here the title 'agrarian poet' seems unsuitable in the context of poems that are no more interested in nature per se than is Jiménez's poem 'Una a una'. The territory is poetic, not natural, and what many of the poems articulate is an uneasy relationship with the tropes of Romanticism and Symbolism, with the idea of the poet's communion with nature or his ability to read and comprehend its mysteries. If, as Salazar (p. 37) suggests, 'para el hombre primitivo, lo mismo que para el poeta simbolista, la tierra es un ser viviente, y las plantas, las rocas, el agua, el fuego y el aire, criaturas vivas que lo observan, se revelan y le hablan, y cuyos designios es posible descifrar y hacer propicios mediante los procedimientos adecuados', *Libro de poemas* evokes the anxiety related to the abandonment of such a world view, even though this abandonment does not mark the end of creativity, nor the diminishment of the poet's powers, but rather their displacement and what the Chilean poet Vicente Huidobro, father of *creacionismo*, considered to be the poet's liberation – or at least in

---

7 Javier Salazar Rincón, *"Rosas y mirtos de luna ..." Naturaleza y símbolo en la obra de Federico García Lorca* (Madrid: Universidad Nacional de Educación a Distancia, 1999), 33.

part – from his indebtedness to the natural world of things. 'No he de ser tu esclavo, madre Natura,' proclaimed Huidobro; 'seré tu amo. Te servirás de mí; está bien. No quiero, y no puedo evitarlo; pero yo también me serviré de ti. Yo tendré mis árboles, que no serán como los tuyos, tendré mis montañas, tendré mis ríos y mis mares, tendré mi cielo y mis estrellas.'[8]

The first five stanzas of 'Invocación al laurel' seem to affirm the primitive-symbolist perspective, although the opening line contains an ominous sign of confusion and pain on the horizon:

> Por el horizonte confuso y doliente
> venía la noche preñada de estrellas.
> Yo, como el barbudo mago de los cuentos,
> sabía el lenguaje de flores y piedras.
>
> Aprendí secretos de melancolía,
> dichos por cipreses, ortigas y yedras;
> supe del ensueño por boca del nardo,
> canté con los lirios canciones serenas.
>
> En el bosque antiguo, lleno de negrura,
> todos me mostraban sus almas cual eran:
> el pinar, borracho de aroma y sonido;
> los olivos viejos, cargados de ciencia;
> los álamos muertos, nidales de hormigas;
> el musgo, nevado de blancas violetas.
>
> Todo hablaba dulce a mi corazón
> temblando en los hilos de sonora seda
> con que el agua envuelve las cosas paradas
> como telaraña de armonía eterna.
>
> Las rosas estaban soñando en la lira,
> tejen las encinas oros de leyendas,
> y entre la tristeza viril de los robles
> dicen los enebros temores de aldea.

The poet-wizard, however – the one who can hear and understand the language of nature and conjure up the verse and legends that dwell there deep within, but whose abilities, significantly, are conveyed in these lines in the past tense – risks being consigned to the pages of story and fable from which he came. For although the poet continues in this poem to cling to his

---

[8]  Vicente Huidobro, *Non serviam* (1914), *Obras completas*, I (Santiago de Chile: Zig-Zag, 1964), 653.

gift of understanding, the subsequent stanzas are invaded by the uncertainty, by that confusion and pain, glimpsed initially on the horizon:

> Yo comprendo toda la pasión del bosque:
> ritmo de hoja, ritmo de estrella.
> Mas decidme, ¡oh cedros!, si mi corazón
> dormirá en los brazos de la perfecta luz.
>
> Conozco la lira que presientes, rosa;
> formé su cordaje con mi vida muerta.
> ¡Dime en qué remanso podré abandonarla
> como se abandonan las pasiones viejas!
>
> ¡Conozco el misterio que cantas, ciprés;
> soy hermano tuyo en noche y en pena;
> tenemos la entraña cuajada de nidos,
> tú de ruiseñores y yo de tristezas!
>
> ¡Conozco tu encanto sin fin, padre olivo,
> al darnos la sangre que extraes de la Tierra;
> como tú, yo extraigo con mi sentimiento
> el óleo bendito que tiene la idea!
>
> Todos me abrumáis con vuestras canciones;
> yo sólo os pregunto por la mía incierta;
> ninguno queréis sofocar las ansias
> de este fuego casto que el pecho me quema.[9]

The poet knows and understands the passion, lyricism, mystery and charm of this sacred wood, but there are some things he does not know or understand, and it is unclear whether the answers he seeks may be found in the qualities of which these plants and trees are emblematic. Thus poetic perfection – the heart's desire to 'sleep in the arms of perfect light' – and the alternative to the lyre, to its lyricism, associated here with old passions ('las pasiones viejas'), remain elusive, while the wood's songs, as overwhelming as the sincere emotion of the lyric subject ('me abrumáis con vuestras canciones'), provide no remedy for the anxieties afflicting the poet. Instead the answers are to be found in another tree, the laurel, an emblem of the poet's possible liberation but also a sign of the limits of his current repertoire, since as a trope it remains attached to the metaphor of the wood which, in theory at least, only the poet-seer – the poet-wizard – has the ability to interpret. The

---

[9]  In Arturo del Hoyo's edition of the *Obras completas*, 'sólo' appears without an accent. I have followed here, and throughout, the accentuation for poems indicated in Miguel García-Posada's edition, *Obras I: Poesía, 1* (Madrid: Akal, 1982).

irony is that, in face of the laurel tree, the abilities of the poet-seer are of no avail and thus the achievement with which laurels are traditionally associated remains, for the time being, beyond the poet's grasp:

¡Oh laurel divino, de alma inaccesible,
siempre silencioso, lleno de nobleza!
¡Vierte en mis oídos tu historia divina,
tu sabiduría profunda y sincera!

¡Árbol que produces frutos de silencio,
maestro de besos y mago de orquestas,
formado del cuerpo rosado de Dafne
con savia potente de Apolo en tus venas!

¡Oh gran sacerdote del saber antiguo!
¡Oh mudo solemne cerrado a las quejas!
Todos tus hermanos del bosque me hablan,
¡sólo tú, severo, mi canción desprecias!

Acaso, ¡oh maestro del ritmo!, medites
lo inútil del triste llorar del poeta.
Acaso tus hojas, manchadas de luna,
pierdan la ilusión de la primavera.

Importantly, the laurel tree embodies the principle of transformation by virtue of its connection in the poem with the myth of Daphne and Apollo. As the object into which Daphne was transformed in order to escape Apollo's amorous advances, the laurel represents a refuge from unwanted passions and by the same token, given Apollo's association with poetry and self-control, a transformation obliged by the pressure of poetic necessity.[10] Thus the laurel is the site of both Daphne and Apollo – 'formado del cuerpo rosado de Dafne / con savia potente de Apolo en tus venas' – and it is conceivable that the appropriation of their myth and its embodiment by the tree which the poet invokes foreshadow the rejection of the lyrical mode, of emotional outpouring, in favour of a more constrained, impersonal aesthetic. Hence the poet's uncertainty about the laurel tree's judgement of the expression of personal feeling ('Acaso [...] medites / lo inútil del triste llorar del poeta'), in contrast, as Walters (2002, p. 81) has noted, to the laurel's fecund association with silence ('Árbol que produces frutos de silencio') – that silence which

---

[10] On Apollo, see Jean Chevalier and Alain Gheerbrant, *Dictionary of Symbols*, trans. John Buchanan-Brown (London: Penguin, 1996), 34–5. See also Gertrude Jobes, *Dictionary of Mythology, Folklore and Symbol*, 3 vols (New York: The Scarewood Press, 1961), vol. 1, 110–11 (Apollo) and 414 (Daphne).

he mourns and lauds, though in an appropriately less effusive manner, in his 1920 poem, 'Elegía del silencio' (*OC*, I, pp. 59–61). For Walters (2002, p. 81), 'Invocación al laurel' 'emerges like a protest at the facile fluency of [Lorca's] juvenilia and sets a higher, more demanding, goal'. But it is still only the recognition of that goal rather than its achievement, and one that is couched in the vocal lyricism of sincere emotion as opposed to the minimalism that the laurel's silence represents. The poem's final stanza, accordingly, is impregnated with ambivalence, the path the poet must take darkened by the approaching nightfall that is both gentle and ominously severe:

> La dulzura tenue del anochecer,
> cual negro rocío, tapizó la senda,
> teniendo de inmenso dosel a la noche,
> que venía grave, preñada de estrellas.

The governing metaphor in the poem 'Encina' is, as Walters (2002, p. 81) has suggested, 'that of self-examination as an act of plumbing the depths of a deep pool in search of precious stones.' Here the poet's pleas for help in the creative process are turned towards the oak, that 'especial indicator of strength, power, longevity and height in both the spiritual and the material senses of the words' (Chevalier and Gheerbrant, p. 709). Although the poet associates himself more closely with the oak than he does with the laurel, he seems for that to be no nearer to receiving its powers, qualities or blessings, perhaps because this age-old tree is emblematic of a continuity in time that is still alien to him, uncertain as he is both of his relationship to the past and of his future trajectory. Like 'Invocación al laurel', 'Encina' self-consciously exposes the limitations of the lyrical mode, though without rejecting the personal altogether, the persona! reconfigured here, as we will see, in terms more profound and less direct than the emotional outpourings associated with the lyric subject:

> Bajo tu casta sombra, encina vieja,
> quiero sondar la fuente de mi viday
> sacar de los fangos de mi sombra
> las esmeraldas líricas.
>
> Echo mis redes sobre el agua turbia
> y las saco vacías.
> ¡Más abajo del cieno tenebroso
> están mis pedrerías!
>
> ¡Hunde en mi pecho tus ramajes santos!
> ¡oh solitaria encina,

y deja en mi sub-alma
tus secretos y tu pasión tranquila!

Esta tristeza juvenil se pasa,
¡ya lo sé! La alegría
otra vez dejará sus guirnaldas
sobre mi frente herida,
aunque nunca mis redes pescarán
la oculta pedrería
de tristeza inconsciente que reluce
al fondo de mi vida.

Pero mi gran dolor trascendental
es tu dolor, encina.
Es el mismo dolor de las estrellas
y de la flor marchita.

Mis lágrimas resbalan a la tierra
y, como tus resinas,
corren sobre las aguas del gran cauce
que va a la noche fría.
Y nosotros también resbalaremos,
yo con mis pedrerías,
y tú plenas las ramas de invisibles
bellotas metafísicas.

No me abandones nunca en mis pesares,
esquelética amiga.
Cántame con tu boca vieja y casta
una canción antigua,
con palabras de tierra entrelazadas
en la azul melodía.

Vuelvo otra vez a echar mis redes sobre
la fuente de mi vida,
redes hechas con hilos de esperanza,
nudos de poesía,
y saco piedras falsas entre un cieno
de pasiones dormidas.

Con el sol del otoño toda el agua
de mi fontana vibra,
y noto que sacando sus raíces
huye de mí la encina.

Cast in the opening lines as a totemic figure under whose shadow self-examination and the poetic creativity consequent upon it may take place, the oak is a spur of creativity ('¡Hunde en mi pecho tus ramajes santos!'), a suffering kindred spirit ('mi gran dolor transcendental / es tu dolor') and a friend ('esquelética amiga'). Its song, were it to sing to the poet, would be an inspiration ('Cántame con tu boca vieja y casta / una canción antigua'), evidence, according to Walters (2002, p. 82), of the poet's understanding that art, not lived experience, should provide the impulse for creativity. Yet the oak's flight in the final stanza as it uproots itself despite the poet's earlier plea that it not abandon him amidst his sorrow ('No me abandones nunca en mis pesares') severs their close relationship and leaves the poet exposed in that liminal space, that void, between the new and the old.

The seeds of novelty are nonetheless planted in this poem, which differentiates between insightful and more superficial modes of personal exploration. For in his development of the metaphor of the catch, which is couched in terms of the precious and the false ('pedrería', 'piedras falsas') and therefore, by association, the valueless and the true, the poet alludes to something that we might call authenticity – an elusive authenticity ('¡Más abajo del cieno tenebroso / están mis pedrerías', 'nunca mis redes pescarán / la oculta pedrería / de tristeza inconsciente que reluce / al fondo de mi vida', 'saco piedras falsas entre un cieno / de pasiones dormidas') of which his awareness is equally an awareness of poetic goals ('las esmeraldas líricas') lying somewhere beyond his grasp or, at the very least, beyond the grasp of sincerity. According to Lionel Trilling (p. 11), authenticity suggests 'a more moral experience than "sincerity" does, a more exigent conception of the self and of what being true to it consists in, a wider reference to the universe and man's place in it, and a less acceptant and genial view of the social circumstances of life'. Authenticity in these terms pertains to a complex conception of selfhood and being which sincerity, or sincere emotion, in simply being and in taking being for granted, need not address. 'A very considerable originative power', writes Trilling (p. 12), 'had once been claimed for sincerity, but nothing to match the marvellous generative force that our modern judgement assigns to authenticity, which implies the downward movement through all the cultural superstructures to some place where all movement ends, and begins.' The key references in Lorca's poem are to the fountain of his life ('la fuente de mi vida'), the muddy depths of his shadow ('los fangos de mi sombra') and a darker place below ('Más abajo del cieno tenebroso'), to his sub-soul ('sub-alma'), his unconscious sadness ('tristeza inconsciente'), the depths of his life ('fondo de mi vida'), and a mire of sleeping passions ('un cieno / de pasiones dormidas'). However difficult it is for him – impossible even – to extract poetic gems from, or beyond, these places, the poet has at least recognized that these places exist, and the downward movement of his net is the very movement of which Trilling writes, towards a deeper understanding of the complexities of the self, of being, and the limitations of the use of sincerity in expressing such depth. The final stanza is appropriately ambivalent, evoking the successes and failures of the poem with the vibrancy of a quivering fountain ('Con el sol del otoño toda el agua / de mi fontana vibra') – creativity achieved – and the emptiness that is a consequence of the oak's flight – creativity frustrated. The uprooted tree marks a juncture in the poet's development and the severance of the simplistic relation between self and expression.

It is not difficult to see how, in 'Encina', the suggestion of a hidden authenticity along with the metaphor of the failure to net the elusive catch might lead us to inquire into the personal circumstances of the poet's creative concerns and to consider these in the context of his homosexuality – the love that dare not say its name. The perceived limitations or superficiality of the lyric mode might thus acquire significance beyond aesthetic considerations and be understood instead in terms of the clear disparity between the sincere, effusive evocation of sentiment and the concealment, tantamount to self-censorship, to which the origins of that sentiment are subjected. It might also explain the endurance of the lyric subject within this poem and the collection as a whole, the lyrical mode – however crude or superficial – providing evidence of the importance attributed by the poet to evoking his emotional life despite the pull he felt towards more impersonal forms of expression together with the extinction of personality that these implied. It is more difficult, however, to set the silence that is so valued in 'Invocación al laurel' or 'Elegía del silencio' within the logic of self-censorship, whether this be voluntary or imposed, conscious or unconscious. For silence is given a positive connotation and is perceived as a goal – a poetic relative of the azure – that in 'Elegía del silencio' is obstructed by sonorous nature and the intrusion of human passion:

> El aire del invierno
> hace tu azul pedazos,
> y troncha tus florestas
> el lamentar callado
> de alguna fuente fría.
> Donde posas tus manos,
> la espina de la risa
> o el caluroso hachazo
> de la pasión encuentras.
>
> Si te vas a los astros,
> el zumbido solemne
> de los azules pájaros
> quiebra el gran equilibrio
> de tu escondido cráneo.

> Huyendo del sonido
> eres sonido mismo,
> espectro de armonía,
> humo de grito y canto.
> Vienes para decirnos
> en las noches oscuras
> la palabra infinita
> sin aliento y sin labios.

Of course, there is no obligation to ally all the poems of *Libro de poemas* to a single interpretative logic or subject, and so the readings of different poems need not cohere, nor need we consider their distinct interpretations as undermining one another. Yet there are sufficient examples of the poet's self-conscious investigation of his medium for us to be able to see poetry itself as a primary concern. Thus we can concur with Walters' view that the poem 'Encina' is, overall, 'conceived in poetic, not psychological, terms' (Walters 2002, p. 81) and, indeed, extend this view to many other poems in the collection. Whatever the origin or nature of the sentiments conveyed in the poems of *Libro de poemas*, the emphasis, for whatever reason, generally seems to be on the poet's approach to these sentiments, on the art of poetry itself and on the poet's very own abilities.

'¡Sé árbol!' says a distant voice in the poem 'Manantial' (*OC*, I, pp. 124–7), dated 1919 and subtitled 'fragmento'. In 'Manantial' the poet is confronted by the mysteries of nature in the form of a spring whose songs he fails to understand. The secrets of nature to which the poet-seer would have had access are beyond his reach, and he is thus left to ponder on questions for which he has no ready answers:

> Frente al ancho crepúsculo de invierno
> mi corazón soñaba.
> ¿Quién pudiera entender los manantiales,
> el secreto del agua
> recién nacida, ese cantar oculto
> a todas miradas
> del espíritu, dulce melodía
> más allá de las almas …?

The response might once have been 'the poet', but now the question, like so many others that punctuate these lines of verse, is left unanswered. '¿Qué alfabeto de auroras ha compuesto / sus oscuras palabras?' asks the poet in respect of the water's songs, '¿Qué labios las pronuncian? ¿Y qué dicen / a la estrella lejana?' He then points to his own, sinful condition in lines which, according to C. Brian Morris, are an example of the way in which Lorca employs 'religion [...] and a consciousness of sin [...] as a fundamental theme that generates and licenses overstatement and dramatic treatment':[11]

> ¡Mi corazón es malo, Señor! Siento en mi carne
> la inaplacable brasa
> del pecado. Mis mares interiores
> se quedaron sin playas.
> Tu faro se apagó. ¡Ya los alumbra
> mi corazón de llamas!

Here the drama surrounds the poet's fallen condition: his interior is no longer illuminated by God ('Tu faro se apagó') and instead it is his own personal crisis, the flames of his own hell ('mi corazón en llamas'), that provides the light – an allegory which in the context of the poem's creative concerns may stand in for the poet's alienation from the poetry of the spirited natural world and the anxieties now fuelling his creative quest. Such is his feeling of alienation that he is forced even to ask the ultimate question: '¿Es sonido tan sólo esta voz mía? / ¿Y el casto manantial no dice nada?'

Yet 'Manantial' is no less ambivalent than the other poems we have looked at so far. Deaf to the meaning of the spring's songs beyond the vaguest of intuitions ('Mas yo siento en el agua / algo que me estremece ..., como un aire / que agita los ramajes de mi alma'), the poet manages nonetheless to hear another voice, although its origins are distant and unclear: '¡Sé árbol! / (Dijo una voz en la distancia.)' – the prompt for the poet's fusion with the age-old black poplar in an attempt to come in from the outside and hear the spring's song as one of nature's own:

> Yo me incrusté en el chopo centenario
> con tristeza y con ansia.
> Cual dafne varonil que huye miedosa
> de un Apolo de sombra y de nostalgia.
> Mi espíritu fundióse con las hojas
> y fue mi sangre savia.
> En untosa resina convirtióse
> la fuente de mis lágrimas.
> El corazón se fue con las raíces,

---

[11] C. Brian Morris, *Son of Andalusia: The Lyrical Landscapes of Federico García Lorca* (Liverpool: Liverpool University Press, 1997), 175. For Morris, 'the stage-management of emotions and situations and the ability to act out large problems in grand gestures and resonant language' was a lesson Lorca learnt from the Andalusian poet Francisco Villaespesa (p. 175).

> y mi pasión humana,
> haciendo heridas en la ruda carne,
> fugaz me abandonaba.

Whereas the principle of similarity governs the poet's affinity with the oak in 'Encina' ('Mis lágrimas resbalan a la tierra / y, como tus resinas, / corren sobre las aguas del gran cauce / que va a la noche fría') or even with the poplar in an earlier stanza in 'Manantial', via the use of the demonstrative pronoun 'mi' ('Mi chopo centenario de la vega / sus hojas meneaba'), here the governing principle is transformation, metamorphosis, metaphor. Yet the transformation remains unconvincing because of the predominating narrative mode. What we have is an account of a past transformation. Here telling takes precedence over being as the poet looks back – and in – from a perspective that is now external even though the poem's images might evoke a place within. As in 'Invocación al laurel', the recourse to the myth of Apollo and Daphne may allude to the creative impulse of the transformation, metamorphosis representing a dehumanization of sorts: blood becomes sap, tears become resin, the heart disappears into roots, and human passion takes flight. But as long as the assumption behind the transformation is allied to the perspective and ambitions of the poet-seer, there can be no creative satisfaction from this communion with nature. 'Mis mares interiores', the poet had confessed, 'se quedaron sin playas', and in this instant the poem seemed for once to coincide with Huidobro's desire to appropriate nature, to make its landscapes truly the poet's own. Not so the majority of its stanzas, witnesses all to the limbo in which the poet finds himself – caught between the pull of an animate landscape that, in his fallen state, he ought not to understand, and the demands of transformation, of renovation, upon which he seems only reluctantly to embark. Unable to accept his fall into language, to turn his back on nature, or abandon his human passions, he continues to search for the origins of his traditional lyric, embodied by the poem's very literal source: the water's spring. And so the questions return to haunt him, the water's song remaining as unintelligible as ever:

> ¿No podrán comprender mis dulces hojas
> el secreto del agua?
> ¿Llegarán mis raíces a los reinos
> donde nace y se cuaja?
> Incliné mis ramajes hacia el cielo
> que las ondas copiaban,
> mojé las hojas en el cristalino
> diamante azul que canta,

> y sentí borbotar los manantiales
> como de humano yo los escuchara.
> Era el mismo fluir lleno de música
> y de ciencia ignorada.

In the poem's final stanza, the distant voice makes itself heard once more, now beckoning another transformation, this time into a nightingale. However, there is little to suggest that this transformation will be more successful than the last, or that this songbird and traditional emblem of the lyric poet will produce anything other than a lament on the subject of the poet's creative predicament. The stars that appear in the last lines of the poem might well be omens of failure rather than success:

> '¡Sé ruiseñor!', dice una voz perdida
> en la muerta distancia,
> y un torrente de cálidos luceros
> brotó del seno que la noche guarda.

The poplars of 'Los álamos de plata' (*OC*, I, pp. 118–19), dated May 1919, inhabit a world of unintelligible murmurs and silence; a world of dignified restraint in contrast to the audible, demystifying voice of humanity:

> Los álamos de plata se inclinan sobre el agua:
> ellos todo lo saben, pero nunca hablarán.
> El lirio de la fuente no grita su tristeza.
> ¡Todo es más digno que la Humanidad!
>
>     La ciencia del silencio frente al cielo estrellado,
> la posee la flor y el insecto no más.
> La ciencia de los cantos por los cantos la tienen
> los bosques rumorosos y las aguas del mar.
>
>     El silencio profundo de la vida en la tierra,
> nos lo enseña la rosa abierta en el rosal.

On the one hand, these lines contain the legacy of that platonic view of the world that distinguishes between appearance and truth, between what is heard and what is meant. But if the poet longs to penetrate the mysteries of animate nature it is not with the aim of uncovering meaning but instead with that of replicating its silence, its murmurings that never reveal what is murmured, its very song for song's sake ('ciencia de los cantos por los cantos') – a rejection of the outbursts of sincerity for something less vocally personal. Yet the subsequent, exclamatory stanzas, far from replicating the virtues of nature

that the poet so prizes, take the form of an exposition of necessity and intent
that emerges from the emotional core of the lyric subject:

> ¡Hay que dar el perfume que encierran nuestras almas!
> Hay que ser todo cantos, todo luz y bondad.
> ¡Hay que abrirse del todo frente a la noche negra,
> para que nos llenemos de rocío inmortal!
>
> ¡Hay que acostar al cuerpo dentro del alma inquieta!
> Hay que cegar los ojos con luz de más allá.
> Tenemos que asomarnos a la sombra del pecho,
> y arrancar las estrellas que nos puso Satán.
>
> ¡Hay que ser como el árbol que siempre está rezando,
> como el agua de cauce fija en la eternidad!
>
> ¡Hay que arañarse el alma con garras de tristeza
> para que entren las llamas del horizonte astral!

The final goal remains but a goal, since the poem does not represent its
achievement. Hence the use of the conditional tense in the final stanza
evoking something of the tranquillity of a new aesthetic, in contrast to the
preceding lyrical bursts:

> Brotaría en la sombra del amor carcomido
> una fuente de aurora tranquila y maternal.
> Desaparecerían ciudades en el viento.
> Y a Dios en una nube veríamos pasar.

The problem for the poet is, as ever, his allegiance to the heart, that reposi-
tory of human emotion and yearning, and the subject of an earlier poem,
'Corazón nuevo' (*OC*, I, p. 74), dated June 1918. This poem turns on a metaphor of change and transformation, the heart shedding its skin like a serpent:

> Mi corazón, como una sierpe,
> se ha desprendido de su piel,
> y aquí la miro entre mis dedos
> llena de heridas y de miel.

What is shed is presumably associated with the old, with what has been, or
has to be, discarded in the process of renewal. In what amounts to a sentimental autopsy, the poet picks through bittersweet feelings and thoughts,
former states of mind and secrets, of which the skin is now but a reminder:

Los pensamientos que anidaron
en tus arrugas, ¿dónde están?
¿Dónde las rosas que aromaron
a Jesucristo y a Satán?

¡Pobre envoltura que ha oprimido
a mi fantástico lucero!
Gris pergamino dolorido
de lo que quise y ya no quiero.

Yo veo en ti fetos de ciencias,
momias de versos y esqueletos
de mis antiguas inocencias
y mis románticos secretos.

The skin marks the line dividing the past and present, the dead and the living, but also concealment and revelation. A connection between what has been cast off – what the poet once loved, but loves no more – and writing is provided by the equation of the skin with parchment ('pergamino'), a connection that is subsequently strengthened by the reference to mummified verse ('momias de versos'). Revealed is the poet's bright star ('fantástico lucero'), the new heart referred to in the title, which the now dead skin once oppressed. Yet what we should make of this new heart is unclear. The final two stanzas take the form of questions about what to do with its discarded skin:

¿Te colgaré sobre los muros
de mi museo sentimental,
junto a los gélidos y oscuros
lirios durmientes de mi mal?

¿O te pondré sobre los pinos
—libro doliente de mi amor—
para que sepas de los trinos
que da a la aurora el ruiseñor?

Although exposure is guaranteed in either place, the museum and the pine represent interiority and exteriority respectively, the former also connoting the preservation and exhibition of objects of the past, the latter, immortality and perpetuity by virtue of the traditional, symbolic associations of its evergreen foliage (see Chevalier and Gheerbrant, pp. 754–6). The choice, then, is between consigning the skin, like a museum piece, to the intimate spaces of nostalgia or resurrecting it amid the trill of the nightingale's – the lyric poet's – song. It is arguably the second option that the poem has taken, it being the lyrical transformation of the dead matter of yesteryear into verse. Yet although the poem alludes to novelty, the subject and rhetoric it employs belong, just like museum pieces, to the past. As Morris (p. 165) writes, Lorca's 'devoting a whole poem to his heart and the changes he visualized in it moors him firmly to the sentimental manner of Andalusian poetry in the early years of this century, which is clearly signposted within the poem by the use of the nouns "lucero," "lirio," and "ruiseñor" and by the adjective "romántico."' At best we can say, as Morris (p. 165) does, that the poem's novelty resides in its 'attempt to cast an old subject in a new metaphoric mould', or else in its self-conscious consideration of the role of lived experience in the production of poetry. Ultimately, however, the heart – both as subject and voice – remains, albeit to question its very place in these lines of verse.

When, in the final lines of 'La sombra de mi alma' (*OC*, I, pp. 32–3), dated December 1919, the poet asks his nightingale whether it is still singing ('¡Ruiseñor mío! / ¡Ruiseñor! / ¿Aún cantas?'), the question remains open-ended. If the nightingale is to be understood as being emblematic of the poetic voice generally, then the answer is clearly yes. If, however, the song-bird is to be associated more specifically with the lyric subject, then the answer, in this poem at least, is far less assured. The uncertainty that pervades the question provides an appropriate conclusion to a poem that is barer and less discursive than many of the poems of *Libro de poemas* and in which lyrical referents quickly dissolve:

> La sombra de mi alma
> huye por un ocaso de alfabetos,
> niebla de libros
> y palabras.
>
>    ¡La sombra de mi alma!
>
>    He llegado a la línea donde cesa
> la nostalgia,
> y la gota de llanto se transforma
> alabastro de espíritu.
>
>    (¡La sombra de mi alma!)

Not the soul, but its shadow. Not the certainty or confidence of the written word, but its capacity to obfuscate (as in this poem) and to embroil. Although the exclamatory refrain (desperate rather than self-affirming) provides a refuge for the lyric subject reluctant to desist, it is trapped between more reflective stanzas (as it is, in the second instance, between parentheses) that embody the rejection of nostalgia and the pain of lived experience (the lament) as contemporary poetic sources, in order to take on, instead, the character of that less emotive place designated in the poem by the fusion of alabaster and spirit. If in the next stanza pain dissolves like a fallen snowflake touching matter, reason by contrast persists, as does the substance, though not the unabashed emotion, of human experience lived before the twilight changes evoked in this crepuscular poem:

> El copo del dolor
> se acaba,
> pero queda la razón y la sustancia
> de mi viejo mediodía de labios,
> de mi viejo mediodía
> de miradas.

Yet the poem is not a treatise proclaiming a new aesthetic. It is the product of the poet's uncertain forays into a literal no-man's land that is no longer illuminated by guiding stars, nor animated by the forthrightness and clearsightedness once provided by the poet's confidence in the value of sincere self-expression, and where even the word 'love', that most sacred of romantic references, has now worn away:

> Un turbio laberinto
> de estrellas ahumadas
> enreda mi ilusión
> casi marchita.
>
> ¡La sombra de mi alma!
>
> Y una alucinación
> me ordeña las miradas.
> Veo la palabra amor
> desmoronada.

Questioning 'the metaphysical theory of the substantial unity of the soul', Eliot, in 'Tradition and the Individual Talent', set out his view that 'the poet has, not a "personality" to express, but a particular medium, which is only a medium and not a personality, in which impressions and experiences combine in peculiar and unexpected ways' (Eliot 1986, p. 56). In 'La sombra de mi alma', if the nightingale has indeed stopped singing it is perhaps because the poet's sense of the medium and its potential for the peculiar and the unexpected (evident in some of the poem's metaphors) is beginning to gain ground on his need to divulge the secrets of his soul.

In poem after poem a pattern of discord emerges that situates the poet of *Libro de poemas* at a crossroads – 'a generational crossroads', as Luis Fernández Cifuentes puts it in respect of Lorca's early prose work, *Impresiones y paisajes.*[12] In this transitional space the poet-seer contemplates shifting his gaze, the personal feels the imperatives of the impersonal, and lived experience begins the process of self-effacement in the name of the higher principle of art-for-art's sake. Still, the crossing has yet to be made, as is the case at the crossroads referred to by the title of the poem 'Encrucijada' (*OC*, I, pp. 99–100), dated July 1920. This poem presents a series of thoughts and feelings that have as their common denominator sorrow, at once the spur of the poet's creativity and the effect of creative difficulty and uncertainty:

> ¡Oh, qué dolor el tener
> versos en la lejanía
> de la pasión, y el cerebro
> todo manchado de tinta!
>
> ¡Oh, qué dolor no tener
> la fantástica camisa
> del hombre feliz: la piel
> —alfombra del sol—curtida!
>
> (Alrededor de mis ojos
> bandadas de letras giran.)
>
> ¡Oh, qué dolor el dolor
> antiguo de la poesía,
> este dolor pegajoso
> tan lejos del agua limpia!
>
> ¡Oh dolor de lamentarse
> por sorber la vena lírica!
> ¡Oh dolor de fuente ciega
> y molino sin harina!
>
> ¡Oh, qué dolor no tener
> dolor y pasar la vida
> sobre la hierba incolora
> de la vereda indecisa!
>
> ¡Oh el más profundo dolor,
> el dolor de la alegría,
> reja que nos abre surcos
> donde el llanto fructifica!
>
> (Por un monte de papel
> asoma la luna fría.)
> ¡Oh dolor de la verdad!
> ¡Oh dolor de la mentira!

---

[12] Luis Fernández Cifuentes, '1918: García Lorca at the Crossroads', in Delgado and Poust, pp. 66–85 (p. 75).

The creative difficulty deplored in the opening stanza, where an ink-stained mind connotes the inability to extract lines of verse from the passions in which they are alienated, is echoed, further down, in the parenthetical references to flocks of letters swirling around the poet and, in the final stanza, to the mountain of paper from behind which a cold, and possibly deathly, moon appears. Sorrow is associated with the character of poetry in the fourth stanza, in accordance with the perspective and principle of the melancholy poet, yet it is endowed with a negative aspect by virtue of the unfavourable juxtaposition of its adherent nature ('este dolor pegajoso') with the limpidity of water. In the following stanza, sorrow, lamentation and lyricism are bound together in the first two lines, but the negative metaphors in the subsequent couplet – the blind fountain, the flourless mill – are suggestive of creative block rather than free-flowing lyricism. The sorrow of not being a happy man ('no tener / la fantástica camisa / del hombre feliz'), with its allusion to a body exposed to the sun ('la piel / —alfombra del sol—curtida'), in contrast, perhaps, to the cultured figure of the clothed poet, has as its antithesis, in a later stanza, the sorrow of not feeling any sorrow at all and the anodyne character of indecision; while the paradoxical sorrow of happiness itself (happiness being a prerequisite for the relatively steep fall into the deepest sorrow of all, 'el más profundo dolor') closes the vicious circle from which the poet ultimately can never escape. In responding so emotionally to the subject of sorrow, albeit in fairly general terms and the most formulaic of modes, the poem remains tied to the perspective of personal art. Yet the images of creative difficulty seem to cast a doubt over the practicability of such art. If the poem constitutes a crossroads, it is because it is the point at which paths leading from and to sorrow intersect, but also because it has something of the 'vereda indecisa' – that indecision – about it. Sorrow may always be the point of departure and arrival, but the crises evoked in these stanzas signal the creative problems en route. The sorrow of truth and lies, with which the poem ends, is not a concern of art that strives to be nothing more than itself. It is, however, a concern for the poet who is faced with the sorrow, on the one hand, of being truthfully, or sincerely, himself (personal poetry) and, on the other, of evading his self altogether (impersonal poetry). In its totality, it is at this junction that 'Encrucijada' finds itself: from the standpoint of personal art, somewhere between truth and lie, between the personal and the impersonal.

Something of the visionary desire of the poet-seer lingers in the poem 'Árboles' (*OC*, I, p. 113) of 1919, in which there is a hint at the creative otherworldliness of the azure and an evocation of the divinity in nature. Yet by setting the first stanza in the form of a series of questions and by selecting shape as the founding principle for the construction of its images, the poet exposes the visionary task to the risk of demystification:

> ¡Árboles!
> ¿Habéis sido flechas
> caídas del azul?
> ¿Qué terribles guerreros os lanzaron?
> ¿Han sido las estrellas?

The logic of this questioning derives from the observation of shape and form: the vertical linearity of trees, the implicit likening of their tops to the feathers of arrows, their roots plunging like arrowheads into the ground. The guiding principle is invention not clairvoyance, while the questions offer no certitude and, if anything, reveal the self-conscious workings of a mind seeking associations rather than affirming them or taking them for granted. The next stanza would appear to rectify the noncommittal character of the first were it not for the question with which it and the poem end:

> Vuestras músicas vienen del alma de los pájaros,
> de los ojos de Dios,
> de la pasión perfecta.
> ¡Árboles!
> ¿Conocerán vuestras raíces toscas
> mi corazón en tierra?

The poet connects what he deems perfect in nature with divine perfection – material perfection with the spiritual. Trees, with their vertical symbolism, are the great connectors between Heaven and Earth (see Chevalier and Gheerbrant, pp. 1026–7), but the poet's parting question raises doubts about whether he will be part of that connection. Once more it is the heart, the poet's emotional centre, which is stranded amongst lines of verse whose aspirations seem to be beyond reach.

By contrast, the poem 'Campo' (*OC*, I, p. 110), dated 1920, presents a landscape that is not a frontispiece for the beyond; one where the lyrical first person is absent and whose poetic qualities are a consequence of the poet's evocation of his perception of colour, shape, movement and sound by means of the combined languages of metaphor and fact:

> El cielo es de ceniza.
> Los árboles son blancos,
> y son negros carbones
> los rastrojos quemados.
> Tiene sangre reseca
> la herida del Ocaso,

y el papel incoloro
del monte está arrugado.
El polvo del camino
se esconde en los barrancos,
están las fuentes turbias
y quietos los remansos.
Suena en un gris rojizo
la esquila del rebaño,
y la noria materna
acabó su rosario.

El cielo es de ceniza,
los árboles son blancos.

Here the landscape, impressionistic rather than naturalistic, is placed at the service of poetry, rather than the contrary. Yet 'Campo' is something of an anomaly in *Libro de Poemas*, above all because it is free from the tensions that result elsewhere from the poet's self-conscious engagement and confrontation with the lyrical. There is, moreover, no kinship here between nature and the poet beyond the marriage of its natural, and his imaginative, palette.

The same cannot be said of the representation of the black poplars in the poems 'In memoriam' (*OC*, I, p. 65), dated August 1920, or 'Chopo muerto' (*OC*, I, pp. 108–9), dated 1920 (no month). In 'In memoriam', the relation between poet and tree is conceived in terms of their respective moods and transformations:

Dulce chopo,
dulce chopo,
te has puesto
de oro.
Ayer estabas verde,
un verde loco
de pájaros
gloriosos.
Hoy estás abatido
bajo el cielo de agosto
como yo bajo el cielo
de mi espíritu rojo.
La fragancia cautiva
de tu tronco
vendrá a mi corazón
piadoso.
¡Rudo abuelo del prado!
Nosotros
nos hemos puesto
de oro.

The transformation from green to gold seems, on the face of it, to be a negative one, despite the positive value we might instinctively attribute to the latter colour. It is debatable, though, whether this transformation has anything to do with the changing hues of autumn, particularly if we attach importance to the fact that the poem was written not during the autumn months but a little earlier in August. The golden colour of the tree might actually have its source in the disease commonly afflicting poplars known as yellow leaf blister (*cloque dorée* in French). This reading would cohere, just as well as an autumnal one, with the poem's title and elegiac character. And yet it is difficult to shrug off the very precious associations of gold, the final reaffirmation of the tree's and the poet's mutual transformation offering tones perhaps of resignation but possibly of pride as well. For a poet for whom sadness is still the mainspring of creativity these two sentiments are not incompatible. Instead they are evidence of the ambivalence of the creative act where achievement is allied to the cultivation of painful material. And if yellow leaf blister, which provides in nature the most spectacular of transformations, is indeed the source of the poem's central image, then what 'In memoriam' has in common with a poem like 'Campo', despite its personal references, is that its source lies not in the conception of a spirited land to whose mysteries the poet is privy, but in the act of observation itself, the magical powers of the poet residing in his capacity to find poetry in the mundane rather than in his ability to decipher nature's secrets.

The very same principle governs the poem 'Chopo muerto', a fallen poplar providing a ready motif for the poet's own fallen state. Once again, this fall is not without its positive connotations, despite the predominantly elegiac tone of the poem. Of all the poems we have looked at it is the closest in its conception to Jiménez's 'Una a una', both in terms of its images of sterility and because it marks a turning point that hinges necessarily on the death of the old in anticipation of the new:

> ¡Chopo Viejo!
> Has caído
> en el espejo
> del remanso dormido,
> abatiendo tu frente
> ante el Poniente.
> No fue el vendaval ronco
> el que rompió tu tronco,
> ni fue el hachazo grave
> del leñador, que sabe
> has de volver
> a nacer.

Fue tu espíritu fuerte
el que llamó a la muerte,
al hallarse sin nidos, olvidado
de los chopos infantes del prado.
Fue que estabas sediento
de pensamiento,
y tu enorme cabeza centenaria,
solitaria,
escuchaba los lejanos
cantos de tus hermanos.

What is significant is that the poplar's decline is cast not as the result of external forces ('vendaval', 'hacha') but as a voluntary act ('Fue tu espíritu fuerte') prompted by an awareness of its sterile state and agedness in contrast to the younger poplars on the meadow – the infantes ready to succeed it. Thus the poplar, even in death, cuts a heroic figure against the landscape from which it will inevitably disappear:

En tu cuerpo guardabas
las lavas
de tu pasión,
y en tu corazón,
el semen sin futuro de Pegaso.
La terrible simiente
de un amor inocente
por el sol del ocaso.

¡Qué amargura tan honda
para el paisaje
el héroe de la fronda
sin ramaje!

Ya no serás la cuna
de la luna,
ni la mágica risa
de la brisa,
ni el bastón de un lucero
caballero.
No tornará la primavera
de tu vida,
ni verás la sementera
florecida.
Serás nidal de ranas
y de hormigas.

Tendrás por verdes canas
las ortigas,

y un día la corriente
sonriente
llevará tu corteza
con tristeza.

If the reference to Pegasus makes possible the connection of the tree's condition with the death of poetic inspiration (or even, more precisely, the death of the *modernista* style with which the winged horse is associated), the destinies of the tree and poet are brought firmly together in the final stanza:

¡Chopo viejo!
Has caído
en el espejo
del remanso dormido.
Yo te vi descender
en el atardecer
y escribo tu elegía,
que es la mía.

It might seem strange that a poet so young and in the early stages of his poetic journey should think to compare himself to this decrepit tree, unless of course we recognize that he is reworking a familiar, established trope which in this version presages, or contains, its own death. The poem is a testimony to the poet's awareness of his place within the life cycle; a cycle in which letting go, however difficult it may be, is a necessary condition for renewal.

# 2

# *Poema del cante jondo* and the Suite*s*:
# The Riddles of the Sphinx

> el poeta erudito se ha hecho realmente hombre
> del pueblo, se ha desposeído de su personalidad y
> pensamiento proprio ...
> > (Antonio Machado y Álvarez ['Demófilo'],
> > *Poesía popular*)

'Ya vengan del corazón de la sierra, ya vengan del naranjal sevillano o de las armoniosas costas mediterráneas, las coplas,' explained Lorca in his lecture 'El cante jondo. Primitivo canto andaluz' (*OC*, III, pp. 195–222), 'tienen un fondo común: el Amor y la Muerte ..., pero un amor y una muerte vistos a través de la Sibila, ese personaje tan oriental, verdadera esfinge de Andalucía' (*OC*, III, p. 205). To his references to the Sibyl and the Sphinx he then added riddles:

> En el fondo de todos los poemas late la pregunta, pero la terrible pregunta que no tiene contestación. Nuestro pueblo pone los brazos en cruz mirando a las estrellas y esperará inútilmente la señal salvadora. Es un gesto patético, pero verdadero. El poema o plantea un hondo problema emocional, sin realidad posible, o lo resuelve con la Muerte, que es la pregunta de las preguntas. (*OC*, III, pp. 205–6)

And he continued, eventually bringing into the equation the decipherer of riddles, Oedipus himself:

> La mayor parte de los poemas de nuestra región (exceptuando muchos nacidos en Sevilla) tienen las características antes citadas. Somos un pueblo triste, un pueblo estático.
> Como Iván Turgueneff vio a sus paisanos, sangre y médula rusas convertidos en esfinge, así veo yo a muchísimos poemas de nuestra lírica regional.
> ¡Oh esfinge de las Andalucías!
>
> > A mi puerta has de llamar,
> > no te he de salir a abrir
> > y me has de sentir llorar.

Se esconden los versos detrás del velo impenetrable y se duermen en espera del Edipo que vendrá a descifrarlos para despertar y volver al silencio. ...     (*OC*, III, p. 206)

The fact that Lorca in this lecture, which he delivered on 19 February 1922 to the Arts Club in Granada, should have conceived of *cante jondo* in terms of riddles has significance, as we shall see, beyond judgements about the true nature of Andalusian popular song: one that relates specifically to avant-garde influences on the development of his own poetry. But before examining the relevance of riddles to his poems, let us dwell for a while on the meta-phorical allusion to the Oedipus myth in the passages from his lecture cited above. We should, of course, first mention its orientalist thrust, the Sibyl and the Sphinx becoming bywords for that inscrutable Orient whose mysteries are in stark opposition to the rationality associated with the Occident. As Edward Said notes in his seminal work, *Orientalism*, accepting 'the basic distinction between East and West' is 'the starting point for elaborate theories [...] concerning the Orient, its people, customs, "mind," destiny, and so on'.[1] But what is of most interest to me here is the appearance of the figure of Oedipus himself, to whom I ascribe that most Western of guises as initi-ated by Freud in his reworking of the myth and his definition of the complex bearing the hero's name. And in my reading the Oedipus to whom Lorca (self-consciously) refers in his lecture is none other than the poet himself.

The connection between Lorca and the Oedipus in his lecture can be made in the context of the confidence and purpose that permeate his text. As Stainton (p. 97) notes, the lecture was received well not only by the Arts Club but also by the press, thus increasing Lorca's stature in Granada.[2] The positive response it provoked was no accident but the result of careful, even masterly calculations on Lorca's part. 'It is', writes Brian Morris (p. 187), 'an impressive achievement, studious in its range and astute in its strategy, which relies on a number of masterstrokes that subtly identify [Lorca] both as an authority and an individual poet.' Morris's praise for the lecture serves, in great part, as a corrective to the negative reaction of critics and flamencolo-gists who quite rightly, as Morris himself concedes, take issue with Lorca's idealization of *cante jondo* and its performers, and highlight a number of erroneous assertions, such as the distinction the poet makes between *cante*

---

[1]   Edward W. Said, *Orientalism* (London: Penguin Books, 2003), 2–3.
[2]   Stainton (p. 97) notes also that the lecture was pronounced a success by the *Noticiero Granadino*, which published it in serial form, and by the *Defensor de Granada*, while *El Sol*, in Madrid, published a short synopsis.

*jondo* and *cante flamenco* and his insistence on the purity of the former, or the fact that he attributes the development of *cante jondo* exclusively to Spain's gypsies. Timothy Mitchell, in *Flamenco Deep Song*, is particularly critical of Lorca, of his orientalist primitivism, and of avant-garde primitivism generally, and sees the lecture as part of a misguided, elitist project to sanitize and elevate a popular art form.[3] 'The whole point of avant-garde primitivism,' writes Mitchell (p. 169), 'was to shun history, to escape urban society, to flee the pollution of modernity.'[4] William Washabaugh, in *Flamenco. Passion, Politics and Popular Culture*, has added his voice to the criticism, reproaching Lorca for portraying *cante jondo* 'as a popular development whose roots extend backwards to "time immemorial" while simultaneously deprecating its professionalization'.[5] Yet these criticisms, however valid, do not detract from the purpose and impact of the lecture. In Said's view (2003, p. 21), the Orientalist 'is never concerned with the Orient except as the first cause of what he says'. What Said signals as an obvious fault compels us, somewhat paradoxically, to consider the possibility that judgements about Lorca's treatment of his subject are less important than our arriving at an understanding of why he embarked on it in the first place, thus shifting our attention away from what Lorca says to why he chose to say it at all.

The Oedipus in the lecture who will come to decipher the riddles of the verse of *cante jondo* is, in one sense, akin to the 'Orientalist, poet or scholar' who 'makes the Orient speak, describes the Orient, renders its mysteries plain for and to the West' (Said 2003, pp. 20–1). By taking it upon himself to explain *cante jondo*, Lorca does no less than adopt the role of the decipherer, who sets about unlocking the mysteries of *cante jondo* for his audience at the Arts Club, albeit with substantial help from a pamphlet written by the composer Manuel de Falla (see Gibson, p. 112, and Stainton, p. 96). But this Oedipus is also akin to the boy who wishes to replace the father, a wish that corresponds here to an emerging poet's desire to establish his own individuality and assert himself via the authority he claims over his subject, his rebellious

---

[3]  See Timothy Mitchell, *Flamenco Deep Song* (New Haven and London: Yale University Press, 1994), 38–50.

[4]  By contrast, Alice J. Poust, in her essay 'Federico García Lorca's Andalusia in Light of Oswald Spengler's Theory of Magian Cultures', in Delgado and Poust, pp. 175–190, provides a positive interpretation of Lorca's exaltation of *cante jondo*, gypsies and Andalusia generally, seeing in his work a more radical ambition, namely the alignment of Andalusia 'with a contemporary tendency to question and even oppose the construct "Western civilization"' (p. 175).

[5]  William Washabaugh, *Flamenco. Passion, Politics and Popular Culture* (Oxford: Berg, 1996), 61.

aspect manifest in his promotion of an art form which at the time had many detractors. This is why, contrary to the misgivings of Mitchell (p. 167) who homes in on what he terms Lorca's 'othering discourses', namely *'pollution,* that is, infectious urban music, pseudoflamenco included, and *purity,* that is, deep song redefined in accordance with orientalist primitivism à la Debussy', we should instead take heed of Morris (p. 187) when he emphasizes Lorca's use of erudition 'to rise above the detractors of *cante jondo* and flamenco whose contemptuous views are [...] brought into the open and shown to be both small-minded and short-sighted.' If Lorca makes reference to an impressive array of musicians, musicologists and writers (Turguenev included), if he cites Persian, Arabic, Asturian and Andalusian verse, it is to gather about him evidence of his erudition and worth, just as his reservations about the *coplas* of previous generations of poets – Melchor de Palau, Salvador Rueda, Ventura Ruiz Aguilera and Manuel Machado – serve to distinguish him from his predecessors, his forefathers (and herein is revealed the patricidal instinct), as much as they serve to exalt, by contrast, the purity of truly popular verse: '¡qué diferencia tan notable entre los versos de estos poetas y los que el pueblo crea! ¡La diferencia que hay entre una rosa de papel y otra natural!' (*OC*, III, p. 208). And if, as Stainton (p. 96) notes, the voice in the lecture was 'unmistakably Lorca's', 'seasoned' as it was 'with personal anecdotes and allusions', it is because his lecture was as much a vehicle for himself – for his own poetic artistry and sensibilities – as it was an exposition of the artistic value of *cante jondo*. For this reason we should not underestimate the importance of the general references Lorca makes to art in the course of his lecture, whether it be in terms of the struggle of young artists 'por lo nuevo, la lucha por lo imprevisto, el buceo en el mar del pensamiento por encontrar la emoción intacta' (*OC*, III, p. 203) or in terms of his own self-inclusion in the number of poets 'que actualmente nos ocupamos, en más o menos escala, en la poda y cuidado del demasiado frondoso árbol lírico que nos dejaron los románticos y los postrománticos' (*OC*, III, p. 205). Ironically, a lecture which traced the origins of *cante jondo* to 'los primitivos sistemas musicales de la India' (*OC*, III, p. 197) had something significant to say, although not always overtly, about the poets and poetry of the day. If anything, Lorca's lecture served to identify him among the 'amantes de la tradición engarzada con el porvenir' (*OC*, III, p. 216).

In the months preceding his lecture, Lorca had been putting the finishing touches on a new collection of poems entitled *Poema del cante jondo*. These poems, along with his lecture on *cante jondo*, were the fruit of a period of seemingly intense fascination on his part with the popular song of his region, a period dating back at least to the moment in which he struck up a friendship with Falla, who had moved to Granada in 1920.[6] Acting upon an idea that has been attributed to Miguel Cerón Rubio, a local businessman (see Gibson, p. 109), Lorca and Falla were soon involved in planning and staging a *cante jondo* competition, which was eventually held on 13 and 14 June 1922 in the Alhambra's Plaza de los Aljibes (see Gibson, p. 115). As is the case with Lorca's lecture, the *Concurso del cante jondo* has provoked negative criticism because of its misguided attempt to promote purity and authenticity, the desire to find the true, untainted voice of the people leading organizers to exclude from the competition professional performers over the age of twenty-one (see Mitchell, pp. 165–77, and Walters 2007, p. 75). And yet, whether or not self-promotion can be counted as one of his aims, the competition represented for Lorca a personal success, earning him rave reviews in the press, as did his first recital of *Poema del cante jondo* at Granada's Alhambra Palace Hotel only a week before (see Gibson, p. 115, and Stainton, p. 102).

It is just as easy to romanticize Lorca's interest in *cante jondo* as it is to see flaws in his approach, tempting as it is to put a romantic gloss on his excursions to the caves of Sacromonte in search of the authentic experience of *cante* (see Stainton, p. 92), or to idealize his friendship with gypsies who, as he told his friend, the music critic and composer Adolfo Salazar in August 1921 (*EC*, p. 123), taught him to play flamenco guitar. Yet there is sufficient reason also to resist connections between our poet and popular song based on notions of some common racial or regional heritage or passionate disposition. To begin with, novelty was, as ever, of paramount importance to the poet, as we have seen in his lecture on *cante* (that 'lucha por lo nuevo'). In another letter to Salazar, from January 1922, Lorca comments on the Andalusian evocations, the allusions to the songs of *cantaores* and the popular style of *Poema del cante jondo*. And yet despite citing these traditional aspects he emphasizes that the collection, which he characterizes as a jigsaw puzzle ('*puzzle americano*'), represents a new direction both for him personally and in more general terms: 'El poema está lleno de gitanos, de velones, de fraguas [...]. Es la primera cosa de *otra orientación mía* y no sé todavía qué decirte de él ... ¡pero novedad sí tiene! [...] Los poetas españoles nunca han *tocado* este tema' (*EC*, p. 137). It is significant that Lorca, before embarking on *Poema del cante jondo*, had already been busy working on another series

---

6   For details of Lorca's personal and working relationship with Falla, see D. Gareth Walters, 'Parallel Trajectories in the Careers of Falla and Lorca', in Federico Bonaddio and Xon de Ros (eds), *Crossing Fields in Modern Spanish* (Oxford: Legenda [European Humanities Research Centre], 2003), 92–102; his chapter 'Music', in Federico Bonaddio (ed.), *A Companion to Federico García Lorca* (Woodbridge: Tamesis, 2007), 63–83; also Gibson, pp. 108–16, and Stainton, pp. 89–109.

of poems, his Suites (to whose composition he would subsequently return). There is a clear relation between his *cante*-inspired series and the Suites (André Belamich refers to them as 'el laboratorio del *Poema del cante jondo*'[7]), even though direct references to *cante jondo* at the level of theme or influence are mostly absent from them. Indeed, in his letter to Salazar of August Lorca distinguishes *Poema del cante jondo* from his Suites on this very basis (see *EC*, p. 136). The points they do have in common, however, are formal and aesthetic, and central to both is the endeavour, or at least the awareness of the need, to create non-referential, independent poems in line with the precepts of the avant-garde.

The influence of the avant-garde on the Spanish literary scene in the 1920s is summarized in an essay by Manuel Durán, with particular emphasis on the work of Lorca. Durán pinpoints the importance of Futurism, both as it was interpreted by Ramón Gómez de la Serna in the form of his *greguerías* and in terms of its aesthetic principles, which were sustained into the 1920s by the movements of *creacionismo* and *ultraísmo*.[8] Although aspects of Futurism, such as the cult of violence, speed and the machine, may not always be directly relevant to practitioners of the new literary mode in Spain – Lorca being a case in point – its literary style most certainly was. As Durán (p. 765) explains, Futurism 'tiende a la frase breve, a eliminar adjetivos, a suprimir transiciones y conjunciones: es un estilo "telegráfico," económico, de pocas palabras'. And he continues:

> Hay que desprenderse de lo inútil, de todo posible lastre, para que el globo, es decir, la frase redonda y de gran fuerza, pueda elevarse. La velocidad requiere aligerar el peso. Se simplifica la sintaxis, e incluso, más tarde, la puntuación. Y, al perder lo accidental, lo descriptivo y discursivo, el lenguaje poético se contrae hasta quedar desnudo, en carne viva, en los puros huesos, es decir en la metáfora o en la greguería. (Durán, pp. 765–6)

---

[7] André Belamich, 'Presentación de las *Suites*', in Federico García Lorca, *Suites*. Edición crítica de André Belamich (Barcelona: Ariel, 1983), 9–26. As Belamich (p. 9) explains, Lorca began writing his Suites at the end of 1920 and completed them in July 1923. Neglected for some length of time, a number of Suites were published in 1935 under the title *Primeras canciones* (Belamich, p. 16).

[8] See Manuel Durán, 'Lorca y las vanguardias', *Hispania*, 69.4 (December 1986), 764–70. As Andrew A. Anderson points out in his essay 'Ramón Gómez de la Serna and F. T. Marinetti: Epistolary Contacts and the Genesis of a Manifesto', in Harris 1996, 19–31 (p. 19), Ramón produced a translation of a version of Marinetti's Futurist Manifesto as early as April 1909 in *Promoteo*. Huidobro, the father of *creacionismo*, had, as Gibson (pp. 84, 221) notes, spent five months in Madrid in 1918 where he made a considerable impact, while Guillermo de Torre published the first *ultraísta* manifesto in 1920 (see Gibson, p. 84).

To this economical approach to lexis, syntax and punctuation, which is
the very basis for non-discursiveness, non-referentiality and the creation of
metaphors, we should add the eradication of excessive sentimentality and
emotionalism. One of the consequences of the new style and emphasis was
a re-evaluation of the lyric subject, the controlling first person no longer a
constant at the centre of the work or the manifest origin of all comment,
experience and emotion. Durán (p. 766) already sees traces of the influence of the new aesthetic in some poems of *Libro de poemas*, but where it
would really begin to take hold is in the Suites. And yet even if stylistically
the Suites mostly embody the element of simplification so characteristic of
contemporary trends, we can still detect, here and there, an air of reservation
about new directions, particularly in respect of the status of the first-person,
lyric subject.

The Suite 'Pórtico' (*OC*, I, p. 649), written in early 1921, is an example
of the adoption of the ethos of simplification and the creation of independent,
non-referential poems based on metaphor and an eradication of emotionalism. The source of its images in reality is not totally beyond our grasp, and
yet its metaphors deflect our attention away from that place of origin onto the
intricate details of colour, shape, smell and form that are bound together by
the processes of personification, synaesthesia and visual distortion:

> El agua
> toca su tambor
> de plata.
>
>   Los árboles
> tejen el viento
> y las rosas lo tiñen
> de perfume.
>
>   Una araña
> inmensa
> hace a la luna
> estrella.

If there is anything approximating to emotion here, it takes the form of intimacy and wonder and is not vocalized via a first-person subject. What Alan
Hoyle has to say about Ramón's *greguerías* is useful for an understanding
about what is, in effect, a displacement in the Suite of the presence of the
first-person subject. To borrow from Hoyle, 'Pórtico' creates 'significant fragments of space and time, details disconnected and heightened, moments of

intensity in which the self loses itself ecstatically, momentarily, in the objects of perception';[9] indeed,

> the transcendent universe [is] reduced to a fragmentary here and now, in which the self is lost, temporarily, in the contemplation of its immediate surroundings, producing a confusion of subject and object, the disappearance of normal human feeling and its reappearance (by imaginative projection) in inanimate reality, now animated by the human consciousness of it.
> (Hoyle, p. 10)

Consciousness is revealed in 'Pórtico' in the creation of metaphors, which is at the heart of the process of rendering poetic that which has been observed. The real elements alluded to in the Suite ('agua', 'árboles', 'viento', 'rosas', 'perfume', 'araña', 'luna') are subsumed into the poetic logic of the metaphorical ('toca', 'tambor', 'plata', 'tejen', 'tiñen', 'inmensa', 'estrella') and set in a configuration in which the function of describing a real scene – a porch on a rainy, wind-swept night – is secondary to the poetic effects of metaphorical construction. The definition Hoyle (p. 9) supplies for Ramón's *greguerías* – 'self-contained [...] poems that poeticize ordinary everyday reality' – seems also to apply to 'Pórtico', although it is important to emphasize that the poetic result takes precedence over the everyday observation that may have been its origin.

There are Suites that sidestep referentiality altogether, that is, by turning the word into the referent, into the very thing that is being referred to. The Suites 'Sol' (*OC*, I, p. 683), 'Pirueta' (*OC*, I, p. 684) and '[Árbol]' (*OC*, I, p. 685), collected together under the title 'Caprichos' from July 1921, do just that:

> SOL
>
> ¡Sol!
> ¿Quién te llamó
> sol?
>
> A nadie le extrañaría,
> digo yo,
> ver en el cielo tres letras
> en vez de tu cara
> de oro.

---

[9]  Alan Hoyle, 'Ramón Gómez de la Serna and the Avant-Garde', in Harris 1996, 7–16 (p. 10).

PIRUETA

Si muriera el alfabeto,
morirían todas las cosas.
Las palabras
son las alas.

La vida entera
depende
de cuatro letras.

[ÁRBOL]

Árbol,
la *ele* te da las hojas.
Luna,
la *u* te da el color.
Amor,
la *eme* te da los besos.

The ludic character of each of the above Suites is apparent. Walters (2002, p. 110) relates a later set of Suites, 'Cuco-cuco-cucó' (*OC*, I, pp. 765–72), from July 1923, to 'the childish word-games indulged in by Lorca and his fellow students at the Residencia de Estudiantes', the institution in Madrid where Lorca resided periodically between 1919 and 1928 and which provided him with the base from which to explore the latest literary trends in the capital. For Walters, a set like 'Cuco-cuco-cucó' 'illustrates how fine is the line dividing lightness and frivolity from insignificance and nonsense'. The set 'Caprichos', I would suggest, falls into the former category, but does not lack significance for appearing to be light or frivolous. Each Suite tackles the relationship between words and reality and emphasizes the fact that the world is ultimately mediated by language. By suggesting, humorously, that we would not be surprised to see three letters in the sky rather than a fiery globe, 'Sol' makes the point that, however arbitrary the noun that gives the sun its name, the word has attained iconic status, is inseparable from its referent, the signifier and the signified having become inextricably bound. 'Pirueta' spins a similar theme, stating that the world exists for us only through language. Life at the level of noun ('vida'), but also signifying everything that the world contains, is literally dependent on the letters that spell it out. '[Árbol]' provides a final twist. By relating the function of letters to those of material objects ('hojas'), properties ('color') and acts ('besos'), this Suite alludes to the autonomous life of signs which embody a range of associations independently from any specific referents in the real world. It also demonstrates that nature can be put at the service of art, employing leaves, colour and kisses to describe the three signs' linguistic composition.

These Suites, because they focus on words, the very building blocks of poems, and because they touch upon the fundamental relationship between language and reality, continue that line of self-conscious enquiry so evident in *Libro de poemas*, albeit in a language and form more exposed to the influence of avant-garde trends. Indeed, their humour and playfulness mark a shift in tone from the sorrowful voice that traversed so many of the poems of Lorca's first collection. Humour, of course, was a characteristic of much avant-garde production. Ramón, for example, defined his own inventions with the formula 'Humorismo + metáfora: *greguerías*' (see Hoyle, p. 8), while Ortega y Gasset (pp. 381–3), in his 1925 essay 'La deshumanización del arte', would argue that irony and farce were characteristics of the avant-garde style.[10] And yet it is impossible to make sweeping statements about the Suites as a whole since they differ not only in quality but also in tone and, importantly, in terms of the extent to which they embrace the new aesthetic. A number of Suites do not seem to have escaped the angst accompanying the difficult artistic transition expressed in *Libro de poemas*, as is the case in two which Lorca himself discarded from his original collection: 'Caracol' (*OC*, I, p. 1073), from the set entitled 'Estampas del mar' (*OC*, I, pp. 603–9), supposedly written towards the end of 1920, and 'Parque' (*OC*, I, p. 1077), from the set 'Sombra' (*OC*, I, pp. 699–708), dated July 1921.

The opening line of 'Caracol' may provide a clue as to why it was removed from 'Estampas del mar'. The direct reference to the lyric poet distinguishes it from the remaining Suites in the set:

> Poeta lírico,
> descubre la civilización
> de las perlas
> y propaga la música del mar
> tierras adentro.
> Pone un raro turbante
> de nácar a la espuma
> y rima con el mar
> tanto como la vela.

[10] Hoyle (p. 11), in discussing Ramón's *greguerías*, provides a corrective to Ortega's negative take on the ludic character of avant-garde art, that is, that it did not take itself seriously, by arguing that '[w]hat this art takes very seriously is its ability and duty to invest the trivial experience of the everyday with transcendence, a heightened sense of significance, which involves irony, not in the sense that art is a joke. But if life plays the dirty trick of condemning men to mortality, then the writer can play jokes on life, play around with our conventional categories, in order to recreate and enjoy the paradoxical and very human sensation of being simply alive.'

The idea, no doubt, is that the poet is like a seashell through which you can hear the sea. Thus the Suite affirms a well-established model for poetic creation, the poet cast in the role of a medium through which are revealed the sea's music and hidden treasures. Not only is he in tune with the sea (as suggested by the final simile) but he also, via his lyrical craft, embellishes its mundane appearance ('Pone un raro turbante / de nácar a la espuma). Already we can see a degree of confusion about the poet's role, for it is not the same to uncover hidden secrets as it is to augment appearance through embellishment. But even more problematic in the context of the new aesthetic is the decision to identify the poet's role at all. It goes without saying in the Suite 'Pórtico' that it is the poet who mediates experience. To mention him in 'Caracol' and, what is more, to identify him as the lyric poet, is to undermine the goal of creating independent poems, even though the reference here is not in the first person but in the third. Although there are first-person references in two other Suites in the set, 'Contemplación' (*OC*, I, p. 606) and 'Nocturno' (*OC*, I, p. 607), these do not emphasize the role, presence or centrality of the poet in the way that 'Caracol' does. In 'Contemplación', the 'Yo' is quickly rid of its agency by virtue of its objectification on the basis of its geometric associations with the shape of Corinthian capitals, columns and pine trees:

> Yo evoco
> el capitel corintio,
> la columna caída
> y los pinos.

The subsequent sudden shift to the third person brings into the equation the sea, the subject of the verb *cantar*, coaxing us into drawing associations between it and the first-person subject of the first four lines, although the precise nature of their relationship remains enigmatic:

> El mar clásico
> canta siempre en Estío
> y tiembla como el
> capitel corintio.

In 'Nocturno', on the other hand, although there is something more integral about the first-person subject of the verb *mirar*, the exclamatory responses to what is seen imply surprise rather than either the visionary prowess or controlling hand of the poet:

> Miro las estrellas
> sobre el mar.

¡Oh, las estrellas son de agua,
gotas de agua!

Miro las estrellas
sobre mi corazón.
¡Las estrellas son de aroma,
núcleos de aroma!

The stars seen by the subject are subsumed into enigmatic metaphors that empty them of their reality as heavenly bodies in the night sky, and the final couplet brings the Suite to a dead end, creating a contrast between the sparkling metaphors of the previous two stanzas and the stark reality of the shadowy ground: 'Miro la tierra / llena de sombra.' Both these poems differ from 'Caracol' in terms also of how they treat the sea. If in 'Caracol' the sea was put at the service of a metaphor of poetic discovery and creation, in 'Contemplación' and 'Nocturno' it seems to have a life of its own and is set in a relation of interaction with the first-person subject (with enigmatic consequences) rather than one of subservience to the goal of lauding the abilities of the poet. In the opening Suite of the set, '[El mar]' (*OC*, I, p. 605), the sea takes on a similarly autonomous aspect, acquiring volition and a seascape that reworks traditional mythological associations:

El mar
quiere levantar
su tapa.

Gigantes de coral
empujan
con sus espaldas.

Y en las cuevas de oro
las sirenas ensayan
una canción que duerma
al agua.
¿Veis las fauces
y las escamas?

Ante el mar
tomad vuestras lanzas.

Proposing menace, as opposed to the lyrical treasures of 'Caracol', the sea is set in an antagonistic relationship with the reader ('tomad vuestras lanzas'), which also reflects the difficulty of our penetrating the metaphor to arrive at the reality from which it sprang. In this respect, the mythological references to giants and mermaids, as well as playing on the shape of aquatic forms and the unreliability of our subaqueous vision, secure the independence of the poem from the sea as worldly reality.

The problem with the Suite 'Parque', ejected from the set 'Sombra', is, I would suggest, that it harks back to the sincerity and tropes of *Libro de poemas*. Walters (2002, p. 115) has seen the influence of the *greguería* in the eccentric images of other Suites in the set, where, for example, a bat is cast as 'the elixir of a shadow biting the heel of day' ('Murciélago', *OC*, I, p. 703) or a weeping willow is compared to Jeremiah ('Sauce', *OC*, I, p. 708). In 'Parque', by contrast, we have the reappearance of Pegasus, the most cherished of *modernista* symbols:

> Entre los árboles tronchados
> estaba el Pegaso muerto;
> en cada ojo tenía
> una flecha de sombra.
>
> Enorme araña tocaba
> la mandolina rota
> de aquella … ¡Oh Dios mío!
> ¡Es mejor guardar
> silencio!
>
> Y al pasar por las frondas
> del *Tú*, perdí mi anillo
> y mi corazón.

Rather than invention or play, we have here sorrow at the death of the winged horse, symbol of poetic flight and, of course, associated closely with the aestheticism of *modernismo*. In the second stanza, the broken mandolin presents yet another allusion to the silencing of creativity, echoed in the lyric subject's own calls for silence in lines 8 and 9. The elision of the noun in line 7 to convey emotional difficulty, along with the subsequent exclamation ('¡Oh Dios mío!'), is over-dramatic and forced, and yet consistent with the ethos of sincere self-expression that pervades the poem. To the loss expressed in the first two stanzas is added a loss associated even more closely with the poet in the third, that of his ring (symbolic of duty or vocation?) and his heart, that familiar romantic trope. To whomever we attribute the second-person pronoun '*Tú*', the expression of sorrow in the midst of images of creative loss is reminiscent of the uncertainties surrounding the abandonment of first-person lyricism in *Libro de poemas*, this Suite conveying nothing of the self-effacement required to allow poetry to speak for itself.

We need not, however, look only to rejected poems for evidence that Lorca was still in a transitional phase at the time he embarked on the project of his Suites or that he had misgivings about the self-effacement required to make that transition complete. The set '[Yo]' (*OC*, I, pp. 641–6), from December 1920, engages directly with the contentious figure of the first-person subject, and in so doing resists referentiality, like the set 'Caprichos', by focusing on the word, on the pronoun itself, while at the same time seeming to champion the first person which is cast as being under threat:

> YO
>
> ¡Ah fantasma esquelético,
> árbol lleno de nieve,
> chopo de todas
> las pasiones!
>
> No hay hacha que logre
> talar tu Madera,
> ni llama que abarque
> tus brazos enhiestos.
> Continúas siempre.
> Eres magnífico.
> Eterno.
>
> YO
>
> ¡Guardián de la humanidad!
> Espantaquerubes
> y espantavirtudes.
> Debieras llevar sable
> y casco.
>
> YO
>
> Imperativo.
> Nido
> del águila del Más.
>
> YO
>
> Me siento atravesado
> por la grave *Y* griega
> (bieldo de académicos,
> toro del alfabeto)
> y la *O* cual corona
> de tinta en mis pies.

All these Suites are, in effect, riddles, providing definitions or descriptions of an object not referred to by name in the text. The object is, however, referred to in the titles, the purpose of the game – and here it is a most serious game – not to guess its identity but instead to arrive at an adequate definition of it and thereby recognize the value of something which is in itself a riddle, so simple at the level of its two-letter sign and yet so enigmatic and complex in terms of what lies behind and beneath it: identity, desire, volition, the self, and so forth. In this way, the importance of all that the pronoun stands for is underscored, the point being perhaps that whether or not the first-person subject figures in a text, what is undeniable is that the consciousness it signals always plays its part, be it in life or in the creative act. Each Suite plays on the visual aspect of 'Yo'. The 'Y' is skeletal, tree-like, with two branches and a trunk; it has the form of a scarecrow or, by contrast, provides a nesting place for birds; it brings to mind the prongs of a rake or a bull's horns; its accompanying 'O' is presented as a crown. But beyond these formal associations lie more serious points.

In the first Suite of the set, the 'Yo' is a ghost, pointing to the intangible nature of consciousness, and in its tree-like form, associated with emotion ('las pasiones'), it is indestructible. Despite the material connotations of the tree-sign, neither axe nor flame can bring it down. It is magnificent and, significantly, eternal. In the second Suite, in the guise of scarecrow, what the 'Yo' guards is humanity, denoting all that pertains to the human realm, including, we might presume, emotion. Its adversaries are cherubim and virtues, the 'Yo' set in opposition to the heavenly, and the moral, the human, in opposition to the divine: an ironic allusion, perhaps, to the self's dogged resistance to precepts and maxims imposed from above. For this reason, it had better protect itself with a sabre and helmet. In the third Suite, the 'Yo' is an imperative, perhaps authoritative but most definitely essential, and the nesting place for the majestic eagle, the imperial bird whose empire here evokes transcendence and infinite possibilities, in recognition of the potentiality of human consciousness: 'el Más'. The final Suite differs from the others in the set because of its use of the first-person voice. The letters 'Y' and 'O' are cast as accoutrements in the martyrdom of the subject, with allusions to Christ's crucifixion: 'Me siento atravesado / por la grave *Y* griega'; 'y la *O* cual corona / de tinta en mis pies.' The first-person pronoun is a burden for the poet, but not necessarily one that he either wants or is able to shrug off. For if it weighs down on him it is precisely because he is aware of its significance as the sign, however arbitrary or vague, of all that he really is, and because it is central to his relationship with reality and art; an art which increasingly demands that modern poets turn away from reality and from the personal, the poet's engagement with which was hitherto epitomized by the self-affirming first-person 'I'. And so each of these Suites affirms the importance of the first-person subject, the pronoun that denotes it cast as eternal, terrestrial and imperative, a burden only because of the weight of its significance and because its status as the starting point for creative expression is under attack.

In a letter to his friend Melchor Fernández Almagro, dated 17 February 1922, just two days before he gave his lecture on *cante jondo* to the Arts Club in Granada, Lorca wrote of his desire to return to Madrid, but expressed his reservation, nonetheless, about the literary trends in the capital: 'Deseo ardientemente estar en la villa y corte,' he explained, 'aunque el actual ambiente literario me asquee terriblemente. Me siento muy lejano de la actual descomposición poética y sueño con un amanecer futuro que tenga la emoción inefable de los cielos primitivos. Me siento Ecuador entre la naranja y el limón' (*EC*, p. 143). Together in this letter we find Lorca's misgivings about current literary trends, but also what he has in common with them. His disparaging comments refer, perhaps, to the ludic excesses of the avant-garde, his own, more moderate, approach indicated by the metaphor in which he situates himself at a half-way point between sweetness and bitterness ('Ecuador entre la naranja y el limón'). The primitive skies that he mentions prefigure the subject matter of his lecture and are also in keeping with the trajectory of his collection *Poema del cante jondo* in as much as it centres on what he would describe in his lecture as the primitive song of Andalusia. But I would suggest that another key term here is 'inefable', as it points to the artistic endeavour of describing the indescribable, thus alluding both to the limitations of language and to the paradoxical attempt nonetheless to surpass them, a constant of the various -isms that held sway in the first decades of the twentieth century. In this context, the musical origin of the term 'suite' is significant. Walters (2002, pp. 102–3, and 2007, p. 80), after Belamich (p. 19), notes two musical models which Lorca had in mind when inventing his Suites: an eighteenth-century composition, with a variety of mood, whose movements are only loosely linked together; and an earlier version, 'the theme and variation', or 'diferencias' to use the Spanish term employed by Lorca, which possesses a greater sense of continuity and development. It is possible to see their respective influences in different Suites (see Walters 2002, p. 103, and 2007, p. 80), but what is most significant in the context of our discussion is that Lorca should have sought to adopt musical models at all. It is evidence, I would suggest, of his desire to find forms of organization for his poems that did not rely on conventional discursive and referential modes. To adopt a musical model was to aspire to capture for poetry something of the openness, elusive quality and evocative range of an art form which was not bound by the material fact of language: the word. The

Suites, in turn, provided a model for the poems of *Poema del cante jondo*. By describing his collection as a jigsaw puzzle (*'puzzle americano'*), in his January letter to Salazar, Lorca was highlighting that he had chosen for it a similarly alternative mode of organization; but with this collection he goes further still by making a musical art form its very subject, the poet's gaze, and the reader's, planted firmly not on the objects, emotions and events of the real world, at least not directly, but on the world of song and dance – a barrier, if you like, between us and the reality that inspired the verse of *cante jondo* in the first place. In any case, the themes treated by *cante jondo* form part of a well-established tradition that has emptied them of their historical specificity. It is with this tradition that Lorca engages, not as a means to convey anything about the present in respect of himself or anyone else, but quite simply as an end in itself, although it goes without saying that his endeavour, like his lecture, and the *Concurso* too, may have been designed to serve some purpose in terms of personal recognition and the advancement of his career.

In an article on the subject of Lorca's view of communication, Dennis Perri argues that in the 1920s 'the deep commitment to refashioning the language of poetry should not [...] imply that [...] artists denied or ignored the receptive pole of the aesthetic experience'.[11] 'I do not seek to reject', writes Perri, 'the presence of an intense desire by these artists to emphasize the formal features of their craft; rather I wish to demonstrate that this stress does not negate the presence of an equally persistent attention to the receptive pole of communication' (Perri 1992, p. 484). Whether or not we agree with him – and his is perhaps a valid point given Lorca's natural inclination to give recitals of his work – two observations emerge from his argument, which are particularly relevant to our discussion. Firstly, he attributes Lorca's fascination with *cante jondo* to the 'terseness and purity which differentiated it from the exaggerated expression of Romanticism' (Perri 1992, p. 485), reminding us of Lorca's self-inclusion in his lecture among the number of poets preoccupied with 'la poda y cuidado del demasiado frondoso árbol lírico que nos dejaron los románticos y los postrománticos' (*OC*, III, p. 205). Secondly, he argues that Lorca '[c]ommitted to avoiding the Romantics' reliance on the direct expression of subjectivity by the poetic "*yo*," [...] finds in the *cante jondo* a poetic voice who is able to communicate with the audience in a special way' (Perri 1992, p. 485). It is not that either the first-person voice or its subject pronoun are absent from *Poema del cante jondo*, but rather that that the 'yo' has been reconfigured. For Perri, the nature of this

---

[11]  Dennis Perri, 'Fulfillment and Loss: Lorca's View of Communication in the Twenties', *Hispania* 75.3 (September 1992), 484–91 (p. 484).

reconfiguration can be comprehended in the following extract from Lorca's lecture: 'El «cantaor», cuando canta, celebra un solemne rito, saca las viejas esencias dormidas y las lanza al viento envueltas en su voz ..., tiene un profundo sentimiento religioso del canto. La raza se vale de ellos para dejar escapar su dolor y su historia verídica' (*OC*, I, p. 215). What Perri (1992, p. 485) concludes is that '[t]he art of *cante jondo* which Lorca admired presents a reciprocal relationship in which the singer both embodies and recasts the values and beliefs of the audience', the implication being that voice in *Poema del cante jondo* does the same thing.[12] In effect, the poetic voice and language of *cante jondo* are, according to Perri (1992, p. 485), 'the model of a religious ritual which touches the very soul of its participants' and not, importantly, 'the model for the ironic, modern voice of the "new" poetry'. Therefore, although Perri relates Lorca's fascination with *cante jondo* to the avant-garde rejection of the verbosity and sentimentality of subjective, romantic lyricism, the connection between the traditional and the modern seems less secure in the context of what he deems to be the communal character of the former. And yet a slight shift in emphasis demonstrates that there are connections even in this respect. For what *cante jondo* provides Lorca with is a voice that is not specific to one body; one that is dispersed, subsumed into the tradition of an art form that has been passed down over generations. The poet, to borrow a phrase from Antonio Machado y Álvarez, 'desaparece [...] para confundirse en las multitudes de voces anónimas'.[13] This is not to say that the voice in *Poema del cante jondo* is not Lorca's at the point of articulation, but rather that it is not wholly his, so identified is it with songs that are in the public domain. Thus, somewhat paradoxically, the communal aspect of *cante jondo*, along with the economical character of its expression, allows Lorca to connect with the modern, impersonal ethos of the avant-garde via the traditional art form of his native land.

Lorca's claim that other poets had never dealt with the theme of *cante jondo* seems to have been more than a little disingenuous. The inevitable point of comparison, as Morris (p. 192) indicates, is Manuel Machado's *Cante hondo* (1912), but whereas Machado's work tends to remain faithful to the topics and form of *cante jondo*, thus producing, in Morris's opinion (p. 193), a poetry that is contrived, pedestrian and often limited to listing

---

[12] Rob Stone, in his *The Flamenco Tradition in the Works of Federico García Lorca and Carlos Saura: The Wounded Throat* (Lewiston, Queenston and Lampeter: The Edwin Meller Press, 2004), 52, responds to the same extract from Lorca's lecture by suggesting that 'Lorca's vision of himself adhered to his definition of the *cantaor* as *portavoz* for the common people.'

[13] Antonio Machado y Álvarez (Demófilo), *Poesía popular* (Seville: Francisco Álvarez, 1883), 67.

the components of *cante* styles, what Lorca does in *Poema del cante jondo* is evoke its spirit, and in this respect his claim to novelty is at least partially justified. As Walters (2002, p. 122) explains, 'despite his high regard for the poetry of *cante jondo* [Lorca] never incorporates it verbatim in his book. Only occasionally does he adopt its lexical mannerisms or turns of phrase.' Morris and Walters both identify melisma – vocal modulation on a single syllable, characteristic of *cante jondo* – as a precedent and prompt for the 'repetition, variation and irregularities of meter and form' (Morris, p. 212) in Lorca's collection, a key example of the poet's interpretative approach to *cante jondo*'s style and technique. What he aims for is 'an equivalence of effect', which is 'another way of saying that detail matters less than impact: that we should acquire an experience from reading the poetry akin to that of hearing song, or, better, witnessing the spectacle, of *cante jondo*' (Walters, 2002, p. 122). What is significant too, in the context of contemporary trends, is that this experience should be an artistic one: one that is removed, as I have already argued, from the worldly experiences which inspired the songs of *cante jondo* in the first place.

Four sets of poems in *Poema del cante jondo* focus on specific forms, or styles, of *cante jondo*, namely the *siguiriya gitana*, *soleá*, *saeta* and *petenera* respectively. Each set presents an array of moments, images, themes and moods that convey the character and spirit of the songs they allude to. Their poems correspond to the pieces of puzzles which in their entirety depict the styles in question, kinds of extensions to the riddles which we saw in the Suites. Fittingly, the first set, 'Poema de la siguiriya gitana' (*OC*, I, pp. 155–63), is devoted to the style which Lorca singles out in his lecture on the grounds of its authenticity and primary status among other styles of the genre: 'Se da nombre de *cante jondo* a un grupo de canciones andaluzas cuyo tipo genuino y perfecto es la siguiriya gitana, de las que derivan otras canciones aún conservadas por el pueblo' (*OC*, III, p. 196).[14] Norman Miller provides a description of the *siguiriya* which, as we will see, demonstrates that Lorca took into account the structure of its performance when piecing his puzzle together:

> The *siguiriya gitana* begins with a guitar introduction that helps establish the mood of the song. The guitar prelude, called a *temple*, is followed by a prolonged *quejío* or *grito* of the singer who dramatizes the emotions to

---

[14] For Walters (2002, p. 125), '"Poema de la siguiriya gitana" is the evocation of performance, "Poema de la soleá", the evocation of narrative, and "Poema de la saeta", the evocation of festivity.'

be expressed in the lyrics. The *quejío* is often [...] succeeded by a silence which is then followed by two *coplas* [...]. These are generally sung on an emotionally ascending scale and may be interrupted at any point by exclamations, cries of *¡ay!*, or by sudden, unexpected silences which often come after the moments of greatest emotional intensity [...]. The song ends with the gradual fading away of the singer's voice and the guitar accompaniment.[15]

Miller (p. 28) also points out that its lyrics 'are especially noted for their tragic content, for the *siguiriya* is, above all, a song of despair'. 'Las más infinitas gradaciones del Dolor y la Pena', declared Lorca, 'laten en los tercetos y cuartetos de la siguiriya y sus derivados' (*OC*, III, p. 205). It is perhaps no coincidence, then, that the poet of *Libro de poemas*, a collection which he declared to be laden with emotion that sprang from 'mi tristeza y el dolor que siento ante la naturaleza' (*EC*, p. 50), should have become fascinated with a genre so closely associated with sorrow. Significantly, however, the expression of sorrow is no longer verbose, nor is its vehicle the singular voice of the poet.

In 'Paisaje' (*OC*, I, p. 157), the first poem of 'Poema de la siguiriya gitana' – the first piece of the puzzle – the subject of emotion is not human, but an animate landscape of sunken skies, cold stars, trembling reeds, grey air, captive birds, twilight, shadow and bitter olives:

> El campo
> de olivos
> se abre y se cierra
> como un abanico.
> Sobre el olivar
> hay un cielo hundido
> y una lluvia oscura
> de luceros fríos.
> Tiembla junco y penumbra
> a la orilla del río.
> Se riza el aire gris.
> Los olivos
> están cargados
> de gritos.
> Una bandada
> de pájaros cautivos,
> que mueven sus larguísimas
> colas en lo sombrío.

---

[15] Norman C. Miller, *García Lorca's 'Poema del cante jondo'* (London: Tamesis Books, 1978), 28.

Sentiment, however, is at most only an equal partner of invention, which manifests itself in the poem's construction of simile and metaphor. Of particular significance is the poem's initial simile, which compares olive fields to the opening and closing of a fan, a familiar folkloric motif. The effect is to imbue the land with movement, an allusion, perhaps, to an undulating terrain. This movement is taken up later in the poem by the verbs *temblar*, *rizarse* and *mover*, echoes which contribute to a confusion of the natural and the artificial, of the landscape and the fan. On the one hand, the self-contained images divided into punctuated groups of between one and four lines are reminiscent of the fan's folds; on the other, the movements these images convey are evocative of the fan's swaying. Thus we are taken to and away from the world via an object closely associated with Andalusian custom. Rather more than a setting for what is about to come, 'Paisaje' is a prelude in its own right. It is one that is filled with feeling and invention, a twist of the hand twinning the movement of nature with the movement of a fan – an object which we might readily associate with the audience or performers of *cante jondo*.

In the next poem, 'La guitarra' (*OC*, I, p. 158), we find the *temple*, to which Miller refers. The guitar, emblematic of the *siguiriya* and of *cante jondo* more generally, replaces the first-person lyric subject in the expression of sadness and pain:

> Empieza el llanto
> de la guitarra.
> Se rompen las copas
> de la madrugada.
> Empieza el llanto
> de la guitarra.
> Es inútil
> callarla.
> Es imposible
> callarla.
> Llora monótona
> como llora el agua,
> como llora el viento
> sobre la nevada.
> Es imposible callarla.
> Llora por cosas
> lejanas.
> Arena del Sur caliente
> que pide camelias blancas.
> Llora flecha sin blanco,
> la tarde sin mañana,

> y el primer pájaro muerto
> sobre la rama.
> ¡Oh guitarra!
> Corazón malherido
> por cinco espadas.

Through a process of personification, the guitar transcends its character as inorganic object, as mere instrument, and becomes the very mouthpiece of sorrow and the subject of the verb *llorar*, the claim 'Es imposible / callarla' similarly endowing it with an aura of autonomy. The similes comparing it with natural elements ('el agua', 'el viento') also contribute to its transcendence of the inorganic and the functional. In his lecture, Lorca spoke of how the *siguiriya* evoked for him 'el camino donde murió el primer pájaro y se llenó de herrumbre la primera flecha' (*OC*, III, p. 198). These images are present here too, augmenting the personality of the guitar by suggesting that pain and frustration are both the origin and end of its song. In the final two lines, a human subject – the guitar player – is introduced, but only indirectly via metonymy and metaphor. The five swords are the five fingers of the playing hand, making the association between artistic creation and the opening of wounds, although the dominant aesthetic prevents this from giving rise to the first-person lyrical outpourings we once saw in *Libro de poemas*. Indeed, it is not the emotions of either the poet or the guitarist that are on display, but instead those of the guitar itself, defined in these lines as the heart. Suffering is thus displaced from its human origin onto the realm of song and the body of the guitar, just as the emotional world of the poet is subsumed into impersonal images and metaphors in a poem which at best speaks for, but never as, him.

The third poem in the set presents us with the shout, the *quejío* or *grito*. In his lecture, Lorca describes how the *siguiriya* proper begins with 'un grito terrible, un grito que divide el paisaje en dos hemisferios ideales. Es el grito de las generaciones muertas, la aguda elegía de los siglos desaparecidos, es la patética evocación del amor bajo otras lunas y otros vientos' (*OC*, III, p. 198). This shout, then, signifies for him more than a vocalization in the present by a specific body; indeed, it broadens the notion of communality to include past generations, combining, in an instant, performance, history and tradition. The shout in 'El grito' (*OC*, I, p. 159) is appropriately, therefore, not tied to a specific individual. The repetition of the exclamatory '¡Ay!' is disembodied and although human figures do make an appearance, it is as spectators, not performers:

> La elipse de un grito
> va de monte
> a monte.
>
> Desde los olivos
> será un arco iris negro
> sobre la noche azul.
>
> ¡Ay!
>
> Como un arco de viola
> el grito ha hecho vibrar
> largas cuerdas de viento.
>
> ¡Ay!
>
> (Las gentes de las cuevas
> asoman sus velones.)
>
> ¡Ay!

The shout is disconnected from an articulating subject by virtue of the poem's focus not on any point of origin but on shape. It is described in terms of an ellipse travelling from hill to hill, a geometrical form which is recast first as a rainbow, its black colour consistent with its sorrowful character, and then as the bow of a viola. Here both the shout and the wind, which is plucked like the strings of a musical instrument, are associated with the musical domain, thus shifting the emphasis away from the representation of nature onto that of art.

In the remaining four poems of the set, the focus on the art form is maintained. As pieces of the puzzle, they continue to complete the picture of the *siguiriya*, which in its totality conveys the song's constituent elements, alluding to its structure, progression and dramatic moments. Although in 'El silencio' (*OC*, I, p. 160), the first-person subject appears initially to be more intrusive than in previous poems of the set, its intrusion represents no more than a fleeting moment in a poem that centres on the paradoxically replete character of silence:

> Oye, hijo mío, el silencio.
> Es un silencio ondulado,
> un silencio,
> donde resbalan valles y ecos
> y que inclina las frentes
> hacia el suelo.

The silence corresponds to the dramatic pause following the first sounds of the guitar and the opening cry, and is therefore meaningful by virtue of being integral to the performance. Human figures ('frentes') are alluded to only in terms of their reaction to the moment, and not at the level of either performance or self-expression. In the next poem, 'El paso de la siguiriya' (*OC*, I, p. 161), the human is put at the service of art, a young girl serving to personify the *siguiriya*:

> Entre mariposas negras,
> va una muchacha morena
> junto a una blanca serpiente
> de niebla.

> *Tierra de luz,*
> *cielo de tierra.*

> Va encadenada al temblor
> de un ritmo que nunca llega;
> tiene el corazón de plata
> y un puñal en la diestra.

> ¿Adónde vas, siguiriya,
> con un ritmo sin cabeza?
> ¿Qué luna recogerá
> tu dolor de cal y adelfa?

> *Tierra de luz,*
> *cielo de tierra.*

Just as in 'El grito' we found a black rainbow, here we have black butterflies, the unreality of this image consistent with the aim of evoking the tone and mood of the *siguiriya*, which are plainly sombre. The image of an accompanying 'white snake of mist' has an ominous feel about it, as does the reference, in the second stanza, to the dagger the young girl is holding and, in the third, to her pain, associated here with lime and the poisonous oleander, in a phrase which perhaps has its origin in *una de cal y otra de arena*, a saying evoking sets of opposites or incongruous elements. The refrain '*Tierra de luz, / cielo de tierra*', a stock device of *cante jondo*, is equally paradoxical, reinforcing the unreality of other images while also having a rhythmic function, rhythm itself being a thematic concern of the poem. The notion of a rhythm 'que nunca llega' may allude to the way in which the *siguiriya*'s rhythm is broken up by its disparate metre or its many constituent parts, while its association with a tremor, to which the *siguiriya* is captive, reminds us of the use of *temblar* in 'Paisaje' and *vibrar* in 'El grito', underscoring the visceral character of the song and of the responses it induces. This aspect is picked up also by the 'headless' rhythm in the third stanza, a rhythm that is instinctual, not cerebral. Altogether this poem is a good example of the way in which Lorca attempts the impossible: to convey a sense of the character of *cante jondo*, here the *siguiriya*, by alluding to its mood, themes and rhythm in imagistic terms. What is more, although he brings a young girl into view, or even butterflies, a snake, a dagger or oleander, we soon realize, once again, that he is inviting us to gaze not upon reality but on art.

'Poema de la siguiriya gitana' is brought to an end by two poems which together reflect the characteristic fading away of the song. In the first, 'Después de pasar' (*OC*, I, p. 162), the end is signalled by a point in the distance upon which all looks are fixed:

> Los niños miran
> un punto lejano.
>
> Los candiles se apagan.
> Unas muchachas ciegas
> preguntan a la luna,
> y por el aire ascienden
> espirales de llanto.
>
> Las montañas miran
> un punto lejano.

The sense of ending is conveyed also by the extinguishing of oil lamps, situating the performance at night, as did the lamps in 'El grito', while the spirals of cries cohere with the motif of undulation and reverberation echoing throughout the set. The final poem, 'Y después' (*OC*, I, p. 163), brings the performance to a close, emphasizing the evanescence of the elements integral to the reality of the song:

> Los laberintos
> que crea el tiempo,
> se desvanecen.
>
> (Solo queda
> el desierto.)
>
> El corazón,
> fuente del deseo,
> se desvanece.
>
> (Solo queda
> el desierto.)

> La ilusión de la aurora
> y los besos,
> se desvanecen.
>
> Solo queda el desierto.
> Un ondulado
> desierto.

If in 'El silencio', the adjective 'ondulado' suggested the replete character of the pause in proceedings, here, in its qualification of 'desierto', it conveys, at most, the traces left by song. The desolation for which the desert is a sign emphasizes, by contrast, the power and reality of the performance: a parenthesis to the humdrum of everyday life, with its own sense of time ('laberintos / que crea el tiempo'), and a space for emotion ('corazón') and hope ('ilusión'). Given that 'Y después' is a final note not only to the performance of the *siguiriya* but also to the poems of the set, one wonders whether poetry and the poetic process themselves are just as powerful and real, experiences just as parenthetical, in the mind of the poet.

In addition to the sets of poems evoking specific *cante jondo* styles, *Poema del cante jondo* contains other groupings that bring together variations on the setting, personalities, objects, motifs and mood of deep song. Among them is the set entitled 'Seis caprichos' (*OC*, I, pp. 215–22). In its six poems there is clearly a ludic aspect as well as the by now familiar privileging of artifice over the depiction of reality. Although the Spanish for riddle (*adivinanza*) appears only in the title of the first poem, 'Adivinanza de la guitarra' (*OC*, I, p. 217), all six have the quality of riddles, albeit riddles already deciphered, the emphasis being not on our guessing but rather, in a thoroughly self-conscious twist, on the poetic accomplishment inherent in the invention of similes and metaphors. In 'Adivinanza de la guitarra', the metaphor centres on the relation between the guitar's sound hole and its strings:

> En la redonda
> encrucijada,
> seis doncellas
> bailan.
> Tres de carne
> y tres de plata.
> Los sueños de ayer las buscan,
> pero las tiene abrazadas
> un Polifemo de oro.
> ¡La guitarra!

The place where strings and sound hole intersect is conveyed by the oxymoron 'round crossroads' ('redonda / encrucijada'), while the reverberation of plucked strings is evoked by the appropriately musical and rhythmic act of dance ('bailan'). More striking is the way in which the strings are embodied by six dancing maidens in the clutches of a gold Polyphemus. The Cyclops' inferred single eye is an unspoken allusion to the sound hole, while his golden colour evokes the gloss finish of the body of the guitar.

Whether 'Adivinanza de la guitarra' is anything more than a clever conceit based on the imaginative treatment of the relation between the shapes of the guitar's constituent parts is debatable. Beyond the geometrical, the image of a one-eyed monster guarding maidens from the dreams of yesteryear ('sueños de ayer') may serve to make a philosophical point by emphasizing the physicality and immediacy of performance in contrast, or even as an antidote, to the immaterial and ephemeral character of dreams. Equally we might claim that the image communicates something of the tension and anxiety of the sad songs of *cante jondo* centring on love and death. And yet the poet's very recourse to a classical figure, somewhat out of place in the context of *cante jondo*, seems to me to suggest that the dictates of metaphorical invention were more pressing even than the desire to convey something specific about the nature of the musical art form itself.

There are other places in *Poema del cante jondo* where the poet employs references that lie outside the ambit of what we might readily associate with either Andalusia or *cante jondo*. A case in point is the poem 'Procesión' (*OC*, I, p. 182), from the set 'Poema de la saeta' (*OC*, I, pp.177–86), in which mythological and literary figures combine in an unconventional treatment of a typical Holy Week scene:[16]

> Por la calleja vienen
> extraños unicornios.
> ¿De qué campo,
> de qué bosque mitológico?
> Más cerca,
> ya parecen astrónomos.
> Fantásticos Merlines
> y el Ecce Homo,
> Durandarte encantado,
> Orlando furioso.

---

[16] For a history of the *saeta* and Lorca's interpretation of this religious song, see Edward F. Stanton, *The Tragic Myth: Lorca and 'Cante Jondo'* (Lexington: University of Kentucky, 1978), 90–111.

The references to unicorns, astronomers and to Merlin pick up on the pointed shape of the hoods of the penitents accompanying the float bearing the figure of the suffering Christ ('Ecce Homo') and lend a fabulous air to the moving procession, as do the noble, if unusual, associations of Christ's figure with Roland and his sword, Durendal. For Morris (p. 254), this and other poems of *Poema del cante jondo* are examples of how the collection 'demonstrates repeatedly that the key to Lorca's treatment of Andalusia is adaptation and interpretation: of words, songs, and spectacles. Too many writers', adds Morris, 'have focused on its surface: Lorca saw through it, beneath it, using it as a starting-point rather than an end in itself.' We might go further still and argue that what poems like 'Procesión' or 'Adivinanza de la guitarra' demonstrate is that the reality which inspired their images is less important than the resultant images themselves. The poet, in his pursuit of ingenious metaphors, thus makes use of the full range of references he has at his disposal, even though they may be extraneous to the specific cultural context of the subject at hand. For this reason, we should not be surprised to find Daphne and Attis in the poem 'Chumbera' (*OC*, I, p. 220), another of the 'Seis caprichos', in which a prickly pear is cast both as Laocoön and as a player of the Basque ball game known as *pelota vasca*:

> Laoconte salvaje.
>
> ¡Qué bien estás
> bajo la media luna!
>
> Múltiple pelotari.
>
> ¡Qué bien estás
> amenazando al viento!
>
> Dafne y Atis,
> saben de tu dolor.
> Inexplicable.

It has been suggested that the origin of the association of a prickly pear with the Trojan priest is actually an art work: the group representing Laocoön and his sons sculpted by Athenodoros of Rhodes, the outline of which apparently resembles the wild cactus.[17] The multitudinous pears attached to the cactus are, in turn, at the source of the connection with the game *pelota*, each becoming a ball thrown and struck by the *pelotari* whose movement is

---

[17] See the edition of *Poema del Cante Jondo* and *Romancero gitano* by Allen Josephs and Juan Caballero, 7th edn (Madrid: Cátedra, 1984), 202, n. 1.

frozen in time and space, as still in the image as the cactus's multiple arms raised menacingly against the wind. Lorca has invented his own myth, that of Laocoön's transformation into a prickly pear, thus resurrecting the priest from the waters where he and his sons were killed by the two monstrous sea serpents that also figure in Athenodoros's sculpture. The metamorphosis is mirrored by the presence of Daphne and Attis. Just as Daphne was transformed into a laurel tree to escape Apollo's advances, the Phrygian deity was himself reborn as an evergreen pine after his brutal murder near that very tree (see Jobes, vol. 1, p. 154). Implicit in each of these mythological transformations is a release from emotional turmoil, which is recast in the tree-metamorphoses of *Libro de poemas* as the expurgation of lyrical sentiment en route to creating dehumanized art. In 'Chumbera', to single out Daphne and Attis as having the ability to understand Laocoön's pain is to acknowledge that the poem's metaphorical images are the product of such an expurgation. For what is left clearly privileges visual associations (Athenodoros's statues, prickly pears, *pelotari*) over the human stories connected with the figures. If the poem ends with the single-word line 'Inexplicable', it is perhaps to emphasize that it invents images not explanations. The poet's work is to imagine, while it is up to the reader to piece the images together.

The remaining four poems of 'Seis caprichos' are equally concerned with inventing images. In 'Candil' (*OC*, I, 218), the simile which compares the flame of an oil lamp to an Indian fakir can be understood in the context of the connections Lorca made between *cante jondo*, a mystical Orient and primitive Indian culture ('los primitivos sistemas musicales de la India') in his lecture on the subject:

> ¡Oh, qué grave medita
> la llama del candil!
>
> Como un faquir indio
> mira su entraña de oro
> y se eclipsa soñando
> atmósferas sin viento.
>
> Cigüeña incandescente
> pica desde su nido
> a las sombras macizas,
> y se asoma temblando
> a los ojos redondos
> del gitanillo muerto.

In the final stanza, the fakir's disappearing trick is followed by another metaphorical image as the flame is cast as a stork, its colour, shape and movement now rendered by the bird's yellow and pecking beak. The fact that it should light up the face of a dead gypsy boy adds a further twist by virtue of the poem's manipulation of the stork's popular associations, the bird now becoming a witness not to maternity, as is the convention, but to death.

'Crótalo' (*OC*, I, 219) is the appropriately onomatopoeic title of the next poem, which conjures up the sound and also the shape and colour of traditional castanets:

> Crótalo.
> Crótalo.
> Crótalo.
> Escarabajo sonoro.
>
> En la araña
> de la mano
> rizas el aire
> cáildo,
> y te ahogas en tu trino
> de palo.
>
> Crótalo.
> Crótalo.
> Crótalo.
> Escarabajo sonoro.

With its references to living creatures – the rattlesnake ('crótalo'), beetle ('escarabajo') and spider ('araña') – the poem lends the playing of castanets a bizarre and independent life, the only allusion to the human performer coming synecdochically in the mention of a hand which is, in any case, rendered unfamiliar by a metaphorical, arachnidan qualification: 'la araña / de la mano'. If the beetle picks up on the black, rounded shape of castanets, the rattlesnake evokes their sound. The onomatopoeic character of the word *crótalo* is used to maximum effect through its repetition at the start and end. The poem's overall symmetry serves visually and sonorously to frame the movement connected with the central stanza, namely the flourish or gesture by which hands and castanets create the sound that instantaneously surrounds them. 'Pita' (*OC*, I, 221) also makes use of an animal reference, this time to conjure up the form of the agave or pita:

> Pulpo petrificado.
>
> Pones cinchas cenicientas
> al vientre de los montes,
> y muelas formidables
> a los desfiladeros.
>
> Pulpo petrificado.

The succulent is cast as an octopus, the oxymoronic combination of the underwater creature and petrifaction alluding both to the plant's fleshiness and sap and to its rigid forms and immobile state. And in the pursuit of images the agave also becomes other things: at once ash-coloured saddle straps stretched around the bellies of mountains and formidable teeth lining the mouths of ravines.

The final poem of 'Seis caprichos', 'Cruz' (*OC*, I, 222), approaches the symbolism of the cross in specifically literary terms:

> La cruz.
> (Punto final
> del camino.)
>
> Se mira en la acequia.
> (Puntos suspensivos.)

The poem, in just a few meagre lines, combines a number of familiar signs and tropes to create an intriguing conceit. The cross, if it is to be understood as signalling death, does indeed mark the end of the road and serve as a full stop to the text of our lives; yet reflected in an irrigation channel, that full stop becomes a series of dots, an ellipsis, an open ending.... Now the cross seems to signal the possibility of an afterlife, while also, in the context of the poem's literary references, alluding to the open-ended nature of textual practice: 'Cruz', along with the series of caprices that it brings to an end, will be subject to constant re-readings and signification in what might be suitably termed its literary afterlife. The reflection in the water conveys this lack of fixity and limitation, as well as reminding us of the transformative possibilities of art, which takes reality and turns it into an evocative and significant other.

'Me siento Ecuador entre la naranja y el limón,' wrote Lorca to his friend Fernández Almagro, in a letter which perhaps conveyed, as we have already noted, the poet's more balanced approach in face of what he termed 'la actual descomposición poética'. The desire to negotiate rather than plump for one line or another is arguably what characterizes *Poema del cante jondo*, engaging as it does both with local popular culture and with contemporary trends where the latter engagement implies, amongst other things, 'la poda y cuidado del demasiado frondoso árbol lírico'. Consequently this negotiation must also be between life experience and art, the former not rejected out of hand but taking a significantly artistic turn in as much as it enters the collection only in the form of *cante jondo*, by virtue of the treatment of its performance and the evocation of its traditional context and themes. Lorca no doubt benefited personally from this negotiation, and yet the combination of passion and self-control which it implies landed the poet in the strangest of places, one in which not giving oneself over to either could create uneasy tensions. It is this kind of tension which is played out in the section 'Dos muchachas', comprising two poems: 'La Lola' (*OC*, I, p. 199) and 'Amparo' (*OC*, I, p. 200). In the first of these depictions of contrary women and ideas, what is celebrated, it seems, is the experience of the vitality of nature, life and love:

> Bajo el naranjo lava
> pañales de algodón.
> Tiene verdes los ojos
> y violeta la voz.
>
> ¡Ay, amor,
> bajo el naranjo en flor!
>
> El agua de la acequia
> iba llena de sol,
> en el olivarito
> cantaba un gorrión.
>
> ¡Ay, amor,
> bajo el naranjo en flor!
>
> Luego, cuando la Lola
> gaste todo el jabón,
> vendrán los torerillos.
>
> ¡Ay, amor,
> bajo el naranjo en flor!

Lola is tied to nature via her maternity (she is washing nappies and presumably the little bullfighters are her children) and by her place amidst the orange and olive trees, as well as sun-filled irrigation channels and the sparrow's song. Her eyes and her voice are described in vivid colour: green and violet respectively. And yet the poem's refrain, with its ever so poignant cry, although it might at a stretch be read as a reaffirmation of the poem's vital elements, seems rather to have been launched from the perspective of their possible, imminent or actual loss. Amparo's poem goes on to make sense of this ambiguity, for in her world what we find are the actual consequences of removing oneself from the domain of Lola's experiences:

> Amparo,
> ¡qué sola estás en tu casa
> vestida de blanco!

(Ecuador entre el jazmín
y el nardo.)

Oyes los maravillosos
surtidores de un patio,
y el débil trino amarillo
del canario.

Por la tarde ves temblar
los cipreses con los pájaros,
mientras bordas lentamente
letras sobre el cañamazo.

Amparo,
¡qué sola estás en tu casa,
vestida de blanco!
Amparo,
¡y qué difícil decirte:
yo te amo!

Amparo lives in solitude, the whiteness of her dress (in contrast to Lola's colours) conveying coldness rather more than it does either purity or innocence. In lines which echo Federico's words to his friend Melchor, this whiteness is reprised in the mention of jasmine and tuberose. The references here are more subtle than Lorca's equatorial balancing of oranges and lemons, since each flower is the same colour and ambiguous in meaning. As Salazar Rincón (pp. 390, 393) points out, both flowers can allude metaphorically to either coldness or sex and passion, although he adds that in the tuberose such associations may be accompanied by connotations of frustration. The fact that jasmine is also a climbing plant might align it with freedom in relative terms to the less adventurous tuberose. In any event, what is clear from the rest of the poem is that Amparo's associations are with moderation and restraint. She is not totally cut off from the vitality of the natural world, for she can hear the water from the fountains of her patio and the faint trill of a canary. Yet both these sources of sound also connote limitation: the water is subject to the patio's order and design, while the canary conjures up the image of a caged bird. In the afternoon the cypresses and birds which Amparo sees are similarly robbed of their vitality by virtue of these trees' funereal associations (see Chevalier and Gheerbrant, p. 271) and the use of the verb *temblar* to indicate their movement. Amparo most definitely finds herself somewhere between jasmine and tuberose, where these flowers suggest promise and its frustration respectively. Most significantly, Amparo passes the time slowly embroidering letters onto canvas, in contrast to Lola's nappy-washing.[18] This embroidery is, in effect, a form of writing and raises the possibility that Amparo is none other than Lorca's equatorial kin. Her place of containment, moderation and control (the very product of lyricism pruned) is perhaps equivalent to Lorca's compromise, to his negotiation of life and art, which is ultimately a rejection of Lola's openly passionate 'violet' voice in favour of a more restrained and economical approach. It no doubt represents a necessarily contemporary approach, but one with which the poet, as ever, does not seem totally comfortable: '¡y qué difícil decirte: / yo te amo!'

---

[18] In this respect Amparo is perhaps the prototype for the gypsy nun in *Romancero gitano*. See 'La monja gitana', *OC*, I, 404–5.

# 3

# *Canciones*: Autonomy and Self

> the artist seeks his personal authenticity in his entire
> autonomousness – his goal is to be as self-defining
> as the art-object he creates.
> (Lionel Trilling, *Sincerity and Authenticity*)

*Canciones*, published in 1927, contains many poems that are contemporaneous with the Suites. Written between 1921 and 1925 (see Walters 2002, p. 136), they head similarly in the direction of syntactical simplification and the eradication of emotionalism, 'towards an aesthetic', as Walters (2002, p. 137) puts it, 'that implied economy, understatement, detachment'. This minimalist approach contributes, as it did in both the Suites and *Poema del cante jondo*, to the independent character of poems that privilege metaphor over discursiveness. There is, once again, a ludic aspect in all this, combined also with a double perspective characterized by Walters as that of the child and the poet respectively. 'To the child,' writes Walters (2002, p. 143), 'falls the role of sentient observer; to the poet belongs the role of registering, rationalizing, however minimal this may be.' This perspective will no doubt have its psychological aspect, implicit in the collection's 'obsessive regard for the child's world and the problems that arise on departing from it' (Walters 2002, p. 251). Yet it also has important aesthetic consequences. For adopting the simple utterances of children facilitates the minimalist character of poems; while the naivety of the childlike perspective keeps at bay the needs and sensibilities of adult selfhood, thus contributing to the elimination of emotionalism and the project of depersonalization.

It would be a mistake, however, to think that Lorca was any more reconciled in *Canciones* with the precepts of impersonal art than he had been in his previous work. In a reader-oriented approach to the collection, Dennis Perri (1995, p. 190) identifies *Canciones* 'as a space in which heterogeneity and diversity prevail', a contributing factor being the very instability in the distance and tone of the speaker. 'He appears', writes Perri (1995, p. 190), 'to be testing out methods and techniques for talking to the reader without ever sinking into exaggerated sentimentality, or concealing every trace of subjectivity.' However, what Perri attributes to experimentation with method and technique might also be viewed as a struggle. Although there is plenty of evidence to suggest that Lorca was pleased with *Canciones*, in a much cited letter to Melchor Fernández Almagro, dated 9 December 1926, he makes the following damning appraisal of his poetry in general: 'Todo me parece lamentable en mi poesía. En cuanto que *no he expresado* ni puedo *expresar* mi pensamiento. Hallo calidades turbias donde debiera haber luz fija y encuentro en todo una dolorosa ausencia de mi *propia* y *verdadera* persona. Así estoy. Necesito irme lejos' (*EC*, p. 395).[1] It is not easy to hit on the precise meaning of these words, as Walters (2002, p. 139) has pointed out; but what we can say with some confidence is that they reveal a perception of poetry that does not banish notions of self-expression and self. It is an ironic coincidence, no doubt, that Lorca should complain of the absence in his work of his true self precisely when the general predilection is for impersonal art. Eliot (1986, p. 54) wrote that 'the more perfect the artist, the more completely separate in him will be the man who suffers and the mind which creates; the more perfectly will the mind digest and transmute the passions which are its material'. He wrote also that '[t]he progress of an artist is a continual self-sacrifice, a continual extinction of personality' (Eliot 1986, p. 53). With *Canciones*, Lorca continues to make that progress, but he does so, as ever, self-consciously. The result is a work that often displays the very processes of extinction and elimination that are instrumental in depersonalization; a work in which the sacrifice about which Eliot writes is still strangely connected to a traditionally lyrical voice that finds it painful to let go. Perri (1995, p. 176), perhaps, notes something of this in his awareness of the hybridity of a collection which, like Suites and *Poema del cante jondo*, brings traditional elements into contact with the exigencies of avant-garde or, as he puts it, modernist aesthetics:

> *Canciones* can be seen as a point of convergence for several ideological and cultural currents of the twenties. On the one hand, the ironic tone, the attempts at abstraction, the imagistic emphasis in certain sections or

---

[1] Compare the crisis evoked here with his positive outlook in a much earlier letter to Fernández Almagro, from January 1926, when he was planning to publish three collections for the following year – *Suites, Poema del cante jondo* and *Canciones* – of which, of course, only *Canciones* would make publication in 1927 (see Gibson 1989, pp. 168–9): 'He trabajado en el arreglo de mis libros. Son tres. *Depuradísimos*. Las cosas que van en ellos son las que deben ir. El libro que me ha salido de canciones cortas es interesante' (*EC*, p. 318). In another letter to Fernández Almagro, one year later, the poet is equally positive about his work, despite the qualification in brackets: 'este libro de *Canciones* [...] es esfuerzo lírico sereno, agudo, y me parece de gran poesía (en sentido de nobleza y calidad, no de *valor*)' (*EC*, p. 418).

poems correspond to many of the values perceived as modernist. On the other hand, the reworking of traditional, popular sources, the concern for specific regional identification, and lyric intimacy link these poems with values if not at odds with modernism, at least, not always based on the same assumptions.

*Canciones* is a point of convergence, but also one of tension, implicit in which is the concern about where personal authenticity – call it 'the sentiment of being' (Trilling, p. 99) – lies in respect of creativity for which surrender to the principle of self-effacement is paramount. 'Quiero ser un Poeta por los cuatro costados,' had written Lorca in a letter to Fernández Almagro back in January 1926, 'amanecido de poesía y muerto de poesía' (*EC*, p. 319). In *Canciones*, what is vitally important is the relationship between the very life of the poet and the death of the man.

The opening poem of the collection, 'Canción de las siete doncellas (teoría del arco iris)' (*OC*, I, p. 273), is a good example of the double perspective to which Walters refers: childlike, sentient observation combined with adult rationalization. It is a perspective that is manifest across the range of poems in the section entitled 'Teorías' (*OC*, I, pp. 272–88), to which this first poem belongs; a range that blends apparent naivety with conceptual complexity; a blend which is itself conveyed by the combination of frankness, simplicity and intellectual promise in the section's title. As Walters (2002, p. 143) explains, in Lorca's theory of the rainbow, 'the rainbow is perceived as song':

> Cantan las siete
> doncellas.
>
> (Sobre el cielo un arco
> de ejemplos de ocaso.)
>
> Alma con siete voces
> las siete doncellas.
>
> (En el aire blanco,
> siete largos pájaros.)
>
> Mueren las siete
> doncellas.
>
> (¿Por qué no han sido nueve?
> ¿Por qué no han sido veinte?)
>
> El río las trae,
> nadie puede verlas.

The seven maidens, and indeed the poem's entire dramatization and defamiliarization of a commonplace object or phenomenon, call to mind the fantasy of the six maidens – the six guitar strings – in 'Adivinanza de la guitarra' from *Poema del cante jondo*. What is more, there are clearly connections to be made between the notion of the 'riddle' and that of the 'theory', each combining play and knowledge in as much as they offer enigmas to be (or that have been) worked out or divined. In the specific case of this *teoría*, what is true also is that nature has been put at the service of art, the physical reality of rainbows becoming less important than the images and metaphors which the form and logic of the seven coloured bands have proffered: 'ejemplos de ocaso'; 'siete voces'; 'siete doncellas'; 'siete largos pájaros'. This use of metaphor is arguably childlike in its conception, the product of simplistic and whimsical associations. The questions in the penultimate, parenthetical couplet are equally childlike, displaying complete ingenuousness in respect of the laws of physical science and through the random character of the numbers they come up with: '¿Por qué no han sido nueve? / ¿Por qué no han sido veinte?' And yet there are also more serious, profound aspects to these questions which show them to be precisely the kinds of questions befitting a poet. For they point to the limitations that nature presents any poet looking to it for inspiration. Nature's rainbows can provide no more than seven bands and seven colours, and the poem has no doubt made the most of these septuple possibilities. The inference, however, is that poetry can or should provide many more. As Walters (2002, p. 142) points out, the Greek etymology of theory (*theoria*) relates it to sight, to vision. This poem, this *teoría*, is indeed the product of a way of seeing, but one that is poetic rather than objective, offering prismatic effects rather than a realistic picture.

The *teoría* that begins 'El canto quiere ser luz' (*OC*, I, p. 276) presents us with the inverse of 'Canción de las siete doncellas': not a spectrum of light perceived as song, but song desiring to be light and thus itself conveyed in luminous terms:

> El canto quiere ser luz.
> En lo oscuro el canto tiene
> hilos de fósforo y luna.
> La luz no sabe qué quiere.
> En sus límites de ópalo,
> se encuentra ella misma,
> y vuelve.

Formally the poem is as compressed and condensed as it is thematically turned in on itself, replicating at either level the energy concentrated and centred in the incandescent filaments ('hilos de fósforo y luna') that song is said to possess. Form and content combine in the image of light revolving upon itself within opal limits, as poetry in the poem – if we take poetry to be synonymous with song – is lit up and displayed in a spark of self-definition. The crux of the matter is to be found in the poem's central irony: song wants to be light, but light knows not what it wants, suggesting that the aspiration is ultimately for song, and by association poetry, to have no aim other than to be what it is, the poem thus constituting an affirmation of the principle of poetic autonomy. It is precisely its self-consciousness that underscores its independence, the poem's incandescence being nothing other than a vital sign, just as light is nothing other than a sign of its own burning.

'Friso' (*OC*, I, p. 283) is another *teoría* that invites us to look, reaffirming the autonomy of poetry by treating it as an object in its own right. 'Instead of engrossed in a story or dialogue,' writes Perri (1995, p. 182), 'speaker and reader appear much more like two observers of a sculpture.' The effect Perri describes owes itself to the poem's layout which invites us to read horizontally across it as well as vertically from top to bottom:


        TIERRA                      CIELO

   Las niñas de la brisa          Los mancebos del aire
  van con sus largas colas.      saltan sobre la luna.


The gender division highlighted by the heading to each couplet (*tierra* versus *cielo*), subsequently reinforced in each (*niñas*, *brisa* and *largas colas* versus *mancebos del aire*), appeals to our predilection for order and categorization, the two images presented in the frieze being adjacent yet distinct and literally opposite elements. The symmetry, however, in its horizontality, offers possibilities of reading that undermine the monolithic character of each section, leading the eye to stray from their vertical logic. Now our gaze traverses their borders and happens instead upon different configurations: 'TIERRA / CIELO', 'Las niñas de la brisa / Los mancebos del aire', 'van con sus largas colas / saltan sobre la luna'. In this way the eye moves about the poem just as it might move about the form and surface of a sculpted frieze. Any allusion to natural elements ('brisa', 'aire', 'luna') is subordinate to this effect, the focus being on what has been carved out rather than what might have been its inspiration. The dislocation between the art object and nature is accentuated further still by the vaguely mythological resonances of the scene which move us away from objective reality into a world of magic and fable.

In the next *teoría*, 'Cazador' (*OC*, I, p. 284), nature is also less important than the form and effects of the poem itself:

¡Alto pinar!
Cuatro palomas por el aire van.

Cuatro palomas
vuelan y tornan.
Llevan heridas
sus cuatro sombras.

¡Bajo pinar!
Cuatro palomas en la tierra están.

Durán (p. 766) has commented on the play of presence and absence in the poem: 'Tan importante es lo que no se dice como lo que se señala.' There is, as Durán goes on to note, no mention of the hunter's shots. Indeed, apart from the title, there is no direct reference to the hunter either. The vertical and downwards logic of the poem, however, does suggest the doves' precipitous fall – from on *alto* to *bajo*. Yet what is perhaps most significant in the poem is that the birds' wounds have been displaced to their shadows ('Llevan heridas / sus cuatro sombras'). For this manifestly poetic twist does itself shadow the poem's denaturalizing processes, the ways in which the poem shifts our attention from a real event to its elisions, effects and form. The possibility arises that the hunter here is none other than the poet himself, who shoots down these birds as he shoots down nature in the pursuit of art. Of course, Lorca famously employed the hunt as a metaphor in his 1926 lecture entitled 'La imagen poética de don Luis de Góngora' (*OC*, III, pp. 223–47), in which the prey are the very images that poets are bent on seeking out. 'La originalidad de don Luis de Góngora,' explained Lorca, 'aparte de la puramente gramatical, está en su método de *cazar* las imágenes' (*OC*, III, p. 230). Later, in a rather dramatic passage, Lorca is more explicit in his equation of the poetic venture with the hunt: 'El poeta que va a hacer un poema (lo sé por experiencia propia) tiene la sensación vaga de que va a una cacería nocturna en un bosque lejanísimo' (*OC*, III, p. 235). The hunt he goes on to describe is, of course, an interior hunt, of which Góngora is the master – 'no le asombran en su paisaje mental las imágenes coloreadas, ni las brillantes en demasía' (*OC*, III, p. 236) – and which, importantly and paradoxically, despite the obvious associations of hunting with the natural world, is not concerned with capturing nature at all. 'Intuye con claridad', explains Lorca of Góngora, 'que la naturaleza que salió de las manos de Dios no es la naturaleza que debe vivir en poemas' (*OC*, III, p. 236). No surprise, then, that 'Cazador' should distract us from the plight of real birds; what we have instead are pine groves and doves which the poet has made exclusively his own.

The next *teoría*, 'Fábula' (*OC*, I, p. 285), sets the world of the poem in opposition to nature:

> Unicornios y cíclopes.
>
> Cuernos de oro
> y ojos verdes.
>
> Sobre el acantilado,
> en tropel gigantesco,
> ilustran el azogue
> sin cristal, del mar.
>
> Unicornios y cíclopes.
>
> Una pupila
> y una potencia.
>
> ¿Quién duda la eficacia
> terrible de esos cuernos?
>
> ¡Oculta tus blancos,
> Naturaleza!

The opening conjunction allies two mythical beasts, the unicorn and cyclops, who are bound also by an arithmetical similarity – a single horn and a single eye – and by their collective presence on the cliffs overlooking the sea. Their reflection in the sea is recast as their very adornment of this natural element, their physical attributes dominating nature here as they do throughout the poem, in which their traits and potency are brought to the fore to the exclusion of any reference to reality. Whatever the origins of the images conveyed here, it is clear that the poem is now the domain of the fabulous and not the real. The poem's final warning to nature keeps her at bay. If *blanco* is to be taken to retain its literal meaning of target as well as an allusion to the whites of the eyes then the message to nature is clearly for her to avert her gaze and protect her eyes. She must do so because she is under attack and because, quite simply, she cannot be privy to this scene that belongs not to her but to myth and fable.

The final poem of 'Teorías' is 'Cortaron tres árboles' (*OC*, I, p. 288):

> Eran tres.
> (Vino el día con sus hachas.)
> Eran dos.
> (Alas rastreras de plata.)
> Era uno.
> Era ninguno.
> (Se quedó desnudo el agua.)

If in 'Cazador' the subject of the destructive act was not mentioned other than in the title, here the wielders of the axe are absent from that place too. With reference to this poem, Perri (1995, p. 184) writes: 'With more emphasis than in any other poem, [Lorca] continually insists on the progressive and definitive process of elimination.' Perri relates this process to existential themes such as the passing of time, loss, and death, but it is possible also that the reference here, as elsewhere in the collection, may equally be artistic. Clearly, as in 'Cazador', the play of presence and absence is a feature of 'Cortaron tres árboles'. Not only is our attention focused on the decreasing numbers which form the poem's backbone ('tres', 'dos', 'uno', 'ninguno') but we are also made to dwell on the accompanying parentheses whose effect is to fill with poetic substance the spaces left empty by – or rather emptied of – (disappearing) nature.

A similar effect of elimination, coupled with parentheses, can be found in the poem 'Lunes, miércoles y viernes' (*OC*, I, p. 342), from the section entitled 'Canciones de luna' (*OC*, I, pp. 337–46):

> Yo era.
> Yo fui,
> pero no soy.
>
> Yo era ...
>
> (¡Oh fauce maravillosa
> la del ciprés y su sombra!
> Ángulo de luna llena.
> Ángulo de luna sola.)
>
> Yo fui ...
>
> La luna estaba de broma
> diciendo que era una rosa.
> (Con una capa de viento
> mi amor se arrojó a las olas.)
>
> Pero no soy ...
>
> (Ante una vidriera rota
> coso mi lírica ropa.)

It is not clear whether the tripartite journey of the self from the imperfect tense, via the preterite, to the present (and with it, towards absence) correspond to the three days of the week in the title. The title itself toys with presence and absence by virtue of its having leapfrogged Tuesday and Thursday, which are there implicitly within the logical sequence but not actually there to be seen. One wonders whether the parentheses are meant to act similarly – both there and not there; glimpses of a first-person lyric subsumed by the absence which the seemingly concrete but ultimately unstable affirmation 'no soy' conveys. 'Yo' has been deprived of a solid platform in this poem which seems to trace a history of depersonalization. Whereas the parenthetical phrases in 'Cortaron tres árboles' served to fill empty spaces, here their function is to confine. In the second of the poem's four-line stanzas the distinction between what lies inside or outside the brackets is not about plenitude or lack but rather about ironic distance in the form of the moon's flippant joke and uncontrolled sentiment as conveyed by love's dramatic act ('se arrojó a las olas'). This parenthesis, like the first, is not short on poetic substance ('una capa de viento', 'Ángulo de luna llena / Ángulo de luna sola'), but the tone ranges from the passionately effusive ('¡Oh fauce maravillosa / la del ciprés y su sombra!') to the melodramatic, of which the cape ('capa') is recognizably a clichéd prop. 'I am not', as the poem puts it, if the 'I' is taken to be synonymous with the sincere, lyric subject. Yet the 'I' – the personal – is voiced anyway, albeit in an artistically self-conscious context that, while pointing to the exigencies of the self, saves the poem from descending into a lyric outpouring. The final parenthesis is nonetheless disconcerting, for although in the context of impersonal art it might seem logical that the poet's lyrical clothing should be in disrepair, the fact that the window before which the poet is sewing is broken presents the reader with an ironic twist. The poem is not a defence of the new aesthetic which simply discards the old, but nor is it one in which the old remains intact. Ultimately, 'Lunes, miércoles y viernes', with its broken fragments, is the window through which we see the personal becoming depersonalized. Yet there is resistance in the fact that although a fractured window may guarantee that what we see will not be easily recognizable, what it cannot do is completely hide the fact that someone very real is looking into it.

In 'Primer aniversario' (*OC*, I, p. 344), also from 'Canciones de luna', there are glimpses of remembered feelings, but the memory of those feelings is unsettled by a self-conscious question about the usefulness of poetry:

> La niña va por mi frente.
> ¡Oh, qué antiguo sentimiento!
>
> ¿De qué me sirve, pregunto,
> la tinta, el papel y el verso?
>
> Carne tuya me parece,
> rojo lirio, junco fresco.
>
> Morena de luna llena.
> ¿Qué quieres de mi deseo?

Ironically, the lines succeeding the first question and preceding the last might be taken to be evidence of precisely what paper, ink and verse can do, namely invent images which here transpose the addressee to a poetic plane: 'rojo lirio, junco fresco'; 'Morena de luna llena'. Yet the final question brings the poem to a dissatisfying end. Although it mentions desire there is as little sense here or elsewhere in the poem of a desiring voice as there is of a confident speaker; an impression compounded by the lack of first-person subject pronouns and accompanying active verbs.

For Morris (p. 280), 'Primer aniversario' is an example of what he calls Lorca's 'very human expressions of doubt about the value to him of his poetic activity'. We can also view these doubts, as in the case of 'Lunes, miércoles y viernes', as signs of reluctance or resistance. For those self-conscious articulations from which a sense of the human does emerge, however measured and attached they may be to the depersonalizing process, also serve as counterpoints to that process of which the disjointedness and lack of assuredness of a poem like 'Primer aniversario' are symptomatic. Even a poem like 'Cancioncilla del primer deseo' (*OC*, I, p. 369), from the section 'Amor *(Con alas y flechas)*' (*OC*, I, pp. 367–78), which on the surface appears to be an innocent, whimsical reflection on the route towards becoming a poet, cannot help but allude to the loss which that journey involves:

> En la mañana verde,
> quería ser corazón.
> Corazón.
>
> Y en la tarde madura
> quería ser ruiseñor.
> Ruiseñor.
>
> (Alma,
> ponte color naranja.
> Alma,
> ponte color de amor.)
>
> En la mañana viva,
> yo quería ser yo.
> Corazón.
>
> Y en la tarde caída
> quería ser mi voz.
> Ruiseñor.
>
> ¡Alma,
> ponte color naranja!
> ¡Alma,
> ponte color de amor!

Desire develops from morning to evening, from wanting to be the heart to wanting to be a nightingale, which are equated respectively in the fourth and fifth stanzas with the self ('yo quería ser yo') and with voice ('quería ser mi voz'). The heart and nightingale are, of course, familiar clichés, and the progression from one to the other might suggest either a movement away from life to art – from the Dionysian to the Apollonian poles – or from emotionalism towards poetic control. The possessive adjective 'mi', which precedes 'voz', also raises the possibility that the concern is to find an authentic voice, although we cannot be sure whether this authenticity would relate to self-expression, originality or poetic capability. The parenthetical, third stanza introduces another element: the soul. The poet's exhortations to the soul seem to have a purely poetic logic, evidenced by the fact that love is conceived of as a colour. Yet the vivacity of these lines, reprised in exclamatory terms in the final stanza, as well as the very mention of love itself, do not suggest a total detachment from the principle of life embodied by *corazón*. This ambiguity is conveyed also by the common associations of the morning and evening with a new start and inevitable end respectively. What is more, the morning here is qualified by the adjectives 'verde' and 'viva', both attached to life and seeming to have positive connotations. By contrast, although it might be logical to cast the evening as mature ('madura'), this does little to dispel the mood of resignation about it which is compounded by the adjective 'caída'.

In 'Soneto' (*OC*, I, p. 378), the final poem of the section 'Amor *(Con alas y flechas)*', there is, as Walters (2002, p. 240) has noted, a sense of poetry 'transcending emotion'. The emotions otherwise associated with love sonnets become the poem's starting point not its end, reminding us once more of Eliot's account of the transmutation of emotion in the poetic process:

> Largo espectro de plata conmovida,
> el viento de la noche suspirando
> abrió con mano gris mi vieja herida
> y se alejó; yo estaba deseando.
>
> Llaga de amor que me dará la vida
> perpetua sangre y pura luz brotando.
> Grieta en que Filomela enmudecida
> tendrá bosque, dolor y nido blando.
>
> ¡Ay qué dulce rumor en mi cabeza!
> Me tenderé junto a la flor sencilla
> donde flota sin alma tu belleza.

> Y el agua errante se pondrá amarilla,
> mientras corre mi sangre en la maleza
> olorosa y mojada de la orilla.

As with 'Primer aniversario', it is a love remembered which seems to provide the spur. Significantly, memory is conveyed as the reopening of an old wound ('abrió con mano gris mi vieja herida'), a motif which is sustained in the poem in the references to the love wound ('Llaga de amor'), crevice ('Grieta') and myth of Philomela's mutilation in the second stanza, as well as by the image of bleeding in the fourth. At the same time, there is in these elements the implication of transformation too. Firstly, we have Philomela's metamorphosis, changed (so the myth goes) into a nightingale after Tereus, her brother-in-law, cut out her tongue so she could not speak of how he raped her (see Jobes, vol. 2, p. 1263); and secondly, the prediction in the final stanza that the poet-speaker's spilt blood will turn waters yellow. What is being played out here, albeit in quite literal terms, is perhaps nothing other than Eliot's contention that artists progress by virtue of their 'continual self-sacrifice', where sacrifice is equated with the 'extinction of personality'. The idea, of course, that new life can spring out of sacrifice belongs to religious convention, and we are reminded also of Eliot's own reference to Philomela in *The Waste Land* (1922), where the nightingale's song is a redeeming, spiritual response to suffering caused by a violent, physical act: 'The change of Philomel, by the barbarous king / So rudely forced; yet there the nightingale / Filled all the desert with inviolable voice' (Eliot 1985, p. 30). Yet the kind of sacrifice implicit in depersonalization has aesthetic motives and consequences, regardless of whether a poem is born of a painful, personal experience. In this context, the reference to a muted Philomela may be understood as promoting reticence and restraint, the nightingale's voice – by inference, since there is no explicit mention of it here – representing, as in 'Cancioncilla del primer deseo', a counterpoint to the effusions of the heart. The combination conveyed by 'bosque, dolor y nido blando' suggests that Philomela's pain and, by association, the poet-speaker's will be poetically productive, although that conviction does not rescue this text entirely from the ambiguity we have found in other poems. For what we are left with in the final image of the speaker bleeding at the water's edge is something that has a distinctly physical impact – and this despite the evidently figurative character of the references to wounds throughout the poem. This may reveal the limitations of the conceit itself and the difficultly of freeing words from their referents; but it may also be yet another sign of the pull of the human on a poet who still seems to be attracted by the personal.

In 'De otro modo' (*OC*, I, p. 381), from the final section of *Canciones*, entitled 'Canciones para terminar', we have, as Walters (2002, p. 241) notes, 'if not an evacuation of emotion as a lyrical motor then its relegation to an intermittent presence':

> La hoguera pone al campo de la tarde
> unas astas de ciervo enfurecido.
> Todo el valle se tiende. Por sus lomos,
> caracolea el vientecillo.
>
> El aire cristaliza bajo el humo.
> —Ojo de gato triste y amarillo—.
> Yo, en mis ojos, paseo por las ramas.
> Las ramas se pasean por el río.
>
> Llegan mis cosas esenciales.
> Son estribillos de estribillos.
> Entre los juncos y la baja tarde,
> ¡qué raro que me llame Federico!

To begin with, the striking, initial image of the first stanza stands separate from the first-person speaker. His role in instigating the scene can, for the time being, only be discerned in the inventiveness of the imagery; one that diverts attention away from its origins in nature onto the dynamics of the conceit: the use of animal parts ('astas de ciervo', 'lomos') to evoke the impact of the elements (the flames of a bonfire, the air of a breeze) on the evening landscape. It is only in the second stanza that the speaker directly introduces himself, but even here he appears as little more than an item amongst others, limited as he is to a single line and sentence of the entire four which constitute the quatrain. 'The "I",' writes Walters (2002, p. 241), 'is perceived as distant and removed', later commenting on the effect of 'withdrawal' in the poem, which culminates in the final stanza 'in the tentative recognition of self': '¡qué raro que me llame Federico!' This final exclamation both draws attention to the self and undermines its fixity and place within the poem, marking a sudden, self-conscious presence of mind otherwise lost amidst the refrains of refrains ('estribillos de estribillos') and the literary elements of a poem in which knowing who the poet is has become of little or no importance.

A similar lack of fixity permeates the poem 'El espejo engañoso' (*OC*, I, p. 384), whose title indicates the uncertainty of mimetic processes as well as of perceptions of self:

> Verde rama exenta
> de ritmo y de pájaro.

> Eco de sollozo
> sin dolor ni labio.
> Hombre y Bosque.
>
> Lloro
> frente al mar amargo.
> ¡Hay en mis pupilas
> dos mares cantando!

The opening couplet conveys a sense of barrenness which we will find also in 'Canción del naranjo seco'. Whether or not it is meant to convey creative difficulty is another matter, its most probable function here being, I would contend, to contribute to the play of presence and absence which underscores the relationship between the speaker and the text. What we have is a dislocation of associations. Rhythm and the bird are brought together with the green branch only to be excluded from that place. Similarly, there is the echo of a sob, but there is neither the pain nor a pair of lips by which to situate its cause and origin. As Walters (2002, pp. 247–8) puts it, 'the reality of suffering is deprived of its immediate attachment'. In the Man and Woods ('Hombre y Bosque') we no doubt have generic categories for the elements which the poem has provided, or indeed not provided, thus far; categories which, due to the earlier dislocations, are emptied of substance and content. The process continues in the final stanza, even with the introduction of the first-person subject. The initial, solitary verb ('Lloro') seems to stand as an affirmation of emotion felt, only to be undone by the final image – a 'non-reflection' (Walters 2002, p. 248) – which replaces tears with song. Although the poem seems to offer us a glimpse of a man reflected, all it does give us in the end is his song.

Despite its evidently playful aspect, the references to barrenness, sobs, pain and tears give a 'El espejo engañoso' a mournful air which, paradoxically, for all the poem's moments of dislocation or non-reflection, hint once again at a personality: one which is undergoing the process of (self-)effacement but is not yet totally effaced. 'Canción inútil' (*OC*, I, p. 385) presents a similar scenario of absence and presence in which the extinction of personality is conveyed, in accordance with Eliot, as an act of self-sacrifice:

> Rosa futura y vena contenida,
> amatista de ayer y brisa de ahora mismo,
>         ¡quiero olvidarlas!
>
> Hombre y pez en sus medios, bajo cosas flotantes,
> esperando en el alga o en la silla su noche,
>         ¡quiero olvidarlos!

Yo.
¡Sólo yo!
Labrando la bandeja
donde no irá mi cabeza.
¡Sólo yo!

Whatever significance we might wish to give to the rose, vein, amethyst, breeze, man, fish, floating objects, algae, chair or night, what seems clear is that they are set within a configuration of future, past and present which the speaker wants to consign to oblivion: '¡quiero olvidarlos!' What will be left once all these things have been forgotten is the 'I', accordingly assigned a solitary position at the head of the final stanza. Although the first-person subject is singled out and granted agency ('Labrando'), it works to fashion, as Walters (2002, p. 245) has suggested, something that will ultimately not be used: the tray ('bandeja'). There is an allusion, no doubt, to John the Baptist, beheaded on a wish granted to Salome as a reward for her dancing. Here, however, the suggestion is that there will be no reward, since the speaker will not offer his own head on a plate. Yet despite the negation, the image of a severed head and plate, underpinned as it is by our common knowledge of the paradigm, has already, I would suggest, entered our consciousness, rendering a word as tiny as *no* less emphatic and conclusive than it otherwise might have been ('donde no irá mi cabeza'). In fact, if we equate the tray with the poem, as Walters (2002, p. 245) does, then a sacrifice of sorts, where this implies self-effacement and the extinction of personality, has indeed been made. For although there is certainly a strong lyrical presence in the desperate first-person cries to forget, the very act of forgetting serves only to detach the speaker from anything that might lend reality to his emotions. And if he claims that the tray will be empty, it is only because the poem, once the lid is lifted, reveals nothing of the man who has written it; nothing, that is, other than the uncertainties and anxieties accompanying his self-effacement in the first place.

'Canción del naranjo seco' (*OC*, I, p. 389), the penultimate poem of the section 'Canciones para terminar' and therefore of the collection as a whole, is striking for what appears to be its unabashed emotionalism, which is in stark contrast to the reticence – however ambiguous – we have identified in other poems. Walters (2002, p. 248) suggests that were it not for the final poem of the section, 'Canción del día que se va' (*OC*, I, p. 390), in which emotionalism is curtailed once more ('¡Qué trabajo me cuesta / dejarte marchar, día! / Te vas lleno de mí, / vuelves sin conocerme'), 'Canción del naranjo seco' would have brought *Canciones* to an inappropriately emotional end:

Leñador.
Córtame la sombra.
Líbrame del suplicio
de verme sin toronjas.

¿Por qué nací entre espejos?
El día me da vueltas.
Y la noche me copia
en todas sus estrellas.

Quiero vivir sin verme.
Y hormigas y vilanos,
soñaré que son mis
hojas y mis pájaros.

Leñador.
Córtame la sombra.
Líbrame del suplicio
de verme sin toronjas.

Although we might attempt to argue that the device of speaking through a tree is a step, at least, in the direction of depersonalization, the emotional content indicates otherwise, and we are left above all with the curiosity of discovering the human significance of what is, in effect, an extended metaphor. The images of barrenness, along with the self-conscious awareness of that barrenness, appear to hold the key. If we take the tree's fruitlessness to signify creative incapacity, then this might explain why such emotionalism should hold its own in the collection. For amidst the uncertainty and reluctance attached to the move towards the impersonal, this poem acts not so much as a riposte to that process, but rather more as a sign of the fears which that process raises. Alternatively, it might be viewed instead as an exhortation in favour of depersonalization. After all, the tree seeks to be freed from the obligation of having to see its shadow, from having to see a realistic image of itself ('¿Por qué nací entre espejos?'). This way of seeing is associated here with sterility, in contrast to the fertility which the dreams of the imagination could conjure ('hormigas y vilanos, / soñaré que son mis / hojas y mis pájaros'). In this sense, the pleas to the woodsman actually, if somewhat paradoxically, fall within the logic of self-sacrifice that is a prerequisite for dehumanization.

There is a section we have yet to look at which is fundamental to our discussion, both because of the self-conscious character of its poems and because of its engagement with the processes of depersonalization. Entitled 'Tres retratos con sombra' (*OC*, I. pp. 319–26), it consists of three portrait poems (and their shadows): 'Verlaine' (and 'Baco') (*OC*, I, pp. 321–2); 'Juan

Ramón Jiménez' (and 'Venus') (*OC*, I, pp. 323–4); 'Debussy' (and 'Narciso') (*OC*, I, pp. 325–6). One of the first things we note is that each shadow poem appears in a smaller typeface. For Neil C. McKinlay, theses changes 'clearly invite us to assume that the portraits are more important than the *sombras*, although such obviousness is a clue that the real substance lies in what is being overtly hidden'.[2] Walters (2002, p. 228) is of the same opinion and compares the device to the use of parentheses throughout *Canciones* which 'far from containing incidental or marginal material, [often] constitute the crux of the poem'.[3] However, we might want to question the assumptions underpinning such views. Could it not be the case that the change in size serves simply to identify the second poem in each pairing as the first's shadow? Beyond this, any judgements we might make would seem to depend on the importance we attach to the derivative nature of shadows. Size, I would suggest, matters less than the relation between individual portraits and their respective shadows, which is perhaps more important even than the horizontal relationships we might seek to trace across all pairings.[4] Where we certainly can agree with McKinlay is in his contention that the portraits 'lack any definite assertion' (McKinlay, p. 77). As Walters points out, 'Verlaine' begins with 'a categorical negation of speech' (Walters 2002, p. 227); 'Juan Ramón Jiménez', in turn, 'emerges as a symbol of reserve and non-commitment; it appears to say nothing' (Walters 2002, p. 230); while implicit in 'Debussy' is the silence that is so overtly conveyed in the other two portraits (see Walters 2002, p. 231). By contrast, the shadow poems do appear to be more dynamic, although it is only in conjunction with their companion portraits that they acquire their full significance. Taken together, what portrait and shadow offer us is once again that paradigm of reticence and emotion which we have found elsewhere in *Canciones*.

   When approaching each pairing, we might ask ourselves to what extent we need draw upon the real lives and works of the distinguished men whose names sit so weightily at the head of each portrait. Could our engagement

---

   2   Neil C. McKinlay, 'Clues that Confuse: Lorca's *Canciones*', *Romance Studies*, Vol. 17 (I), June 1999, 75–88 (p. 77).
   3   See also D. Gareth Walters' earlier treatment of the three portraits and their shadows in '"Comprendí. Pero no explico". Revelation and concealment in Lorca's *Canciones*', *Bulletin of Hispanic Studies*, 68 (1991), 265–79.
   4   By contrast, Walters (2002, p. 232) argues that the shadow poems 'are only loosely related to their respective companion poems' and are instead 'more closely related to each other through Lorca's personal and unusual treatment of well-known mythological figures'. McKinlay (p. 77), in turn, argues that the fact that in 'Debussy' *sombra* is continually stressed 'suggests that significant information lies in the three shadows, and not in the portraits'.

with the poems be illuminated by our knowledge of their connections with Symbolism? And what of their passionate love affairs? After all, Bacchus, Venus and Narcissus all have erotic connotations.[5] In my opinion, the precise details of either their work or their life are of little help to us.[6] These are clearly not portraits in the conventional sense, nor could we expect them to be, given the movement in *Canciones*, however laboured, towards dehumanization and the extinction of personality. What we cannot ignore, however, is that all the titular figures chosen are artists, and it would seem strange were this fact not to shape our reading of the portraits and their shadows in some way. Indeed, in my reading, it points not only to the self-conscious aspect of the poems but also to the task in which all three, as well as Lorca, share: the transmutation of real-life experience into art. If precise details about the personal lives of these men are of little use, it is because the focus is not on life or personality but on the process of transmutation, in which such things are already lost.

Whereas the principle of 'Verlaine' is silence or reticence – the speaker refers to the song that he will not sing –its shadow, 'Baco', is sonorous:

VERLAINE

La canción,
que nunca diré,
se ha dormido en mis labios.
La canción,
que nunca diré.

---

[5] We might want to think, for example, of Verlaine's tempestuous relationship with Rimbaud, or Debussy's several troubled relationships and affairs. On Verlaine, see Alan English, 'Paul Verlaine', *The Literary Encyclopedia*, 21 July 2004 [http://www.litencyc.com/php/speople.php?rec=true&UID=4536, accessed 5 October 2009]; on Debussy, see Robert Orledge, 'Debussy the Man', in Simon Trezise (ed.), *The Cambridge Companion to Debussy* (Cambridge: Cambridge University Press, 2003), 9–24. On Jiménez, see Javier Herrero's 'Los Lorca y Juan Ramón. Una Amistad poética', in Francisco Javier Díez de Revenga and Mariano Paco (eds), *Pasión de mi vida. Estudios sobre Juan Ramón Jiménez* (Murcia: Fundación Cajamurcia, 2007), 91–111. In his essay, Herrero mentions the flirtatious, if innocent, relationship between the poet (now married) and Lorca's sister Isabel. He explains that 'Juan Ramón había sido en su primera juventud un mujeriego impertinente', but that after his marriage to Zenobia Camprubí in 1916 'se convirtió en un esposo modelo' (Herrero, p. 93). 'Pero claro está,' proceeds Herrero (p. 93), 'que esa fidelidad no había extinguido su sensualidad y consiguientemente ahora se limitaba a admirar, y suponemos que disfrutar, a distancia lo que en el pasado hubiera sido objeto de una acción más directa.'

[6] Worthy of note, in this respect, is McKinlay's warning that we should be careful 'not to confuse Lorca's style in *Canciones* with straightforward, conventional symbolism, where a clearly identifiable "meaning" is projected on to a term or concept' (McKinlay, p. 76).

Sobre las madreselvas
había una luciérnaga,
y la luna picaba
con un rayo en el agua.

Entonces yo soñé,
la canción,
que nunca diré.

Canción llena de labios
y de cauces lejanos.

Canción llena de horas
perdidas en la sombra.

Canción de estrella viva
sobre un perpetuo día.

           B A C O

Verde rumor intacto.
La higuera me tiende sus brazos.

Como una pantera, su sombra
acecha mi lírica sombra.

La luna cuenta los perros.
Se equivoca y empieza de nuevo.

Ayer, mañana, negro y verde,
rondas mi cerco de laureles.

¿Quién te querría como yo,
si me cambiaras el corazón?

… Y la higuera me grita y avanza
terrible y multiplicada.

The effect of the postpositive 'llena de' in the portrait is misleading since the sense is almost immediately undermined by adjectives that empty the song of immediacy and substance ('labios / y […] cauces lejanos', 'horas / perdidas'). There is, then, a tension between plenitude and lack, between presence and absence, which is emphasized in the final line with the idea of a bright star shining over a never-ending day: the star might be there, but daylight will ensure that it will not be seen. Instead, it is the principle of quiet and stillness, conveyed in the moonlit scene of the second stanza, which dominates this portrait. In 'Baco', by contrast, sound remains intact ('Verde rumor intacto'), and is audible in the moon's counting ('La luna cuenta perros') as well as in the fig-tree's shouts ('la higuera me grita'). This menacing tree, which is sacred to Bacchus's Greek incarnation, Dionysos (see Chevalier and Gheerbrant, p. 377), is likened to the equally menacing panther, and in its augmented form in the final line ('terrible y multiplicada') recalls the 'Múltiple pelotari' of 'Chumbera' in *Poema del cante jondo*. This is a poem which counters the reticence of its companion portrait with threat. Moreover, what is threatened is equated with the poetic task, as the fig-tree lies in wait for the speaker's lyrical shadow ('su sombra / acecha mi lírica sombra'), while the laurel, associated with poets and symbolizing Apollonian qualities (see Chevalier and Gheerbrant, p. 593), appears to be besieged ('rondas mi cerco de laureles'). Bacchus might stand for many things in this poem, but I would suggest that, set in contrast to the Apollonian control governing the portrait, his function here is to signify the zest and potential chaos of life. In the context of the self-conscious logic of 'Verlaine' and 'Baco' together, life equates precisely with the personal and worldly material which the poet must sacrifice on the way to achieving impersonality in art: what the poet ultimately will not sing ('la canción, / que nunca diré'). Of course, the poem 'Baco' does itself bear the mark of the impersonal inasmuch as it coheres with its aesthetic, centring on metaphor and eschewing emotionalism. But there is no contradiction here as, after all, it constitutes the very shadow cast by 'Verlaine' and must necessarily resemble it. Furthermore, 'Baco' is not concerned with the specific details of any life in particular, but instead with life as a fundamental (Bacchanalian) principle. It is a principle that shadows the impersonal not because it constitutes what has been discarded, but because it is the thing against which the impersonal defines itself and, as such, is that very thing which the impersonal contains – in the sense of both restraining and holding.

In the pairing 'Juan Ramón Jiménez' and 'Venus', the tension is between, on the one hand, the quiet and stillness evoked by infinite whiteness and, on the other, the stirrings of a passion or eroticism that might have been and which are associated with the Venusian world:

### JUAN RAMÓN JIMÉNEZ

En el blanco infinito,
nieve, nardo, salina,
perdió su fantasía.

El color blanco, anda,
sobre una muda alfombra
de plumas de paloma.

Sin ojos ni ademán
inmóvil sufre un sueño.
Pero tiembla por dentro.

En el blanco infinito,
¡qué pura y larga herida
dejó su fantasía!

En el blanco infinito.
Nieve. Nardo. Salina.

V E N U S

*Así te vi*

La joven muerta
en la concha de la cama,
desnuda de flor y brisa
surgía en la luz perenne.

Quedaba el mundo,
lirio de algodón y sombra,
asomado a los cristales,
viendo el tránsito infinito.

La joven muerta,
surcaba el amor por dentro.
Entre la espuma de las sábanas
se perdía su cabellera.

This tension, however, is not neatly played out by contrasting poems. Instead, the shadow resembles its portrait arguably even more than 'Baco' does its own. The emotions attached to gazing upon the young girl are tempered, of course, by her lifelessness and remain as contained as she is within her shell ('en la concha de la cama') or as love is within her ('surcaba el amor por dentro'), just as emotion stirs but is contained all the same in the portrait ('sufre un sueño', 'tiembla por dentro'). Walters notes that the shell suggests Botticelli's painting *The Birth of Venus*, the dead girl of the poem now supplying an ironic and 'savage demythification' (Walters 2002, p. 234). But her death is in keeping with the logic of the portrait, where personality cannot make its mark ('Sin ojos ni ademán / inmóvil') amidst the blankness conveyed by white images (snow, lily, salt flats) which constitute the limits to – and of – fantasy and the imagination: 'En el blanco infinito, / nieve, nardo y salina, / perdió su fantasía'; 'En el blanco infinito, / ¡qué pura y larga herida / dejó su fantasía!' Even in the reference to doves' feathers, where there might be some opportunity for sound and movement, colour and texture take precedence as the birds are stilled and silenced: 'El color blanco, anda, / sobre una muda alfombra / de plumas de paloma'. Similarly, the promise of eroticism and love which Venus might evoke is withdrawn no sooner than it is offered. As Walters (2002, p. 234) has suggested, 'desnuda' in the shadow's third line 'is likely to catch the reader out', as it soon becomes apparent that it does not indicate the girl's nakedness but is instead 'part of an adjectival phrase with the meaning of "deprived of"'. In the last line, the eroticism which the girl's hair might otherwise connote disappears amidst the sea waves as do the equally connotative bed sheets contained within the final, double image. This image leaves us, above all, with poetic invention in mind, a fitting ending to a shadow of a portrait in which artistic control appears to have the upper hand over life.

The portrait 'Debussy' in the final pairing of 'Tres retratos con sombra' seems to differ from its predecessors in the way it constantly refers to its shadow, while its shadow poem, 'Narciso', evokes not a shadow but, as we might expect from the title, a reflection:

DEBUSSY

Mi sombra va silenciosa
por el agua de la acequia.

Por mi sombra están las ranas
privadas de las estrellas.

La sombra manda a mi cuerpo
reflejos de cosas quietas.

Mi sombra va como inmenso
cínife color violeta.

Cien grillos quieren dorar
la luz de la cañavera.

Una luz nace en mi pecho,
reflejado, de la acequia.

NARCISO

Niño.
¡Que te vas a caer al río!

En lo hondo hay una rosa
y en la rosa hay otro río.

¡Mira aquel pájaro! ¡Mira
aquel pájaro amarillo!

Se me han caído los ojos
dentro del agua.

¡Dios mío!
¡Que se resbala! ¡Muchacho!

... y en la rosa estoy yo mismo.

> Cuando se perdió en el agua
> comprendí. Pero no explico.

The difference, however, is ultimately superficial, as 'Debussy' and 'Narciso'
replicate the paradigms already established by the other pairings. Indeed,
the silence implicit in the opening couplet of 'Debussy' is soon followed by
a reference to privation in the second and then to stillness in the third. The
later mention of crickets refers not to any sound they might make but to their
colour. The water to which there are both direct and indirect references ('el
agua de la acequia', 'ranas', 'cañavera', 'acequia') links the portrait with its
shadow poem, as do the references to shadows in the first four couplets and
to reflection in the third and sixth. Just as there were stirrings of emotion
in 'Juan Ramón Jiménez' that were immediately contained, so in the final
couplet of 'Debussy' the sentimental connotations of 'luz' and 'pecho' seem
to dissipate once we realize we are dealing not with reality but with a reflection: 'Una luz nace en mi pecho, / reflejado, de la acequia.' The shadow poem
is perhaps the site of this deflected emotion. After all, the sensations in it,
with its personae and dialogue, do seem more immediate and dramatic in
contrast to what we find in the portrait. Yet 'Narciso' is as elliptical as was
'Baco' (if not more so); just as in preceding shadows, the emotion it conveys
has been transmuted by the processes of depersonalization. Although we
might look to psychoanalysis for the answers to Narcissus's riddle, the poem
itself gives us no clear explanation as to the meaning of the boy's fall into the
river. The notion of reflection is, of course, evocative in the context of self-
conscious, or self-reflective, production, and the mise-en-abîme of the rose
within a river within a rose ('En lo hondo hay una rosa / y en la rosa hay otro
río') might, along with the Narcissistic gaze and the subsequent, inevitable
fall ('... y en la rosa estoy yo mismo'), suggest art's very concern with itself
along with the artist's immersion in it at the expense of his own personality.
In the end, the poem leaves us only with an enigma: 'Cuando se perdió en
el agua / comprendí. Pero no explico.' In this final act of elusion, the speaker
affirms the poem's autonomy, but not without acknowledging his own part in
it. The 'I' will not explain, but it did understand and, albeit in the service of
art – and impersonal art to boot –it did and still does exist.

# 4

# *Romancero gitano*: Culture versus Nature

The fine delight that fathers thought; the strong
Spur, live and lancing like the blowpipe flame,
Breathes once and, quenchèd faster than it came,
Leaves yet the mind a mother of immortal song.
(Gerard Manley Hopkins, 'To R. B.')

'Childless couples, orphaned children, aborted childbirths, and unregenerately celibate men and women,' writes Edward Said, 'populate the world of high modernism with remarkable insistence, all of them suggesting the difficulties of filiation.'[1] For Said, 'filiation', as Abdirahman A. Hussein explains, 'is premised on narrative linearity, familial procreation, biological succession, and the "vertical" transmission of traditionary authority. Said allegorizes it into the authority of an immediate community or specific culture to which one belongs "by birth, nationality, profession."'[2] The difficulties of filiation that Said perceives in modernism constitute for him the first in a three-part pattern originating in this 'large group of late nineteenth and early twentieth-century writers, in which the failure of the generative impulse – the failure of the capacity to produce or generate children – is portrayed in such a way as to stand for a general condition afflicting society and culture together, to say nothing of individual men and women' (Said 1983, p. 16). The second part of this pattern, 'immediately consequent upon the first, [is] the pressure to produce new and different ways of conceiving human relationships' (Said 1983, p. 17); to move, in other words, 'from a failed idea or possibility of filiation to a kind of compensatory order that, whether it is a party, an institution, a culture, a set of beliefs, or even a world-vision, provides men and women with a new form of relationship' (Said 1983, p. 19) – what Said calls 'affiliation'. The third and final part of the pattern is 'the deliberately explicit

---

[1]   Edward Said, *The World, the Text, and the Critic* (Cambridge, Mass.: Harvard University Press, 1983), 17.
[2]   Abdirahman A. Hussein, *Edward Said. Criticism and Society* (London and New York: Verso, 2002), 167.

goal of using that new order to reinstate vestiges of the kind of authority associated in the past with filiative order' (Said 1983, p. 19). As Said (1983, pp. 19–20) explains,

> if a filial relationship was held together by natural bonds and natural forms of authority – involving obedience, fear, love, respect, and instinctual conflict – the new affiliative relationship changes these bonds into what seem to be transpersonal forms – such as guild consciousness, consensus, collegiality, professional respect, class, and the hegemony of the dominant culture. The filiative system belongs to the realms of nature and of 'life,' whereas affiliation belongs exclusively to culture and society.

Of course, Said's conception of the dynamic between filiative and affiliative orders is not restricted to the regenerative concerns he detects in modernism; nor is it limited to an analysis of modernism in particular.[3] Yet the observations that he makes in respect of modernism specifically, as well as his general conception of affiliation, have an especial resonance for our discussion of Lorca and for our treatment in this chapter of his collection of poems entitled *Romancero gitano*.

To begin with, the notion of affiliation provides a suitably affective basis for our understanding of Lorca's personal and professional relationships in the context of the proliferation of groups, manifestos, reviews and journals that characterized the early decades of the twentieth century, and the artistic collaboration to which it gave rise. What is clear from, amongst other things, Lorca's correspondence is that so many of those he regarded to be his closest friends were actively involved, at some time or other, in the development, promotion or dissemination of his work, and together seem to represent the very plane of 'horizontality' upon which the affiliative process functions.[4] What is more, Lorca's disenchantment with what has been described as

---

3  What concerns Said above all is how, as Hussein (p. 167) notes, 'In the context of modernity, [filiative] authority is gradually eroded and transformed into "horizontal" or spatialized structures premised on adjacency, parallelism, and complementarity.' 'It is these lateral, affiliative structures', adds Hussein, 'that Said broadly characterizes as system or method – namely, a theoretical model that one affirms "by social and political conviction, economic and historical circumstance, voluntary effort and willed deliberation."'

4  See, for example, the discussion of Lorca's drawings in the context of his relationship and correspondence with the art critic Sebastià Gasch, in Jacqueline Cockburn, 'Gifts from the Poet to the Art Critic', in Bonaddio and de Ros (eds) (2003), 67–80, and Jacqueline Cockburn and Federico Bonaddio, 'Drawing', in Bonaddio (ed.) (2007), ch. 4, 84–100.

the ambiguous success of *Romancero gitano*[5] is a sign that his priority was perhaps not to secure the positive reception of his work by a general readership (although this is what occurred even before his ballads were first published as a collection in 1928, as well as after; indeed, *Romancero gitano* is arguably still his best-known and best-loved book of poems), but instead to receive the approval of his peers and their recognition of the contemporariness of his poetic endeavour. Of utmost importance to Lorca was the sense – the very real sense – of belonging to, of being accepted by, the community of artists.

Moreover, it is perhaps not insignificant that *Romancero gitano*, which opens with a poem on the death of a child ('Romance de la luna, luna', *OC*, I, pp. 393–4), should be populated by, among others, characters that transgress or suffer aggression; characters that are solitary, marginalized, frustrated or martyred – all of which points to a fundamental unease, a discontinuity, at the heart of human relationships. There are scenes of a gypsy girl, in 'Preciosa y el aire' (*OC*, I, pp. 395–7), fleeing from 'the sexual menace embodied in the wind' (Harris, p. 9); of bloody encounters between feuding gypsies, in 'Reyerta' (*OC*, I, pp. 398–9) and 'Muerte de Antoñito el Camborio' (*OC*, I, pp. 120–1); of a death foretold by cards, in 'Romance del emplazado' (*OC*, I, pp. 423–5); of the massacre of gypsies by civil guards, in 'Romance de la Guardia Civil española' (*OC*, I, pp. 426–30), or of the torture, mutilation and death of a young woman, in 'Martirio de Santa Olalla' (*OC*, I, pp. 433–5); of lovers who seek but fail to be reunited, in 'Romance sonámbulo' (*OC*, I, pp. 400–3); of women who suffer frustration, either as a result of their vocation, in 'La monja gitana' (*OC*, I, pp. 404–5), or in spinsterhood, in 'Romance de la pena negra' (*OC*, I, pp. 408–9); scenes of adultery, in 'La casada infiel' (*OC*, I, pp. 406–7), and of rape and incest, in 'Thamar y Amnón' (*OC*, I, pp. 439–42).

This is not to say, however, that any of these ballads should be read specifically as depicting the life experience of real or imagined people. In a 1926 recital of his ballads, Lorca was happy to admit that his book was 'un retablo de Andalucía con gitanos, caballos, arcángeles, planetas, con su brisa romana, con ríos, con crímenes, con la nota vulgar del contrabandista, y la nota celeste de los niños desnudos de Córdoba que burlan a San Rafael' (*OC*, III, p. 340). Yet he was by no means focused on the exercise of *costumbrismo*, insisting that his book was one 'donde apenas si está expresada la Andalucía que se ve, pero donde está temblando la que no se ve' (*OC*, I, p. 340). An admirer

---

[5] See Miguel García-Posada, *Lorca: interpretación de 'Poeta en Nueva York'* (Madrid: Akal, 1981), 55–6.

of Góngora and participant in the celebration of the Cordovan poet on the tercentenary of his death in 1927, Lorca had allied himself with the goal of creating pure and independent poetry. What he had to say about the work of the poet in his 1926 lecture, 'La imagen poética de don Luis de Góngora', might equally have been applicable to his own conception of *Romancero gitano*. In terms that contain reminiscences of Vicente Huidobro's *creacionista* proclamation, he declared that Góngora

> no crea sus imágenes sobre la misma Naturaleza, sino que lleva el objeto, cosa o acto a la cámara oscura de su cerebro y de allí salen transformados para dar el gran salto sobre el otro mundo con que se funden. Por eso su poesía, como no es directa, es imposible de leer ante los objetos de que habla. Los chopos, rosas, zagales y mares del espiritual cordobés son creados y nuevos. (*OC*, III, p. 235)

It is in relation to the very goal of producing independent poems that we can understand Lorca's use of myth in his ballads, whether biblical, classical or folkloric, invented or borrowed. Already removed from the plane of reality, myth provides a ready source of metaphor by which to enhance the independence of the poems, rendering it difficult, undesirable even, to penetrate with absolute certainty to their source in a real place, event or person. 'Desde los primeros versos,' explained Lorca in his recital of his work, 'se nota que el mito está mezclado en el elemento que pudiéramos llamar realista, aunque no lo es, puesto que al contacto con el plano mágico, se torna aun más misterioso e indescifrable, como el alma misma de Andalucía' (*OC*, III, p. 342). And yet the characters that inhabit the ballads do take on a life as we see them suffer, dream, struggle and desire, but it is a life always restricted to the domain of the myth that has engendered them. They move in a world of extended metaphors, which is why their experiences and interactions may be read in terms other than those that are tied directly to their literal activity on the page. 'These ballads', writes Harris (1991, p. 13), 'are an extraordinarily ambitious attempt to synthesise a wide variety of sometimes disparate elements which are brought together in the dimension of myth at the centre of the book, where the narrative figures are embodiments or explanations of metaphysical experiences and problems.' Indeed, as the readings that follow will suggest, the life of the characters is even bound up with aesthetic concerns, their actions and dilemmas corresponding, in some cases, to the very endeavour of creating independent poems, to the schism between lived experience and artistic creation that such an endeavour presupposes. Their frustrations and loneliness thus become emblematic of the poet's own artistic need and creative quest to reach out to another community: an artistic community where belonging is dependent on recognition and acceptance, and consequently on one's own submission to the dominant aesthetic of the day.

In 'Preciosa y el aire' we find, as in so many of the ballads, a tension between the anecdotal thrust of the story line and the elaborate images which force us to dwell on their elaboration at the expense of our desire to find out what happens. In addition, we glimpse something of that fundamental dichotomy between nature, or reality, on the one hand, and art, on the other, which manifests itself in the reference to objects belonging undisputedly to the world outside of the poem and in their poeticization, which claims them solely for the world of art itself. It is possible to summarize the scene depicted in the opening stanza in purely realistic terms. A gypsy girl, called Preciosa, playing a tambourine, walks along a path that borders laurel trees on one side and the sea on the other. It is a dark, starless night where the only sounds to be heard are those of Preciosa's playing and the crashing of waves on the beach. There, in the distance, rise mountains where Englishmen live in their lime-washed homes guarded by policemen who are now asleep. On the shore gypsies pass the time assembling shelters out of seashells and branches from pine trees.

> Su luna de pergamino
> Preciosa tocando viene
> por un anfibio sendero
> de cristales y laureles.
> El silencio sin estrellas,
> huyendo del sonsonete,
> cae donde el mar bate y canta
> su noche llena de peces.
> En los picos de la sierra
> los carabineros duermen
> guardando las blancas torres
> donde viven los ingleses.
> Y los gitanos del agua
> levantan por distraerse,
> glorietas de caracolas
> y ramas de pino verde.

Such literal readings, however, do little justice to the verse, failing as they do to take into account the mystery evoked by its images. What we infer to be a tambourine is conveyed in terms of a 'parchment moon'; the path is described as 'amphibious', the water, denoted by 'crystals'; it is the silence that is starless, not the sky – a silence to which is attributed the human activity of fleeing; the sea 'sings', its song being the night itself, which is described

as laden with fish; synecdoche, in the shape of white towers, denotes the
Englishmen's homes, while the preposition 'del', denoting origin, draws an
intimate relationship between the gypsies and the water. The first stanza, in
other words, conjures up far more mystery than any literal reading will allow,
and the reader is distracted from the anecdotal by the combined effect of
colour, shape and sound, and by the possibility that the figures and objects
depicted, as well as the relationship between them, may actually have some
other meaning.

The process of undermining literal meaning continues in subsequent stanzas.
The wind that rises to harass Preciosa is personified as a satyr and as *San
Cristobalón*, a name which, as Ramsden (p. 11) explains, alludes to a number
of traditional elements: 'the Spanish folklore view of Saint Christopher [...]
as a hefty, rugged, muscular being'; 'the *cante jondo* tendency to personify
the wind as a giant'; and 'the Punch-like puppet Cristóbal'. 'The augmenta-
tive *Cristobalón*', adds Ramsden, 'serves to emphasise the paganised saint's
lumbering loutishness':

> Su luna de pergamino
> Preciosa tocando viene.
> Al verla se ha levantado
> el viento, que nunca duerme.
> San Cristobalón desnudo,
> lleno de lenguas celestes,
> mira a la niña tocando
> una dulce gaita ausente.
>
> Niña, deja que levante
> tu vestido para verte.
> Abre en mis dedos antiguos
> la rosa azul de tu vientre.
>
> Preciosa tira el pandero
> y corre sin detenerse.
> El viento-hombrón la persigue
> con una espada caliente.

The dramatic qualities of these stanzas are self-evident: a young girl flees
from the lascivious attentions of the wind whose sexual menace is clear
enough to see in the desire to peek under her dress. The whole episode could
be explained away as being merely the product of Preciosa's imagination, the
reality of events being no more than a conflation of a young woman's fears of
sexual awakening and the very real threat posed by an overpowering gale. But
this would be to treat Preciosa as a real person and lend psychological depth

to a character whose own name denotes the unreality of her origins, having as she does a precedent in the heroine of the same name in Cervantes's exemplary novel *La gitanilla* (see Harris 1991, p. 20, and Ramsden, pp. 8–9). It would also be to ignore the precedents for the episode in classical and popular myth – in the tale of Boreas and Oreithyia (see Harris 1991, p. 20, and Ramsden, p. 8) or, as Harris also suggests, in the folktale of Cinderella, with its own sources in the myth of Isis: 'Isis […] is the veiled goddess whose veil no man ever lifted. If someone does try to lift her veil then her reaction is to flee, just as Preciosa flees when the giant tries to lift her dress.' It is myth, not reality, which offers the pattern for the events of this and other ballads as well as the canvas upon which Lorca may make his embellishments and elaborate his images. Art, if you like (and, what is more, timeless art), is put at the service of Lorca's own artistic endeavour, a procedure which is significant at a time when art was not supposed to present a reflection of the world. Were the wind to have had its way, it would have got its hands not on Preciosa's body but on the 'blue rose' of her belly ('la rosa azul de tu vientre), an image taking precedence in the poem over carnal reality, as is the case too with the phallic allusions in the bawdy references to the wind's 'hot sword' ('espada caliente') and the 'sweet absent pipe' ('dulce gaita ausente') that it is playing. This bawdy humour, no doubt consistent with the origins of the wind's name in puppet theatre, arguably diffuses the menace that can otherwise be sensed in the poem, shifting it into the domain of parody and irony and away from the all too literal fears it might otherwise inspire.[6]

The reaction of the natural surroundings in the following stanza is further testimony to the way objects in the poem have been abstracted from their source in the real world:

> Frunce su rumor el mar.
> Los olivos palidecen.
> Cantan las flautas de umbría
> y el liso gong de la nieve.

The anthropomorphic reactions of the sea, olive trees, shade and snow provide an aptly concerned and urgent backdrop to unfolding events, but importantly

---

[6]   Harris (1991, p. 11) points to the playful element in *Romancero gitano*, noting its lightening and restraining function in conjunction with other elements pervading the ballads: 'the *Romancero gitano* sounds a very grim book, yet it is exactly the opposite. Death, violence and sexual repression are lightened by the techniques of popular song, and then overlaid and restrained with complex and ingenious imagery. This is very attractive poetry […] moving deftly between the serious and the playful, suggesting weighty intentions while subjecting such high import to ironic mockery.'

they do so as ingenious images in their own right – a synaesthetic mixture of colour, shape and sound, particularly surprising in terms of the combination of shade and sound in the third line, texture, sound, colour and temperature (the cold, white snow) in the fourth, and in the way it ascribes noise to the sea's act of frowning, in the first. The concern and urgency is subsequently expressed in more direct terms in the next stanza:

> ¡Preciosa, corre, Preciosa,
> que te coge el viento verde!
> ¡Preciosa, corre, Preciosa!
> ¡Míralo por donde viene!
> Sátiro de estrellas bajas
> con sus lenguas relucientes.

Commenting on these lines, Ramsden (p. 13) suggests that here 'the poet himself intervenes, with admonitions that are also joyous taunts appropriate to an ostensible gypsy narrator', while Harris (1991, p. 19) writes of the introduction of '[a] sudden change of point of view [...] with the appearance of an interlocutor urging Precisosa to flee'. But we could also argue that these lines merely vocalize (translate, if you will) the sentiments expressed by the natural elements in the previous stanza; sentiments which, in any case, permeate a poem whose dramatic aspect centres on the menace of the chase and which are dispersed more widely throughout its stanzas than might otherwise be suggested by the ascription of these warning cries to any particular body.

As things turn out, Preciosa does manage to escape, finding refuge in the home of the English consul:

> Preciosa, llena de miedo,
> entra en la casa que tiene,
> más arriba de los pinos,
> el cónsul de los ingleses.

> Asustados por los gritos
> tres carabineros vienen,
> sus negras capas ceñidas
> y los gorros en las sienes.

> El inglés da a la gitana
> un vaso de tibia leche,
> y una copa de ginebra
> que Preciosa no se bebe.

> Y mientras cuenta, llorando,
> su aventura a aquella gente,

en las tejas de pizarra
el viento, furioso, muerde.

These stanzas are clearly more prosaic than those which have preceded them, thus giving the impression that anecdote has finally gained the upper hand over poetry. And yet there is a specifically poetic rationale for this shift which is consistent with the poetic logic of the ballad in its entirety. For if the prosaic serves any purpose here, it is to emphasize order over chaos now that Preciosa appears to be out of harm's way. The trajectory of Preciosa's flight from the outdoors to indoors – away from nature with all its perils to the refuge of the Englishman's home and all its connotations of convention and restraint – lends itself, no doubt, to Freudian readings in which the 'carabineros', now very awake, are the super-ego to the wind's id, and where Preciosa, as ego, suffers from a neurosis that is self-evidently sexual in nature. But this offers too narrow an explanation of a poem that draws our attention to how things happen as much as to what happens; a poem that presents us with Dionysiac and Apollonian extremes, not only in terms of the polarity between chaotic nature, embodied by the wind, and the order to which a terrified Preciosa flees, but also in terms of the way the things of the world, whether it be people, objects, feelings or natural phenomena, have been controlled and transformed in the production of verse and the elaboration of images.

There are possible allusions to Dionysian rites in the musical instruments referred to in the poem,[7] but whatever its source, music is clearly associated in this ballad with natural phenomena, whether it be in the sea's song ('el mar bate y canta'), the wind's pipe-playing ('tocando / una dulce gaita ausente') or the flutes and the gong associated with shady places and the snow respectively ('Cantan las flautas de umbría / y el liso gong de la nieve'). True, Preciosa does herself appear wielding a tambourine, but she discards her instrument as soon as she begins to run away from the wind ('Preciosa tira el pandero / y corre sin detenerse'). (No wonder, then, that her retreat to safety should be recounted in terms that contain none of the flourishes of previous stanzas.) In addition to music, there are also a number of references to language and words: in the use of the term 'parchment' to evoke the taut

---

[7]  'While the tambourine is closely associated with gypsies, it is also a very ancient instrument closely linked with Dionysian rites. The playing of drums was part of the rites, and maenads, the handmaidens of god, are usually depicted on Greek friezes wielding tambourines. The flute and the gong [...] could, in the classical context, provide echoes of the hollow cymbals and boxwood flutes played during the Bacchic rituals recounted at the beginning of Book IV of [Ovid's] *Metamorphoses*' (Harris 1991, p. 20).

skin of the tambourine; in Preciosa's retelling of her adventure once she
has reached the safety of the consul's home; but not least in the mention of
the wind's tongues ('San Cristobalón desnudo / lleno de lenguas celestes';
'Sátiro de estrellas bajas / con sus lenguas relucientes'). Beyond their erotic
connotations, these tongues acquire significance in the context of traditional
wind-symbolism:

> wind is synonymous with breath and consequently with the Spirit, a
> heaven-sent spiritual influx. This is why both the Book of Psalms and the
> Koran equate winds with angels as God's messengers. Wind even gives its
> name to the Holy Spirit. The Spirit of God moving across the face of the
> primordial waters is called *Ruah*, 'Wind', and it was a wind which brought
> the Apostles the tongues of fire of the Holy Spirit. In Hindu symbolism,
> the wind, personified as the god (Vāyu) is cosmic breath and the Word.
> (Chevalier and Gheerbrant, pp. 1110–11)

The wind is bound up with language, with divine messages and with speaking
in tongues; a language that is other-worldly and beyond human control; a
language that can be as chaotic and emotive as the sentiments which nature
inspires. In running from the wind, Preciosa runs from this kind of language
too. Encapsulated in the final stanza of the poem, where Preciosa recounts
her story within the house and furious nature is kept without, is the trajectory
of her flight from natural forces and, most significantly, the trajectory of the
poetic endeavour itself – namely, that of keeping nature at bay and ordering
and fashioning its raw material into a work of art. The events of the ballad
embody the poem's very principle, as does casting the wind as a satyr, or
the use of other mythical or literary references, and, of course, the crafting
of ingenious images, or the variation between poetic and prosaic language.
If 'Preciosa y el aire' tells any story it is the story of why it is impossible to
read the ballad – as it is also with the poetry of Góngora – 'ante los objetos
de que habla'. Although this story is clothed in sexual allusion and eroticism,
we need not consider sex, either as it relates to neuroses or to unacceptable
sexual behaviour, as the subject of the poem. For this natural phenomenon
has also been appropriated by poetry for poetry, the sexual act, or indeed its
evasion, standing for the way art ought not to allow itself to be consumed
by the principles of nature. This is the poem's self-conscious message, and
if there is no sexual union (whether forced or consensual) in the poem, it is
because it seeks to evoke the tension, not the collusion, between the natural
world and the denaturalizing practices of art; a tension which demonstrates
itself to be a potently creative source. And yet the fact that there should
be any tension at all – that art should have failed to dispense with nature

altogether – is itself something to bear in mind. On the one hand, it serves
to remind us of the difficulty of the (creative) task. On the other, it raises
the possibility that the poet is still working certain issues through, that what
the poem is registering is the endeavour to create independent poetry, but
in terms that suggest that this project still has something of the status of a
work in progress about it; or even the possibility – and this is perhaps what is
most intriguing – that the poet (regardless of the benefits) only ever engaged
reluctantly with the task in the first place.

Although the fragments which combine to produce the ballad 'Romance
sonámbulo' present us with the semblance of a very different anecdotal
context from that of 'Preciosa y el aire', it is interesting that it too should be
suggestive of a union (in this case, we might presume, one that is mutually
desired) that never actually takes place. It is a poem which also employs the
fundamental masculine/feminine, male/female binary oppositions articulated
in 'Preciosa y el aire' through the gypsy girl and the wind. In 'Romance
sonámbulo' these opposite poles are occupied respectively by yet another
gypsy girl and by a wounded man (one of two *compadres*) who goes in
search of her. These characters, along with the promise or suitability of their
union, or re-union, are prefigured in accordance with the thoroughly poetic
logic of the ballad by the masculine and feminine association of complementary objects (boat/sea, horse/mountains) in the opening stanza, which
begins, quite appropriately, with an evocation of desire. Here is the ballad
in its entirety:

> Verde que te quiero verde.
> Verde viento. Verdes ramas.
> El barco sobre la mar
> y el caballo en la montaña.
> Con la sombra en la cintura
> ella sueña en su baranda,
> verde carne, pelo verde,
> con ojos de fría plata.
> Verde que te quiero verde.
> Bajo la luna gitana,
> las cosas la están mirando
> y ella no puede mirarlas.
>
> \*
>
> Verde que te quiero verde.
> Grandes estrellas de escarcha,
> vienen con el pez de sombra
> que abre el camino del alba.
> La higuera frota su viento

con la lija de sus ramas,
y el monte, gato garduño,
eriza sus pitas agrias.
¿Pero quién vendrá? ¿Y por dónde ...?
Ella sigue en su baranda,
verde carne, pelo verde,
soñando en la mar amarga.

*

Compadre, quiero cambiar
mi caballo por su casa,
mi montura por su espejo,
mi cuchillo por su manta.
Compadre, vengo sangrando,
desde los puertos de Cabra.
Si yo pudiera, mocito,
este trato se cerraba.
Pero yo ya no soy yo.
Ni mi casa es ya mi casa.
Compadre, quiero morir
decentemente en mi cama.
De acero, si puede ser,
con las sábanas de holanda.
¿No veis la herida que tengo
desde el pecho a la garganta?
Trescientas rosas morenas
lleva tu pechera blanca.
Tu sangre rezuma y huele
alrededor de tu faja.
Pero yo ya no soy yo.
Ni mi casa es ya mi casa.
Dejadme subir al menos
hasta las altas barandas,
¡dejadme subir!, dejadme
hasta las verdes barandas.
Barandales de la luna
por donde retumba el agua.

*

Ya suben los dos compadres
hacia las altas barandas.
Dejando un rastro de sangre.
Dejando un rastro de lágrimas.
Temblaban en los tejados
farolillos de hojalata.
Mil panderos de cristal,
herían la madrugada.

*

Verde que te quiero verde,
verde viento, verdes ramas.
Los dos compadres subieron.
El largo viento, dejaba
en la boca un raro gusto
de hiel, de menta y de albahaca.
¡Compadre! ¿Dónde está, dime?
¿Dónde está tu niña amarga?
¡Cuántas veces te esperó!
¡Cuántas veces te esperara,
cara fresca, negro pelo,
en esta verde baranda!

*

Sobre el rostro del aljibe,
se mecía la gitana.
Verde carne, pelo verde,
con ojos de fría plata.
Un carámbano de luna
la sostiene sobre el agua.
La noche se puso íntima
como una pequeña plaza.
Guardias civiles borrachos
en la puerta golpeaban.
Verde que te quiero verde.
Verde viento. Verdes ramas.
El barco sobre la mar.
Y el caballo en la montaña.

What becomes apparent through a closer inspection of the ballad is that the principal male and female figures are kept apart not only at an anecdotal level in terms of the failure of their (re)union, but also by the way in which they are made to occupy distinct and separate stanzas, the gypsy girl inhabiting the first, second and fifth stanzas, the wounded *compadre*, the third and fourth. It is this structural separation that is most significant since it moves us into a metapoetical domain where poetic processes and strategies are everything, and where the anecdotal, with its alliance to the real things and events of the world, is once more relegated to a secondary place. Indeed, 'Romance sonámbulo' is perhaps the best example in *Romancero gitano* of Lorca's anti-anecdotal stance.[8]

---

[8] See also Federico Bonaddio, 'Lorca's "Romance sonámbulo": the Desirability of Non-Disclosure', *Bulletin of Hispanic Studies*, 72 (1995), 385–401. The present discussion of the ballad reworks some of the ideas contained in this article.

Nevertheless, despite what is by now the familiar notion that the story line of 'Romance sonámbulo' resists reconstruction (a resistance acknowledged by Lorca when he spoke of his own inability to explain what happens in the poem: 'nadie sabe lo que pasa ni aun yo' [*OC*, III, p. 341]), critics have not been deterred from hazarding their own reconstructions. Tales of a wounded smuggler seeking refuge from civil guards in the house of his lover who, anxiously awaiting him and under the entrancing influence of the moon, drowns (either voluntary or involuntarily) before the young man can reach her, no doubt touch upon the poem's folkloric sources of inspiration, but also underestimate the very significance of the poem's disruption of discursive processes.[9]

In his 1926 recital Lorca signalled, if not strictly speaking a method, at least a specific intention in the composition of his ballads, namely the fusion of narrative and lyric ballad modes:

> El romance típico había sido siempre una narración y era lo narrativo lo que daba encanto a su fisonomía, porque, cuando se hacía lírico, sin eco de anécdota, se convertía en canción. Yo quise fundir el romance narrativo con el lírico sin que perdieran ninguna calidad y este esfuerzo se ve conseguido en algunos poemas del *Romancero* como el llamado *Romance sonámbulo* […]. (*OC*, III, p. 341)

In 'Romance sonámbulo', the distinctive quality of the respective ballad modes seems to be maintained by the apparent predominance of one over the other in particular sections of the poem. The account of the *compadres*' climb ('Ya suben los dos compadres / hacia las altas barandas'), the inclusion of their dialogue and the reference to the civil guards ('Guardias civiles borrachos / en la puerta golpeaban') all seem to be consistent with the predominantly impersonal, sequential and dramatic mode of the narrative ballad. In contrast, aspects of the lyric ballad mode are maintained through the incorporation and repetition of the emotional opening refrain ('Verde que te quiero verde'), the descriptive and contemplative passages relating to the gypsy girl, and the employment of a language of association and allusion, as in the use of the word 'green' or the descriptions of an animate landscape.[10] The fusion of narrative and lyric modes to which Lorca referred might be understood, therefore, in terms of the poem's embodiment of the characteristics of both.

---

[9]   See Ramsden (p. 29) for a summary of a series of interpretations that emphasize 'underlying narrative'

[10]   See Mercedes Díaz Roig's introduction to her edition of *El Romancero Viejo* (Madrid: Cátedra, 1992), 9–57, for a description of the narrative *romance* and its lyric influence.

Yet given that the narrative ballad has traditionally always displayed characteristics of lyric influence and that the distinction between narrative and lyric ballads could be said to rest principally upon the extent to which lyric devices are incorporated in each, to restrict our interpretation of the notion of fusion in this way is neither helpful nor remarkable.[11] Instead we might understand the fusion of narrative and lyric modes in terms of a reciprocal semantic contagion resulting from the cohabitation of lines and passages whose voices, because they are either preponderantly narrative or lyrical, are essentially at odds. In other words, narrative and lyric characteristics do not simply coexist or cooperate within a poem clearly indebted to both ballad modes. Rather, they actually intrude upon the nature and function of one another, an intrusion that is instrumental in the subversion of clear and coherent story telling. Indeed, language serving narration and appearing to function on a literal plane becomes, by association with the lyrical, figurative; whilst lyric descriptions that are profoundly allusive become strangely entangled in the narrative thread. Lorca's declaration that not even he understood what 'happens' in the poem is itself recognition of the success of fusion: 'hay una gran sensación de anécdota, un agudo ambiente dramático y nadie sabe lo que pasa ni aun yo, porque el misterio poético es también misterio para el poeta que lo comunica, pero que muchas veces lo ignora' (OC, III, p. 341).

The temptation of critics, however, has been to attribute greater significance to one or other mode in an attempt to impose on the poem a unitary, anecdotal interpretation rooted in the perspective of either the third-person narrator or the lyrical 'yo'.[12] The discrepancies in the story line may be smoothed over for the sake of totalizing meaning by seeing *fragmentismo* as the source of narrative disorientation or the basis for mapping a dream narra-

---

[11] Díaz Roig (*El Romancero Viejo*, p. 24), in discussing views on the origins of the *romance*, explains that today 'casi todos piensan que el Romancero nació como una simbiosis entre la lírica y la épica'. She adds that, even where the subject matter is strongly related to the epic, 'no faltan abundantes muestras de caracteres líricos como son la expresividad, el deleite en el adorno, multiplicidad de recursos formales de orígen lírico, emoción y acentuación de la emotividad' (p. 25).

[12] For example, Beverly J. DeLong-Tonelli, in 'The Lyric Dimension in Lorca's "Romance sonámbulo"', *Romance Notes* 12 (1971), 289–95, identifies a 'basic speaker', 'the smuggler-speaker [who] has done nothing more than admit to himself, in a moment not measured by time, that his beloved is dead' (p. 295). DeLong-Tonelli concludes that the poem 'is fundamentally lyric rather than narrative, [although] what the speaker has communicated to himself has never been explicitly stated. He has externalized himself as listener to the point where he could even assume a pseudo-narrative role as he recounted the climb up to the balcony, but the narrative flash does not constitute the basic situation of the poem' (p. 295).

tive onto the poem.[13] Yet what seems clear from the at once differential and interactive relationship between lyric and narrative modes is that the former is not the subordinate of the latter. If anything does happen or is said in the poem, it is as a result of their relationship, as a result of anecdotal disruption, and not in spite of it.

Considering that the poem's depiction of the gypsy girl encompasses two locations – the railings ('Con la sombre en la cintura / ella sueña en su baranda') and the water tank ('Sobre el rostro del aljibe, / se mecía la gitana') – it is perhaps significant that her movement from one place to another is not graphically conveyed. This hiatus in the depiction of her physical actions is consistent with the non-physical activity she is said to be engaged in: dreaming. What is more, her cerebral activity and corporeal inaction are in stark contrast to the motion attributed to the *compadres* ('Ya suben los dos compadres'); a contrast compounded by the way in which the gypsy girl and the wounded *compadre* are kept apart by the poem's structure. One critic has suggested that it can be inferred from the poem's title that the girl is a sleepwalker.[14] However, such an inference does not take into account the absence of detail regarding her movement in sleep from one place to another. In effect, it is the *compadres* who are seen to do the walking, not the girl, and it could be argued, therefore, that these female and male figures are involved jointly in the activity of sleepwalking, which the title, in any case, relates not to the girl but to the ballad itself. The role of each in this joint participation is clearly defined: she does the sleeping and/or dreaming; they, on the other

---

[13] As Robert G. Havard points out in his *From Romanticism to Surrealism. Seven Spanish Poets* (Cardiff: University of Wales Press, 1988), 198, the term *fragmentismo* may refer either to the natural process by which fragments of an original long poem from which a *romance* evolved were forgotten over generations of oral transmission; or to the consequent technique, 'later cultivated by more sophisticated poets who realized that abruptly excerpted sequences often made intriguing, enigmatic poems'. It is this technique which Havard believes Lorca exploits in order to create 'the texture of dream' in his poem. For Havard, if the poem is to be read as a dream, then it is perhaps the poet who is the dreamer, a view that allows the critic to 'penetrate the objective superficies of narrative and characterization by seeing the poem as an imagistic presentation of the poet's own psychic dichotomy' (p. 202). Although this approach maintains an awareness of divisions or oppositions within the text, it arguably seeks also to iron them out by having recourse to dream logic and to the unitary perspective of the dreamer. If Havard finds his speaker in the mind's eye of the dreamer, Harris conveys his sense of an impersonal narrator through an analogy with film technique. By interpreting the poem in terms of 'narrative *focus*', with long shots, close-ups and flashbacks, Harris alludes to the possible existence of an underlying story line that has been 'reshaped' by something approaching cinematographic *fragmentismo* (Harris 1991, pp. 26–31).

[14] See Lázló András, 'El caso de la gitana sonámbula', in Mátyás Horányi (ed.), *Actas del Simposio Internacional de Estudios Hispánicos* (Budapest: Akadémiai Kiadó, 1978), 181–94 (p. 186).

hand, do the walking and so fill the motional hiatus in the poem's depiction of the girl's activity. The girl and *compadres* are thus linked on a conceptual level even if in structural and anecdotal terms they appear to be kept apart.

There is a correspondence too between the roles of these figures and the style pervading their respective sections. The girl's dreaming and corporeal inaction are complemented by the lyrical tone integral to the descriptive and contemplative nature of her sections of the poem. The movement associated with sections inhabited by the *compadres* is likewise enhanced by the narrative bias. In a sense, the completion of the somnambulant equation by the distinct, though complementary, female and male roles, is synonymous with the achievement of fusing the lyric and narrative ballad modes 'whilst preserving the distinctiveness of each'. Thus the adjective 'sonámbulo', in its qualification of the noun 'romance' in the poem's title, encapsulates the interaction of female and male roles within the poem and, consequently, the fusion of lyric and narrative ballad modes with which these roles are associated and which constitutes the body of the 'somnambulist-poem' itself.

As for the poem's famous refrain, 'Verde que te quiero verde. / Verde viento. Verdes ramas', any attempt to ascribe the voice behind it to any specific figure is inevitably thwarted by absence of detail and by the fact that the refrain appears in the stanzas of both the girl and the *compadres*. Any attempt to identify whom the voice is addressing proves equally frustrating. The only workable approach is to accept the ambiguity of the refrain's origin and direction and to understand it in terms of what it enunciates: desire. The significance of this enunciation of desire would seem to hinge on a prior explanation of the role of the direct object 'te', which might refer directly to the colour green itself or to an as yet unidentified person. The first possibility would suggest that the very attainment of greenness is the goal of desire; the second, that the object of this desire is in fact a transformation: either to turn someone or to have someone turn green.

The symbolic character of the enunciation is enhanced in the second line of the refrain in which the wind, unusually, is qualified by the adjective 'green', although now it seems to have none of the bawdy connotations of the 'viento verde' of 'Preciosa y el aire'.[15] The notion of transformation may be present in the image of 'green branches' ('verdes ramas'), which possibly evokes the change in a tree's appearance occasioned by the growth of foliage. What is more, the idea of turning or having someone turn green might be deemed particularly relevant given that there is indeed some indication in the poem

---

[15] As Harris (p. 20) and Ramsden (p. 13, n. 8) point out, there is an allusion here to 'viejo verde', the Spanish equivalent of 'dirty old man'.

of a colour transformation. On three occasions the gypsy girl's skin and hair
are described as being green ('verde carne, pelo verde', in the first, second
and fifth stanzas), but in the fourth stanza there is a reference to her also as
being fresh-faced and having black hair ('¡Cuántas veces te esperara, / cara
fresca, negro pelo, / en esta verde baranda!').

Critics are well aware of the ambiguous connotations of the colour green
both within and outside the context of the poem.[16] Interpretations vary
between viewing the colour in terms of explainable natural phenomena and
attaching to it a symbolic value. Invariably the former approach is limited
and cannot be applied to all references to the colour.[17] But the latter approach
is also problematic. For green may symbolize life and its various attributes
– fertility, youth, hope – by virtue of the colour's overwhelming presence
in the natural world. Or it may be a symbol of death and its companions –
sterility, frustration, bitterness – by virtue of the connection, for instance,
with putrefaction. Inevitably, in a text fraught with ambiguity, both symbolic
interpretations apply and neither is dominant.

This open interpretation of the value of green is supported by the equally
ambiguous value of the moon, which governs both fertility and sterility by
virtue of its association with, amongst other things, the menses and ocean
tides. The moon, with its waxing and waning aspects, is as much a symbol
of victory over death as it is of death itself, and is perhaps better interpreted
in terms of its cyclical activity: life, death and rebirth.[18] Such an interpretation has important repercussions for the analysis of the final image of the girl
in the water tank. Critics tend to refer to the girl as having drowned (either
accidentally or in an act of suicide), an interpretation revolving primarily
around four indicators: the girl's rocking or swaying movement upon the
surface of the water; the green colour of her flesh and hair; her cold, silvery
eyes and their consequent association with the moon's own appearance; and
the role of the icicle of moonlight in maintaining the girl above water ('Un

---

[16] See, for example, J. M. Aguirre, 'El sonambulismo de García Lorca', *Bulletin of
Hispanic Studies*, 44 (1967), 271–4; Robert G. Havard, 'The Symbolic Ambivalence of "Green"
in García Lorca and Dylan Thomas', *Modern Language Review*, 67 (1972), 810–19; and Derek
Harris, 'Green Death: An Analysis of the Symbolism of the Colour Green in Lorca's poetry',
in Nicholas G. Round and D. Gareth Walters (eds), *Readings in Spanish and Portuguese for
Geoffrey Connell* (Glasgow: Glasgow University, 1985), 89–91.

[17] For instance, Harris accepts that the girl's skin colour might be natural, green denoting
for him 'the olive-green complexion found in Andalusia', but not the colour of her hair (1985,
p. 90).

[18] According to Ángel Álvarez de Miranda, *La metáfora y el mito* (Madrid: Taurus, 1963),
41, '[p]ara la religiosidad primitiva y arcaica la luna contiene en sí la muerte, la sufre y la
trasciende'.

carámbano de luna / la sostiene sobre el agua'). However, since the colour green and the moon have ambiguous symbolic values, their presence need not support this specifically deathly interpretation of the girl's position in the tank. And although the use of the verb *mecerse* to indicate the girl's swaying movements might convey the stillness of a corpse, it might equally evoke associations with the rocking of a sleeping child in its cradle. In this one image, therefore, birth and death are possibly associated, just as they may be in the colour green and in the influence of the moon. The difficulty of opting for one interpretation over the other is aggravated by the very omission of any explicit reference to the girl's death. Events thus become ambiguous, the poem remains open-ended, and linear, anecdotal interpretations are subsequently confounded.

At best what we can say about the refrain is that it is yet another example of how the words of the poem cannot be read with any certainty as referents to phenomena in the real world outside its borders. Weaving its way through the ballad, it stands for the very principle of poeticization, whose effects can be seen in the images of the stanzas belonging either to the girl or to the wounded *compadre* – note, for example, the animate landscape of the second stanza in which animals serve to bring life and form to natural phenomena ('el pez de sombra', 'el monte, gato garduño, / eriza sus pitas agrias'); or the hyperbolic use of flowers to denote wounds in the third ('Trescientas rosas morenas / lleva tu pechera blanca'); or the synaesthetic play on light and sound accompanying the *compadre*'s painful climb ('Temblaban en los tejados / farolillos de hojalata. / Mil panderos de cristal, / herían la madrugada'). In addition, as an enunciation of desire, the refrain provides common ground between the two principal and desiring figures of the ballad. The girl's desire is evoked by her dreaming ('ella sueña en su baranda') and by the claim that she had been waiting for some time ('¡Cuántas veces te esperó! / ¡Cuántas veces te esperara, / cara fresca, negro pelo, / en esta verde baranda!); while the desire of the wounded *compadre* is signalled by his desperate need to reach the high, green railings ('Dejadme subir al menos / hasta las altas barandas, / ¡dejadme subir!, dejadme / hasta las verdes barandas') and by his persistent questions to the other *compadre* ('¿Dónde está, dime? / ¿Dónde está tu niña amarga?'). Yet there is no resolution to their dilemma, at least not one provided by the poem, or one that it seeks to provide, either with any clarity or in anecdotal terms.

Acknowledging both its independence and its source, Lorca said the following of his poem: 'Es un hecho poético puro del fondo andaluz, y siempre tendrá luces cambiantes, aun para el hombre que lo ha comunicado, que soy yo' (*OC*, III, p. 343). What Lorca was signalling here was the poem's independence, one that is bolstered by the subversion of anecdote, itself embodied by the failure of the principal figures to be united other than in terms of what each contributes to the intensely poetic character of the ballad. Had the two figures been shown to meet – whether in life or in death – this might have lent greater emphasis to the anecdotal at the expense of the poetic, which is the very product of the tension between the lyrical and narrative modes with which the gypsy girl and the wounded *compadre* are associated. 'Romance sonámbulo' is not concerned with the process of telling but rather with the process of not telling, and so the very human desires of the poem's figures have been sacrificed in favour of the elusively poetic and transformational desire evoked by the refrain. It is the logic of the refrain that endures, repeated as it is, in one form or the other, five times throughout the poem, including at the end. Thus poetry overlays the anecdotal, a process which is facilitated by the fusion (or mutual contagion) of lyric and narrative ballad modes and which is articulated through the non-union of the girl and *compadre*. It is fitting, therefore, that the final image of the poem should differ from its appearance in the first stanza by virtue of the inclusion of a visibly divisive full stop: 'El barco sobre la mar. / Y el caballo en la montaña.' The human desire for union, for togetherness, both structurally and anecdotally – a desire that becomes emblematic of the human emotion which independent art must resist – is here and throughout the poem subordinated to another desire: the desire – the very real desire – to create (or be seen to create) autonomous poems.

Where in 'Preciosa y el aire' we find the gypsy girl and the wind, and in 'Romance sonámbulo', the gypsy girl and the *compadre*, in 'Thamar y Amnón' we have the two figures from the Old Testament story which recounts the rape by David's favourite son, Amnon, of his half-sister, Tamar. Once the violent deed has been done and Amnon has fled on horseback from the palace and the arrows fired by the palace guards, David's reaction in the poem is to cut the strings of a harp:

> Violador enfurecido,
> Amnón huye con su jaca.
> Negros le dirigen flechas
> en los muros y atalayas.
> Y cuando los cuatro cascos
> eran cuatro resonancias,
> David con unas tijeras
> cortó las cuerdas del arpa.

The cutting of the strings may mark David's anger, desperation or dismay, and the point of culmination of the unbearable tension that has built up throughout the ballad, as well as, quite simply, the end of the poem and, indeed, the end of the collection itself. In this respect, it is fitting that a musical instrument, an object from the domain of art, should have been chosen to bring the poetic process to a conclusion. What is more, the self-reflexive aspect of the object reminds us that what has taken place belongs to the realm of art as much as it does (if not more) to the realm of real actions and emotions associated here with the violent act perpetrated by Amnon who, in any case, like the other figures in the poem, is already once removed from the plane of real beings by virtue of having his source not in a contemporary event but in a text, albeit a biblical one. If it was not apparent in the first reading of the ballad, a rerun in light of the final line reveals that the tension mounting throughout the stanzas is equally that which accrues in the struggle between the demands of poetry and the pull of reality occasioned by the material and physical aspects of the anecdote.

In the opening stanza the poetic once more overlays the anecdotal, the scene that is set serving not to provide a context of time or place but instead an atmosphere of tension anticipating the violence that will surface later. The drama emerges from the play of sound, colour, shape and texture, and the very real things to which the lines refer or allude (moon, sky, land, water, summer, tiger, roofs, metal, air, sheep, wounds, light) are rid of their referential aspect and recruited for the purposes of poetic achievement. With this shift of focus from the real to the poetic, it is the poet's craft that holds our attention, the mood and images which he has created forestalling linear, anecdotal movement:

> La luna gira en el cielo
> sobre las tierras sin agua
> mientras el verano siembra
> rumores de tigre y llama.
> Por encima de los techos
> nervios de metal sonaban.
> Aire rizado venía
> con los balidos de lana.
> La tierra se ofrece llena
> de heridas cicatrizadas,
> o estremecida de agudos
> cauterios de luces blancas.

Tamar and Amnon are introduced in the second stanza. They are set in opposition, not only because one is the object of the gaze and the other, its subject, but also because she is associated with ethereal qualities, while he is firmly grounded in the material processes of carnal desire:

> Thamar estaba soñando
> pájaros en su garganta,
> al son de panderos fríos
> y cítaras enlunadas.
> Su desnudo en el alero,
> agudo norte de palma,
> pide copos a su vientre
> y granizo a sus espaldas.
> Thamar estaba cantando
> desnuda por la terraza.
> Alrededor de sus pies,
> cinco palomas heladas.
> Amnón, delgado y concreto,
> en la torre la miraba,
> llenas las ingles de espuma
> y oscilaciones la barba.
> Su desnudo iluminado
> se tendía en la terraza,
> con un rumor entre dientes
> de flecha recién clavada.
> Amnón estaba mirando
> la luna redonda y baja,
> y vio en la luna los pechos
> durísimos de su hemana.

Tamar's associations are with dream, music and coldness (or frigidity). She dreams of birds (presumably song) in her throat, is accompanied by tambourines and zithers and later sings. The erotic possibilities of her nakedness are off-set by the references to the cold, whether it be in the qualification of the tambourines as 'fríos', or of the zithers as moon-shaped (coldness being a quality of the silvery moon in contrast to the heat of the fiery sun), or in her request that her belly be covered in snowflakes and her back pelted by hailstones (evoking self-flagellation and the purgation of the flesh), or in the image of five frozen doves lying about her feet (her own frigid version of the five stigmata of Christ). Given her self-denial and her preferred activity of song, it is up to Amnon to render her nakedness bodily and sexual through his own desiring gaze. His own worldliness and physicality is evoked in the reference to his virile, bodily excitement ('llenas las ingles de espuma / y oscilaciones la barba') and in his qualification as slender and solid ('delgado y concreto'), which in turn associates him with the (phallic) shape and form of the tower in which he is thinking of his half-sister. Tamar is associated once more with the moon, her nakedness illuminated by its beams, and because it is upon the moon that her half-brother gazes and it is in the moon that he pictures her firm breasts. This lunar image thus encapsulates the polar relation between Tamar's cold, ethereal nature and Amnon's physical desire, as well as its undoing, since Amnon, in accordance with the material principle of his lust, here negates the heavenly to imagine only the body in the shape of Tamar's breasts.

The third stanza, as Harris (1991, p. 79) explains, 'deals with the moment before the rape, following the account in the Book of Samuel which describes how Amnon took to his bed, feigning illness, and asked for his sister to be sent to him':

> Amnón a las tres y media
> se tendió sobre la cama.
> Toda la alcoba sufría
> con sus ojos llenos de alas.
> La luz, maciza, sepulta
> pueblos en la arena parda,
> o descubre transitorio
> coral de rosas y dalias.
> Linfa de pozo oprimida
> brota silencio en las jarras.
> En el musgo de los troncos
> la cobra tendida canta.
> Amnón gime por la tela
> fresquísima de la cama.
> Yedra del escalofrío
> cubre su carne quemada.
> Thamar entró silenciosa
> en la alcoba silenciada,
> color de vena y Danubio,
> turbia de huellas lejanas.
> Thamar, bórrame los ojos
> con tu fija madrugada.
> Mis hilos de sangre tejen
> volantes sobre tu falda.
> Déjame tranquila, hermano.
> Son tus besos en mi espalda
> avispas y vientecillos
> en doble enjambre de flautas.
> Thamar, en tus pechos altos
> hay dos peces que me llaman,
> y en las yemas de tus dedos
> rumor de rosa encerrada.

As yet there is no compromise in the poetic endeavour, the mounting tension being evoked by, and centred in, images whose elaborate character and internal logic seem to run counter to any impulse to complete a linear, anecdotal reading. Despite the prosaic description of time, action and place with which the stanza begins ('Amnón a las tres y media / se tendió sobre la cama'), Amnon, like Tamar, is made to submit to the principle of poetic invention, his lines no less convoluted than those of his half-sister, whether it be the descriptions of his state of mind ('Toda la alcoba sufría / con sus ojos llenos de alas', 'Yedra del escalofrío / cubre su carne quemada') or his entreaties to the object of his lust ('bórrame los ojos / con tu fija madrugada. / Mis hilos de sangre tejen / volantes sobre tu falda', 'en tus pechos altos / hay dos peces que me llaman, / y en las yemas de tus dedos / rumor de rosa encerrada'). If in the second stanza Tamar was associated with music, now her association is with silence ('Thamar entró silenciosa / en la alcoba silenciada'), one which also denotes the increasing tension before the terrible event ('Linfa de pozo oprimida / brota silencio en las jarras'). And if music was once linked to Tamar's purity, it now comes to convey the very menace that threatens her ('En el musgo de los troncos / la cobra tendida canta', 'Son tus besos en mi espalda / avispas y vientecillos / en doble enjambre de flautas'). We might attempt to attribute the 'swarm of pipes' to Pan, thereby making sense of the semantic shift in the use of musical references in terms of the predominance in this stanza of instinctual, dionysiac impulses, in contrast to the controlled and frigid references appearing in the second. And yet this variation in the use of music is no less paradoxical than the undertaking of poetic elaboration on the theme of such a terrible act as rape; a poetic elaboration which draws attention to itself – to the aesthetic experience – at the expense of any moral imperative to voice condemnation of the act constituting its source material. The same paradox appears throughout *Romancero gitano* in which, as we have already noted, difficult and painful experience provides the source for a poetry that is often playful and ingenious. Beauty and form overlay horror and pain, which is why we can be entranced by the rhythm of the final lines of 'Romance de la luna, luna' – 'El aire la vela, vela. / El aire la está velando' – despite the tears shed on the death of a small boy, only moments before, by the gypsies of the forge; which is why it is possible too for Soledad Montoya's withered breasts to produce full and rounded songs – 'Yunques ahumados sus pechos, / gimen canciones redondas' ('Romance de la pena negra') – and why Olalla's gruesome martyrdom ('Martirio de Santa Olalla') can end in triumph, not only by the grace of God, but also by that of poetry, which brings to her charred and mutilated body vivid colours, rhythm and song:

Una Custodia reluce
sobre los cielos quemados,
entre gargantas de arroyo
y ruiseñores en ramos.
¡Saltan vidrios de colores!
Olalla blanca en lo blanco.
Ángeles y serafines
dicen: Santo, Santo, Santo.

The fourth stanza of 'Thamar y Amnón' deals with the rape itself. 'Two parallelistic lines [the fifth and sixth]', writes Harris (1991, p. 80), 'indicate the violence of the rape with a directness free of metaphor, which is reserved for the final two lines [...] that enclose Tamar's blood in a complex conceit, as if its presence could only be tolerated in an oblique expression':

Los cien caballos del rey
en el patio relinchaban.
Sol en cubos resistía
la delgadez de la parra.
Ya la coge del cabello,
ya la camisa le rasga.
Corales tibios dibujan
arroyos en rubio mapa.

Harris is perhaps right. Any direct reference to 'the blood of Tamar's ruptured hymen' ('Corales tibios'), here 'trickling over her white skin' ('dibujan / arroyos en rubio mapa'), must necessarily be relegated to the domain of taboo, metaphor thus effecting a displacement of the crudely prosaic onto the circumlocutory decency of poetic conceit. Indeed, the poem's penultimate stanza embodies similar compromises between the prosaic and the poetic:

¡Oh, qué gritos se sentían
por encima de las casas!
Qué espesura de puñales
y túnicas desgarradas.
Por las escaleras tristes
esclavos suben y bajan.
Émbolos y muslos juegan
bajo las nubes paradas.
Alrededor de Thamar
gritan vírgenes gitanas
y otras recogen las gotas
de su flor martirizada.
Paños blancos enrojecen

en las alcobas cerradas.
Rumores de tibia aurora
pámpanos y peces cambian.

Here the anecdotal and its sublimation converge in lines evoking the chaos and grief that follow Amnon's violent act. On the one hand, shouts can be plainly heard, slaves are seen to run up and down stairwells, and blood-soaked cloths point to the care that Tamar has been given. On the other hand, the movement of bodies – the pistons and thighs ('Émbolos y muslos') – retains a metaphorical aspect that is still sexually charged, while nature continues to play a responsive and dramatic role ('las nubes paradas', 'Rumores de tibia aurora / pámpanos y peces cambian'), and the effects of the violation on Tamar's body are evoked only indirectly ('las gotas / de su flor martirizada').

The final stanza describing Amnon's flight, much like the conclusion to Preciosa's flight, is practically devoid of metaphor altogether, save for the reference to David's cutting of the harp strings. David's act, if placed within the diegesis, is an understandably destructive consequence of a father's anger and dismay. If taken metaphorically, it marks, as we have already noted, the point where tension has reached breaking point and where, as a self-reflexive gesture, the ballad comes to an end along with the poetic proc-esses which gave rise to it in the first place. It also echoes Tamar's violation and the silencing of the music and song with which she was associated at the start. This pure song, like pure poetry, is the half-sister to the emotions and passions evoked by Amnon, each sibling being the embodiment of the controlling principle and raw human material of poetry respectively. And given that David's gesture can sit logically within the diegetic frame, it is a fittingly physical act which underscores the very real force of the violence of rape upon our sensibilities, irrespective of the violation's literary sources or the poetic invention which vies with it for our attention. In this sense too, David's cutting of the strings brings the poetry to an end, and it does so by marking its limits and reminding us of the power – the all too invasive power – of the real.

The force of invasive emotion or reality has a special significance for our understanding of 'La monja gitana', the next and final poem we will look at in this chapter:

Silencio de cal y mirto.
Malvas en las hierbas finas.
La monja borda alhelíes
sobre una tela pajiza.
Vuelan en la araña gris,

siete pájaros de prisma.
La iglesia gruñe a lo lejos
como un oso panza arriba.
¡Qué bien borda! ¡Con qué gracia!
Sobre la tela pajiza,
ella quisiera bordar
flores de su fanatsía.
¡Qué girasol! ¡Qué magnolia
de lentejuelas y cintas!
¡Qué azafranes y qué lunas,
en el mantel de la misa!
Cinco toronjas se endulzan
en la cercana cocina.
Las cinco llagas de Cristo
cortadas en Almería.
Por los ojos de la monja
galopan dos caballistas.
Un rumor último y sordo
le despega la camisa,
y al mirar nubes y montes
en las yertas lejanías,
se quiebra su corazón
de azúcar y yerbaluisa.
¡Oh!, qué llanura empinada
con veinte soles arriba.
¡Qué ríos puestos de pie
vislumbra su fantasía!
Pero sigue con sus flores,
mientras que de pie, en la brisa,
la luz juega el ajedrez
alto de la celosía.

The presence of embroidery and of the figure of the embroiderer in Lorca's poetry (and theatre) – here in the shape of the gypsy nun – has been explored in an essay by Manuel Delgado Morales.[19] He points out that not only Lorca but also Salvador Dalí and Luis Buñuel were drawn by the 'symbolic potential of these artforms normally carried out by women' (Delgado, p. 37), noting how the 'richness and complexity of this symbol was to increase significantly under the influence of Freudian and surrealist ideas', but also suggesting two sources for Lorca's own interest in the figure of the needleworker: Jan Vermeer's painting *The Lacemaker* – a reproduction

---

[19] See Manuel Delgado Morales, 'Embroiderers of Freedom and Desire in Lorca's Poetry and Theater', in Delgado and Poust, pp. 37–51.

of which hung in the Residencia de Estudiantes of Madrid – and the real women of Granada, including the poet's own mother. 'In those years,' writes Delgado (p. 39), 'these women devoted themselves to needlework in order to contribute in some way to the domestic economy or in order to break the monotony and the dead hours of their daily routines', and he adds that 'it is easy to imagine [Lorca] as a young boy or an adolescent among these women, attentively observing their bobbin laces, needles, drums, sewing kits and threads, and listening to their gossip, sighs, frustrations, and desires'. For Delgado, Lorca would transform the instruments of the needleworker 'into symbols (= voices) of desire and sexual liberation', although he also points to the self-reflexive potential of the symbol: 'With these instruments the poet (= needleworker) naturally and artfully will elaborate a text (= fabric)' (Delgado, p. 39). He also makes an important observation about the title of the poem 'La monja gitana', explaining 'that neither the constitutions nor the unspoken law of female religious orders envisaged that a Gypsy would become a nun, just as they never considered that a nun could be a Gypsy. In other words, saying "Gypsy nun" is equivalent to juxtaposing two mutually exclusive words' (Delgado, p. 43). He concludes that 'the word *Gypsy* must be considered a qualifying adjective that describes the mindset and behaviour of a woman who, feeling obligated to repress her desire in an extremely small and suffocating space, tries to overcome her repression by fulfilling her desire' (Delgado, p. 44). Finally, on the content of the poem, Delgado (p. 45) describes how the 'constant movement between repression and the need to satisfy her desire or her sexuality, between the oppressive reality of the convent and the psychological need to escape it, causes the outer world and the inner one to become one in the eyes of the nun'.

It is not difficult to see how the poem may be read as articulating the tension between an oppressive environment and self-repression on the one hand, and the desire for sexual freedom and expression on the other. There is plenty of evidence for such a reading: for example, the oxymoron presented by the title; the disparity between the small, cruciferous wallflowers the nun is embroidering on the altar cloth and the brighter, more expansive sunflowers, magnolias, sequins and ribbons she would like to embroider; the disapproving sounds from the church in the distance, rendered threatening by virtue of the simile comparing it with a bear; the symbols of self-sacrifice in the form of the five grapefruit ripening in the nearby kitchen and their association with Christ's stigmata, or even the altar cloth itself; the illusory male presence of the horsemen galloping across the nun's eyes (or her mind's eye); the heat and eroticism implied by the movement of her clothing, prompted by a mysterious sound; and the nun's broken heart, the reference to the fantasies she half-glimpses, and the possibly phallic imagery presented by the 'steep plain and upraised rivers' (Ramsden, p. 35) that she visualizes. Then there is the dichotomy between the inside and outside, whether it be in terms of the nun's hidden desires and the reality of the convent around her, or the objects from nature she embroiders and nature as it exists in the real world, or the environment inside convent walls and the world that exists beyond them. And yet, at another level, these basic dichotomies appear to be undone in a poem whose fabric contains far fewer of those prosaic threads that weave their way through the tissue of the other ballads we have looked at. Harris (1991, p. 31) remarks upon how the poem contains 'a number of complex metaphors and neogongoresque conceits, some of them of striking ingenuity', noting in particular 'the refracted light's seven colours of the spectrum turned to birds [...] and the final image which transposes the chequered pattern of sun and shade thrown onto the wall of the nun's cell by the shutter at the window into a board on which the wind and light play chess'. Indeed, there are very few images that can be taken at face value in a poem in which an almost relentless poeticization 'causes the outer world and the inner one to become one', where the 'outer' (in this recasting of Delgado's description) corresponds to the objects and emotions of the real world and the 'inner' to the world of poetry itself.

The key to our own reading lies in the self-reflexive value of the symbol of the embroiderer or needleworker (as noted by Delgado). Just like the subject of his poem, the poet is bound to work within parameters and limits (even if he may seek to test them): for example, those that are set by the form he has chosen, those that are presented by the difficulties associated with creativity, and those that relate to the norms of the dominant aesthetic whenever acceptance and recognition by an artistic community are amongst the goals set by the poet for himself. However novel or radical a poet might consider his work to be, at its heart will always lie, in some form and to some extent or other, the principles of negotiation and compromise. Indeed, the very awareness of having to work within limits can itself be productive, as we have seen in poems which thrive upon the tension between poetry and reality in a self-conscious attempt to register the process of creating independent art. In 'La monja gitana', the disparity between what the nun can and might otherwise wish to embroider may allude to the frustrations of a poet caught between the what-might-have-been and the reality of his words on the page. More significantly, the nun's removal from the world, her attachment to artifice (nature embroidered) as opposed to nature, and the channelling of her physical desires into fantasy all correspond to the poet's own banishment of the worldly in his pursuit of independent art and, with it, membership of the artistic community. This is the poet's work, evidenced in the poem by the sublimation of the nun's desires into metaphor: namely, to reject the world in favour of the vitality of neogongorine conceit. Indeed, the discontinuity at the heart of human relationships that is so evident in *Romancero gitano* – the loneliness, frustrations, transgressions and violence – is nothing other than the self-conscious articulation of the necessity to separate poetry from life; it is the very embodiment of the rift between nature and art (or culture). Yet the fact that it is cast in such drastic terms, the fact that the embroiderer (or writer) continues to fantasize in 'La monja gitana', could signal a dissatisfaction on Lorca's part with the very aesthetic enterprise in which he was engaged. For all his apparent efforts to keep reality at bay, his decision to populate his ballads with what can only be described as human forms, even if their sources are often in literature or myth, suggests a reluctance to surrender completely to the norms of dehumanized art. At the very least it makes the attempt to create independent poems that much harder. So it should come as no surprise that the title 'La monja gitana' presents us with an oxymoron conveying both an insider and outsider: one who belongs and one who does not. Lorca may not have liked to be thought of as a gypsy poet, but his approach in the ballads did not guarantee him a place inside, failing as it did to gain him the total recognition that he sought from the community – the Order – of his peers.

To even talk of a community of artists is already to touch upon a fundamental problem which Lorca faced in his quest for recognition. That community was by no means monolithic, as Agustín Sánchez Vidal has shown in his discussion of the Spanish avant-garde in the context of the celebrations on the tercentenary of Luis de Góngora's death and the centenary of Goya's a year later in 1928.[20] Some artists rejected the homage to the Cordoban poet altogether, seeing in Goya's painting a more relevant, 'less sterile and aestheticist' (Sánchez Vidal, p. 111) precedent for their own work, their preference for him over Góngora an indication of their rejection of dehumanization, 'which they tried to fight through expressionism, surrealism, neoromanticism or political commitment. This was the case [for example] with Valle-Inclán, Ramón Gómez de la Serna and Luis Buñuel' (Sánchez Vidal, p. 112). Indeed, Dalí's much cited criticism of Lorca's ballads, in a letter of late August 1928, describing them as traditional, old-fashioned, commonplace and conformist, along with Lorca's own claim that his work had been misunderstood ('Claro

---

[20] See Agustín Sánchez Vidal, 'Góngora, Buñuel, the Spanish Avant-garde and the Centenary of Goya's Death', in Derek Harris (ed.), *The Spanish Avant-Garde* (Manchester: Manchester University Press, 1995), 110–22 (p. 111).

que mi libro no lo han entendido los putrefactos, aunque ellos digan que sí' [*EC*, p. 585]), suggest that each man had a very different perception of what it could mean to be contemporary or modern.[21]

Given the Surrealist trajectory of his work, it was perhaps predictable that Dalí should have responded negatively to *Romancero gitano*. David Vilaseca argues that his letter 'clearly denotes a need on Dalí's part to reject Lorca, and position himself (now that he was about to go to Paris and engage himself completely with the Surrealist movement) against Lorca and his art'.[22] Whatever reason Dalí may have had, Lorca, it seems, was not totally surprised by, nor did he wholly disagree with, his friend's critique (see Gibson 1999, p. 210). Well before its publication, Lorca had already become aware of the limitations of *Romancero gitano*, or at least of the limited interpretations to which it might give rise. And yet he recognized that once in the public domain his ballads could not be guarded from readings that ran counter to his own vision of them. 'Por eso,' he declared in the preamble to his 1926 recital, 'no me quejo de la falsa vision andaluza que se tiene de este poema a causa de recitadores sensuales de bajo tono o criaturas ignorantes', although he added that he believed that 'la pureza de su construcción y el noble tono con que me esforcé al crearlo, lo defenderán de sus actuales amantes excesivos, que a veces lo llenan de baba'. Then in a letter to fellow poet Jorge Guillén, dated January 1927, he suggested that the misunderstandings to which his work had given rise were obliging him to change tack, aware as he was of the negative impact they might have on his ambition to be taken seriously as a novel and modern poet. Indicating to Guillén that he would send him some poems with a view to publishing them in the review *Verso y Prosa*, he insisted 'Y desde luego, no serán romances gitanos' (*EC*, p. 414), adding

Me va molestando un poco *mi mito* de gitanería. Confunden mi vida y carácter. No quiero de ninguna manera. Los gitanos son un tema. Y nada más. Yo podía ser lo mismo poeta de agujas de coser o de paisajes hidráulicos. Además el gitanismo me da un tono de incultura, de falta de educación y de *poeta salvaje* que tú sabes bien no soy. No quiero que me encasillen. Siento que me van echando cadenas.[23]

---

[21] Dalí's letter is reproduced in its entirety in Ian Gibson, *Lorca-Dalí. El amor que no pudo ser* (Barcelona: Plaza & Janés, 1999), 207–10.

[22] David Vilaseca, *The Apocryphal Subject: Masochism, Identification, and Paranoia in Salvador Dalí's Autobiographical Writings* (New York: Peter Lang, 1995), 64.

[23] These sentiments are echoed in the letter he sent the same month to his friend, the critic and historian Melchor Fernández Almagro, in which he emphasizes that his book *Canciones* is not 'gitanístico' (*EC*, p. 418).

Despite what he wrote to Guillén, Lorca was not a poet inclined to write about hydraulics, and yet he would have considered himself no less modern for that. For him, the modernity of *Romancero gitano* originated in the neogongorine invention of its verse, in the creation of ingenious, highly metaphorical images. In *Romancero gitano*, observation submits itself to the imagination so that what is conveyed is precisely the Andalusia which, as Lorca put it, cannot be seen. And yet the very transparent, self-conscious tensions between the poetic and the real that are characteristic of the ballads suggest that he may have been deceiving himself. His achievements in the collection are plain to be seen, but as a vehicle by which to position himself it sent too many mixed messages. In its engagement with the processes of abstracting poetry from reality, in its self-conscious treatment of the tensions between the poetic and the anecdotal, it did not manage, nor perhaps did it seek, to distance itself sufficiently from the real world, whether it be the world of human emotion, nature, locality, folklore or myth – worlds which all had a very real place in the popular imagination. Arguably its liminality is its real strength, what makes it both critically challenging and widely accessible. In this sense Lorca was truly the gypsy poet, where the two terms 'gypsy' and 'poet' present an incongruity: the outsider and the insider, the man and the artist. For this reason alone, irrespective of what it meant for his reputation, Lorca could (or should) have defended his *Romancero gitano* to the hilt and with – and why not? – that same knowing, self-parodying, tongue-in-cheek bravado with which he infused the words of his gypsy macho in 'La casada infiel':

> Me porté como quien soy.
> Como un gitano legítimo.
> Le regalé un costurero
> grande de raso pajizo,
> y no quise enamorarme
> porque teniendo marido
> me dijo que era mozuela
> cuando la llevaba al río.

5

# *Poeta en Nueva York*: Against Modernity

> El Yoísmo es la síntesis excelsa de todos los estéticos
> 'ismos' gemelos que luchan rivales por conquistar la
> heroica trinchera de vanguardia intelectual.
> De ahí que el anhelo máximo del 'Yo' ambicioso,
> consciente e hipervitalista es: ser Original.
>
> (Guillermo de Torre, *Ultra-Manifiestos*)

Lorca's series of poems collected under the title *Poeta en Nueva York* present the reader with an often harrowing condemnation of big city life and its alienating consequences.[1] Yet there is something disconcerting about this outsider's attack on a city he knew relatively little about and in which he resided for less than a year (between June 1929 and March 1930) in circumstances that can only be described as comfortable. The anguished tones of Lorca's New York poems are symptomatic, no doubt, of his outrage at the excesses and injustices of capitalist society – sentiments that are anticipated in his 'Oda al Santísimo Sacramento del Altar' (*OC*, I, pp. 960–9), in which he 'bitterly attacks the ambit of cities, a world against nature, a world of alienation, of massiveness dwarfing the human individual, of moral disorientation and oppression'.[2] We might even attribute his feelings to an intense culture shock experienced by someone for whom life in the vast metropolis was essentially alien; and yet the poet's letters to his family during his stay seem to undermine the image of a lost or outraged soul constantly at odds with a hostile and merciless world.[3] What is more, in a rather ambivalent letter to his friend, the Chilean diplomat Carlos Morla Lynch, written only days before he was due to set off on his travels, Lorca suggests that it was

---

[1] This chapter reworks ideas contained in Federico Bonaddio, 'Lorca's *Poeta en Nueva York*: Creativity and the City', in 'The Image of the City', *Romance Studies*, No. 22 (Autumn 1993), 41–51.

[2] Eric Southworth, 'Religion', in Bonaddio (ed.) (2007), ch. 6, 129–48 (p. 137).

[3] For details regarding Lorca's residence in New York, see Gibson (1989, pp. 245–81), Stainton (pp. 221–50), as well as his letters from New York to family and friends (*EC*, pp. 613–80).

actually his preconceived dislike of New York which had informed his decision to go there in the first place: 'Estoy en Madrid dos días,' he wrote, 'para
ultimar unas cosas y en seguida salgo para París-Londres, y allí embarcaré a
New York. ¿Te sorprende? A mí también me sorprende. Yo estoy muerto de
risa de la decisión. Pero me conviene y es importante en mi vida.' And he
added: 'New York me parece horrible, pero por eso mismo me voy allí. Creo
que lo pasaré muy bien' (*EC*, p. 611).

The pretext for this apparently masochistic inclination might be found in
the personal crisis Lorca seems to have been suffering for at least a year or
so prior to his departure. Evidence of this crisis can be found in a letter he
wrote to friend and art critic Sebastià Gasch, dated August 1928:

> Queridísimo Sebastià: No quiero entrar en explicaciones de por qué no te
> he escrito. Pero no te he escrito. Perdóname. He recordado siempre nuestra
> maravillosa amistad. Pero no te puedes hacer idea lo que he pasado de
> cosas. Mi estado espiritual no es muy bueno, que digamos. Estoy atrave-
> sando una gran crisis *sentimental* (así es) de la que espero salir curado.
> 
> (*EC*, pp. 575–6)

Lorca's decision to go to New York could, then, be interpreted as a flight
from depression and anxieties at home, although this interpretation would
not fully explain why he agreed to accompany his friend Fernando de los
Ríos Urruti, Professor of Law at Granada – invited to lecture at Columbia
University – to a place he had already imagined he would detest.

In his first letter home Lorca describes New York as 'la ciudad más
atrevida y más moderna del mundo' (*EC*, p. 617), a view of the city that
is reflected also in the radical style of his New York poems, which represent a formal departure from the ballads of *Romancero gitano*. The poems
incorporate violent juxtapositions and word associations which are generally
identifiable as Surrealist in their inspiration, a fact that is in itself, as we shall
see, not without significance. As Eric Southworth (p. 136) notes, their style,
like their sentiment, is also anticipated in 'Oda al Santísimo Sacramento del
Altar', a poem which Lorca in fact completed once he was in America. But
what is of interest is the very circumstances of the shift in style and force
of feeling. These may well point to crises of a personal character or even to
heartfelt convictions, but we should not ignore either, concerns that are of a
specifically artistic nature, or the possibility that the personal, the ideological
and the artistic are in some way entwined.

The precise source of the crisis to which Lorca refers in his letter to Gasch
is not altogether clear. Contributing factors may have been his relationship
with the sculptor Emilio Aladrén Perojo (see Gibson 1989, p. 231, and

Stainton, p. 206) or indeed his straining triangular relationship with Dalí and Buñuel (see Gibson 1989, pp. 228–9, and Stainton, pp. 205–6).[4] Buñuel, like Dalí, had been critical of *Romancero gitano* (see Gibson 1989, pp. 220–1). As these two men grew closer, their artistic and personal distance from Lorca became ever more marked by their common enthusiasm for Surrealism and their mutual designs on Paris. There they would shoot their Surrealist film *Un Chien andalou*, which premiered in the French capital in June 1929. Although it is unlikely that Lorca saw the film, he would become convinced, according to Buñuel, that it set out to satirize him, complaining (supposedly) in New York to the philologist Ángel del Río that 'Buñuel has made a tiny piece of shit called *An Andalusian Dog* – and I'm the dog' (cited by Gibson 1989, p. 229). The title of the film no doubt contributed to this impression, *perro andaluz* having been the nickname given jokingly to southern poets in the Residencia de Estudiantes in Madrid – 'poetas simbolistas insensibles a la poesía revolucionaria de contendio social'[5] – amongst whom, of course, we can count Lorca (see Gibson 1989, p. 229).[6] Yet whether or not there was any truth in his suspicion, what is certain is that since the publication of *Romancero gitano* in July 1928, Lorca had seen his work subjected to criticism and become estranged from friends he valued. In all of this, whatever the strains of his emotional ties with Aladrén, his estrangement from Dalí must have weighed particularly heavily; after all, his friendship with the painter was so bound up with his own development as an artist.[7]

It is probable, for instance, that Lorca first started drawing around the time he first become acquainted with Dalí in the Residencia in 1923; the painter 'helped the poet regard his own drawings as an integral part of his poetic world' (Maurer 2007, p. 30) and later gave his encouragement and support to the exhibition of his drawings at the Dalmau Gallery, Barcelona, held between 25 June and 2 July 1927 (See Cockburn and Bonaddio 2007,

---

[4]    See also Antonina Rodrigo, *Lorca-Dalí. Una Amistad traicionada* (Barcelona: Planeta, 1981), 204–23. For a book-length study of the triangular relationship between Buñuel, Lorca and Dalí, see Agustín Sánchez Vidal, *Buñuel, Lorca, Dalí: El enigma sin fin* (Barcelona: Planeta, 1988).

[5]    J. Francisco Aranda's *Luis Buñuel: biografía crítica* (Barcelona: Lumen, 1969), 58, n. 1.

[6]    See also Jenaro Talens, *The Branded Eye: Buñuel's 'Un Chien andalou'*, trans. Giulia Colaizzi (Minneapolis and London: University of Minnesota Press, 1993) and Phillip Drummond, 'Surrealism and *Un Chien andalou*', in Luis Buñuel and Salvador Dalí, *Un Chien andalou* (London: Faber & Faber, 1994), v–xxiii. For a discussion of the title of the film, see Federico Bonaddio, 'What's in the Joke?: Buñuel, Dalí, Lorca and the title *Un Chien andalou*', in Isabel Sataolalla *et al.* (eds), *Buñuel, Siglo XXI* (Zaragoza: Prensas Universitarias de Zaragoza, 2004), 53–8.

[7]    See Christopher Maurer, 'Poetry', in Bonaddio (ed.) (2007), 16–38 (pp. 30–2).

p. 84). Several of Lorca's drawings also formed part of an at once personal and artistic exchange between the two men which included letters, poetry and prose.[8] Yet although, as Maurer (2004, p. 4) puts it, their 'two poetic worlds come so intimately into contact that critics sometimes refer to an "época lorquiana" in the work of Dalí, and an "época daliniana" in that of García Lorca', the two men rarely shared the same style or approach. Indeed, as Maurer (2004, p. 4) rightly adds, '[i]n retrospect their aesthetics seem very different'. The difference is apparent even amidst the predominantly laudatory tones of Lorca's 'Oda a Salvador Dalí' (*OC*, I, pp. 953–7), which appeared in the *Revista de Occidente* in April 1926.

The ode serves at least two purposes: firstly, to describe Dalí's aesthetic position which, as Cecilia Castro Lee explains in her article on the subject, corresponds to his pre-Surrealist, Cubist phase; and secondly, as a vehicle for Lorca to stake his own claim to contemporariness by virtue of his association with, and his comprehension of, his friend's art.[9] '[E]s una acabada pieza de crítica de arte,' writes Castro (p. 61), 'donde Lorca demuestra su capacidad de reflexión estética, nos informa sobre su apreciación del arte contemporáneo y crea una composición poética que es praxis de la teoría que expresa.' From the start Lorca relates Dalí's quest to the pure, rational, dehumanized and geometric aesthetics of Cubism, with its attention to surface rather than interiority, and signals also its clean break with the past:

> Una rosa en el alto jardín que tú deseas.
> Una rueda en la pura sintaxis del acero.
> Desnuda la montaña de niebla impresionista.
> Los grises oteando sus balaustradas últimas.
>
> Los pintores modernos, en sus blancos estudios,
> cortan la flor aséptica de la raíz cuadrada.
> En las aguas del Sena un iceberg de mármol
> enfría las ventanas y disipa las yedras.
>
> El hombre pisa fuerte las calles enlosadas.
> Los cristales esquivan la magia del reflejo.
> El Gobierno ha cerrado las tiendas de perfume.
> La máquina eterniza sus compases binarios.

---

8    See Christopher Maurer (ed.), *Sebastian's Arrows: Letters and Mementos of Salvador Dalí and Federico García Lorca* (Chicago: Swan Isle Press, 2004).

9    See Cecilia Castro Lee, 'La "Oda a Salvador Dalí": significación y trascendencia en la vida y creación de Lorca y Dalí', *Anales de la Literatura Española Contemporánea*, 11 (1986), 61–78.

In these stanzas we see what Castro (p. 65) describes as an iconoclastic desire 'de limpieza, de desnudez y de hygiene'. The rose which Lorca sets as Dalí's goal is associated with the perfect form of a circle. The aesthetics of Cubism are conjured up by a bare mountain on a clear day, free from the fogginess of impressionism; by an aseptic flower, the object of apparently scientific attention in the study rooms of the true moderns; by a cold marble iceberg on the Seine as opposed to the romantic, organic associations of ivy; by mechanical rhythm, precision and durability, and not the sensorial art of *modernismo*, whose perfumeries are now closed (see Castro, p. 66). Later in the poem, these aesthetics are related more concretely to Dalí's own person and practice:

> Alma higiénica, vives sobre mármoles nuevos.
> Huyes la oscura selva de formas increíbles.
> Tu fantasía llega donde llegan tus manos,
> y gozas el soneto del mar en tu ventana.
>
> [...]
>
> Al coger tu paleta, con un tiro en un ala,
> pides la luz que anima la copa del olivo.
> Ancha luz de Minerva, constructora de andamios,
> donde no cabe el sueño ni su flora inexacta.
>
> Pides la luz antigua que se queda en la frente,
> sin bajar a la boca ni al corazón del hombre.
> Luz que temen las vides entrañables de Baco
> y la fuerza sin orden que lleva el agua curva.
>
> [...]
>
> El pez en la pecera y el pájaro en la jaula.
> No quieres inventarlos en el mar o en el viento.
> Estilizas o copias después de haber mirado
> con honestas pupilas sus cuerpecillos ágiles.

Minerva is the Roman name for the Greek deity Athene, associated with the arts but also with intelligence and clear-headedness as opposed to mysticism and mystery or the passion and orgiastic rites connected to Bacchus (Dionysus) (see Chevalier and Gheerbrant, pp. 54–5 and 291–4). Dalí's domain is that of Minerva who returns us to the classical world 'de perfección y equilibrio, mundo racional, hacia el cual retorna la presente estética' (Castro, p. 67). Dalí's artistic soul is so pure as to be termed 'hygienic'; he is associated with intelligence through his connection in these stanzas with light, which is set in opposition to the dark forests of fantastical invention and to the inexact flora of dream, the painter's own 'fantasy' (if it can be called that) tied firmly to what he can touch and see. Elsewhere in the poem, Lorca praises Dalí's 'ansias de eterno limitado', a paradox hinging on the combination of art's transcendental goals with its specific attention in this case to material form. The paradox is revisited metaphorically in the image of the caged bird which is linked to the painter's desire to capture objects (see Castro, pp. 69–70). The image is an uncanny reminder of the canary in the poem 'Amparo', from *Poema del cante jondo*, and of its contrast with the freedom of the sparrow in 'La Lola'. The poles of life and art represented respectively by these two *muchachas* seem to cohere with the distinct approaches implicit in the ode, Dalí choosing the caged bird of observation over the freedoms evoked by self-expression and the imagination.

Castro (p. 61) argues that Lorca's ode to Dalí 'es teoría estética que acompaña la gestación del *Romancero gitano*, y prepara el camino para el surrealismo de *Poeta en Nueva York*'. Indeed, it is possible to draw parallels between the movement towards dehumanization in the ballads and that which is lauded in the ode, just as it is possible to relate Lorca's emphasis on the five senses in his lecture 'La imagen poética de don Luis de Góngora' to what he conceives of as the necessary restriction of Dalí's work to what is palpable or visible. 'Un poeta', explains Lorca in his lecture, 'tiene que ser profesor en los cinco sentidos corporales. Los cinco sentidos corporales, en este orden: vista, tacto, oído, olfato y gusto' (*OC*, III, p. 229). And he adds: 'Para poder ser dueño de las más bellas imágenes tiene que abrir puertas de comunicación en todos ellos y con mucha frecuencia ha de superponer sus sensaciones y aun de disfrazar sus naturalezas.' Indeed, just like Dalí, Góngora needed to resist dark, natural forces in order to prevent his imagination running riot: 'Como lleva la imaginación atada, la detiene cuando quiere y no se deja arrastrar por las oscuras fuerzas naturales de la ley de inercia ni por los fugaces espejismos donde mueren los poetas incautos como mariposas en el farol' (*OC*, III, pp. 231–2). The connections are there to be seen, but perhaps too are the contradictions and moments of self-doubt which manifest themselves in what is, as I have argued, at best an incomplete or ambiguous movement towards dehumanization in *Romancero gitano* as well as in the poet's earlier, but no less relevant, difficulty in loving Amparo.

Certainly, amidst the allusions to the aesthetics of Cubism, we can sense in 'Oda a Salvador Dalí' the poet's desire to be counted amongst the so-called moderns, his use of the first-person plural providing the overt mechanism by which to include himself in their ranks: 'Un deseo de forma y límites *nos* gana'; '¡Siempre la rosa, siempre, norte y sur de *nosotros*!'; 'Rosa pura que limpia de artificios y croquis / y *nos* abre las alas tenues de la sonrisa' (my italics). Yet the final part of the ode moves in a direction that is very personal and, because of that, very telling:

> ¡Oh, Salvador Dalí, de voz aceitunada!
> Digo lo que me dicen tu persona y tus cuadros.
> No alabo tu imperfecto pincel adolescente,
> pero canto la firme dirección de tus flechas.
>
> [...]
>
> Pero ante todo canto un común pensamiento
> que nos une en las horas oscuras y doradas.
> No es el Arte la luz que nos ciega los ojos.
> Es primero el amor, la amistad o la esgrima.

Here the poet admits that something other than art unites the pair, and in so doing unwittingly, or perhaps even intentionally, brings the human element back into the equation: love, friendship and what is presumably their artistic 'fencing'. As Castro (pp. 71–2) also notes, in a letter to Sebastià Gasch, dated 2 September 1927, Lorca expresses his inability to ignore the human even in his most abstract creations:

> Yo nunca me aventuro en terrenos que no son del hombre, porque vuelvo tierras atrás en seguida y *rompo* casi siempre el producto de mi viaje. Cuando hago una cosa de pura abstracción, siempre tiene (creo yo) como un salvoconducto de sonrisas y un equilibrio bastante humano.
>
> (*EC*, p. 518)

In his ode the suggestion seems to be that the human ambit is inferior to what art can hope to achieve by avoiding it:

> El mundo tiene sordas penumbras y desorden,
> en los primeros términos que el humano frecuenta.
> Pero ya las estrellas, ocultando paisajes,
> señalan el esquema perfecto de sus órbitas.

And yet by the end of the poem this hierarchization of the human and the dehumanized is no longer as straightforward as it first seemed. 'Las estrofas', writes Castro (p. 71), 'con las cuales se culmina la "Oda" continúan el tema de la realidad humana como problema del arte. Si bien el arte es artificio, síntesis, abstracción, su tema ideal es el hombre en el mundo.' This idea, as Castro rightly notes, informs the final lines of the ode, in which the advice to Dalí is never to lose sight of a landscape that is peopled: 'Viste y desnuda siempre tu pincel en el aire, / frente a la mar poblada con barcos y marinos.'

As Dalí moved ever closer to Surrealism, Lorca continued to shadow him and engage with his aesthetics. He remained, of course, ambivalent in respect of the artist's approach, even though there is evidence of his own increasing curiosity about the newest of avant-garde modes. In his unfinished dialogue 'Corazón bleu y Coeur azul',[10] which was probably composed in late 1927 or early 1928 and which reproduces phrases and images that had shortly before appeared in a text by Dalí entitled 'Pez perseguido por una uva' (see *PP*, p. 46), the speakers named 'YO' (subsequently 'POETA') and 'MI AMIGO' respectively are clearly recognizable as Lorca and Dalí themselves. The focus of their discussion is the validity of poetry based on rational processes and centring on the construction of metaphors. 'Los poetas,' insists the friend, 'tenéis un miedo horrible a perder la cabeza y un amor incomprensible a [...] la calidad lógica. Es absurdo que te conformes a que el zapato no sirva nada más que de zapato y la cuchara de cuchara. El zapato y la cuchara son dos formas de una extrema belleza y de una vida propia tan intensa como la tuya ...' (*PP*, p. 91). The poet retorts by pointing to the possibilities of metaphor: '¡Ay vamos! Yo puedo convertir el zapato en un barquito o ...', only to be interrupted by the other's adamant claim that '[e]l zapato no es nada más que un zapato, sin inventarle nueva personalidad, zapato que puede ir con una aceituna o con una nariz, por el mar del Sur, en medio de una simple emoción de brisa' (*PP*, p. 92). The poet agrees, but what he terms 'un hecho poético más' his friend instead regards quite plainly as being 'real, realísimo, vivo', although he adds: 'Claro que poético, porque poético es todo, pero vivo, sin fantasía, como una hormiga, como un chorro de agua' (*PP*, p. 92). Despite being unfinished, the dialogue suggests that Lorca is at the very least open to what the 'friend' has to say, given that he allows him to interrupt the 'poet' in the text and impose his views with no little vigour and conviction.

Another text from late 1927 which engages with Dalí's aesthetics is the narrative *Santa Lucía y San Lázaro* (*OC*, III, pp. 143–50), published in the December edition of *Revista de Occidente*, in which, as Maurer (2007, p. 31) explains, Lorca contrasts his and the painter's approaches, represented by Saint Lazarus and Saint Lucy respectively. As Terence McMullan puts it, Saint Lazarus is associated in the narrative with 'the unfathomable depths of human insecurity and vulnerability, a deceptive region of gut responses and raw nerve-ends', while Saint Lucy 'encapsulates an aseptic beauty where bright, pure surfaces, schematic outlines, and transparency combine in the transcendental image of an essential reality, timeless and static, defined with

---

[10] Federico García Lorca, *Poemas en prosa*, ed. Andrew A. Anderson (Granada: Comares / La Veleta, 2000), 91–2. Abbreviated henceforth to *PP*.

geometrical precision'.[11] McMullan (p. 14) sees the work as a synthesis of 'spectacularly incompatible interpretations of life into a total viewpoint' which modifies 'the Cubist stance of a Góngora lecture that had repudiated "las fuerzas oscuras que no tienen límite", and a Dalí ode "donde no cabe el sueño ni su flor inexacta"'.

*Santa Lucía y San Lázaro* and 'Corazón bleu y Coeur azul' provide evidence of the beginnings of Lorca's inquiry, even before the publication of *Romancero gitano*, and the criticism it received, into the value of traditional metaphor and the artistic possibilities of non-rational modes of production. Given that he had already contemplated a change of direction for his work, it is perhaps not surprising that he could at least admit in a letter to Gasch, dated 8 September 1928, that Dalí's letter criticizing the ballads was 'aguda y arbitraria' and that it presented 'un pleito poético interesante' (*EC*, p. 585). If in the ballads we can feel the unresolved tension between the poet's attraction to the emotions of the real world and the prescriptions of dehumanized art, now it is the heart (of sorts) that seems to be gaining the upper hand. Indeed, when he refers to his new tendency in the wake of his ballads (which he had written between 1924 and 1926), he does so in terms evoking the intensely personal. 'A pesar de todo,' he wrote to Gasch in respect of his ballads' reception, 'a mí ya no me interesa nada o casi nada. Se me ha muerto en las manos de la manera más tierna. Mi poesía tiende ahora otro vuelo más agudo todavía. Me parece que un vuelo personal' (*EC*, p. 585). And some days later, to Gasch once again, he referred to two new poems of his new tendency in the following terms: 'Responden a mi nueva manera *espiritualista*, emoción pura descarnada, desligada del control lógico' (*EC*, p. 588). 'Son los primeros', he explained, 'que he hecho. Naturalmente, están en prosa porque el verso es una ligadura que no resisten. Pero en ellos sí notarás, desde luego, la ternura de mi actual corazón' (*EC*, p. 589). The prose poems he mentions are 'Suicidio en Alejandría' (*OC*, III, pp. 156–8) and 'Nadadora sumergida' (*OC*, III, pp. 159–60). Just a few extracts from each are sufficient to demonstrate their departure from the ballads. Whether the claims to novelty he makes for both are totally justified is debatable. The opening of 'Suicidio en Alejandría', for example, is reminiscent, it seems to me, of the images of violence, discord and discontinuity in *Romancero gitano*: 'Cuando pusieron la cabeza cortada sobre la mesa del despacho, se rompieron todos los cristales de la ciudad' (*OC*, III, p. 156). However, the

[11] Terence McMullan, 'Federico García Lorca's *Santa Lucía y San Lázaro* and the Aesthetics of Transition', *Bulletin of Hispanic Studies*, 67.1 (1990), 1–20 (p. 14).

recourse to prose does at least provide the poet with a mechanism by which to begin to untangle the methodical and tightly-knit images and metaphors that are at the heart of the ballads. Forming the backbone of 'Suicidio' is a play with numbers descending from the pairing of 13 and 22 all the way down to zero. This numerical device is in keeping with the linearity of prose narrative and with the endeavour to create enigmas plainly told: 'Pasaba un automóvil y era un 13. Pasaba un automóvil y era un 22. Pasaba una tienda y era un 13. Pasaba un kilómetro y era un 22. La situación se hizo insostenible. Había necesidad de romper para siempre' (*OC*, III, p. 156). This notion of rupture, so significant (at least in principle) in the context of Lorca's claims to be embarking on a new tendency, is taken up again in 'Nadadora sumergida', a text in which are prefigured the stark pronouncements and seemingly illogical, surrealistic images of his New York poems:

> Desde entonces dejé la literatura vieja que yo había cultivado con gran éxito.
> Es preciso romperlo todo para que los dogmas se purifiquen y las normas tengan nuevo temblor.
> Es preciso que el elefante tenga ojos de perdiz y la perdiz pezuña de unicornio.
> Por un abrazo sé yo todas estas cosas y también por este gran amor que me desgarra el chaleco de seda. (*OC*, III, p. 160)

In a lecture delivered at the Athenaeum in Granada on 27 October 1928, entitled 'Sketch de la Nueva Pintura' (*OC*, III, pp. 272–81), Lorca seems to speak promisingly of Surrealism, seeing it as the natural successor to Cubism. 'La lección cubista', explained Lorca, 'está bien aprovechada. Pero un triste cerebralismo, un cansado intelectualismo invade la pintura' (*OC*, III, p. 278). Now the way forward was marked out by the Surrealist tendency: 'Vamos al instinto, vamos al acaso, a la inspiración pura, a la fragancia de lo directo.' Yet in his letter to Gasch regarding his prose poems he made it very clear that he also had misgivings about Surrealism, adamant as he was that his own work, even if it was trying to wrestle free of the grip of logic and reason, should preserve the clarity of consciousness: 'emoción ... desligada del control lógico' perhaps, but '¡ojo!, ¡ojo!, con una tremenda *lógica poética*. No es surrealismo, ¡ojo!, la *conciencia* más clara los ilumina' (*EC*, p. 588). We find the same emphasis in a version of his pivotal lecture, 'Imaginación, inspiración, evasión' (*OC*, III, pp. 258–71), which he first delivered in Granada only a fortnight or so before 'Sketch de la nueva pintura'. The thrust of this lecture, as Andrew Anderson succinctly puts it, is that 'the imagination is inadequate to the poet's ultimate task: it does not permit him to plumb the depths or to capture the nuances of external reality'.[12] The alternative is for the poet to allow his work to be governed by inspiration, characterized as 'un estado del alma', and thus escape the logical control associated with the imagination, characterized in turn as 'un hecho del alma' (*OC*, III, p. 261). The poet who manages this '[p]asa del análisis a la fe' and arrives at a place where 'las cosas son porque sí, sin efecto ni causa explicable. Ya no hay términos ni límites, admirable libertad' (*OC*, III, 261). As Anderson (1991, p. 152) explains, in this context 'evasión' relates both to the rejection and subversion of mimetic conventions (in this sense, literally an 'escape' from the world) and to the resultant poetry's achievement of a certain transcendence: 'El poema evadido de la realidad imaginativa se sustrae a los dictados de feo y bello como se entiende ahora y entra en una asombrosa realidad poética' (*OC*, III, pp. 261–2).

In the September before his first lecture on the subject, Lorca had already referred to 'evasión' in a letter to Jorge Zalamea, where he signals in the most visceral of terms the personal nature of his new artistic direction:

> Después de construir mis *Odas*, en las que tengo tanta ilusión, cierro este ciclo de poesía para hacer otra cosa. Ahora hago una poesía de *abrirse las venas*, una poesía *evadida* ya de la realidad con una emoción donde se refleja todo mi amor por las cosas y mi guasa por las cosas. Amor de morir y burla de morir. Amor. Mi corazón. Así es. (*EC*, p. 587)

However, more significant still for our discussion is Dalí's own use of the term in his August letter to Lorca criticizing the ballads, because it raises the distinct possibility that this was the spur that prompted the poet's subsequent references to 'evasión'.[13] 'Precisamente,' Dalí had written, 'estoy convencido que el esfuerzo hoy en poesía sólo tiene sentido con la evasión de las ideas que nuestra inteligencia ha ido forjando artificialmente, hasta dotar a éstas de su exacto sentido real' (see Rodrigo, p. 79 and Gibson 1999, p. 208). This points to another instance of Lorca's engagement with Dalí's aesthetics and yet the poet, true to form, would not accept his friend's stance without adding a proviso of his own. Although in his lecture on the subject he did

---

[12] Andrew A. Anderson, 'Lorca at the Crossroads: "Imaginación, inspiración, evasion" and the "novísimas estéticas"', *Anales de la Literatura Española Contemporánea*, 16 (1991), 149–73 (p. 152).

[13] Anderson (1991, p. 156) notes that Dalí's letter was almost certainly 'the immediate stimulus for Lorca's utilization of the term "evasion" in the formulation of his new aesthetic', but he also suggests (1991, pp. 155–6) that Lorca may have been aware of the use of the term by others, including Guillermo de Torre and José Ortega y Gasset who refers to it in his essay 'La deshumanización del arte'. See Ortega y Gasset, *Obras completas*, III, 353–86 (p. 374).

acknowledge what we might broadly call the Modernist endeavour to achieve 'evasión' as well as the possibility that it could be arrived at in different ways, in a version of the lecture delivered in Madrid in February 1929 he would make clear his reservations about the specifically Surrealist path towards its achievement:

> Esta evasión puede hacerse de muchas maneras. El surrealismo emplea el sueño y su lógica para escapar. En el mundo de los sueños, el realísimo mudo de los sueños, se encuentran indudablemente normas poéticas de emoción verdadera. Pero esta evasión por medio del sueño o del subconsciente es, aunque muy pura, poco diáfana. Los latinos queremos perfiles y misterio visible. Forma y sensualidades. (*OC*, III, 263–4)

We could understand this and other proclamations by Lorca in his letters and lectures as manifestations of what we might call, after Pierre Bourdieu, 'position-takings'. Bourdieu, in his seminal essay 'The Field of Cultural Production, or: The Economic World Reversed', explains the notion of position-taking specifically in the context of the field of literary and artistic production:

> The *space of literary* or *artistic position-takings*, i.e. the structured set of manifestations of the social agents involved in the field – literary or artistic works, of course, but also political acts or pronouncements, manifestos or polemics, etc. – is inseparable from the *space of literary positions* defined by possession of a determinate quantity of specific capital (recognition) and, at the same time, by occupation of a determinate position in the structure of the distribution of this specific capital.[14]

As I have suggested elsewhere, Lorca's 'position-taking is synonymous with both the dynamics of association – the adoption of the principles that hold sway – and differentiation, by which the artist stakes his claim to the established and indispensable virtues of originality'.[15] This model reinforces the notion that his engagement with Dalí's aesthetics, as in the case of his ode to the painter, can be seen as a means of associating himself, whether in the context of Cubism or beyond, with what he had identified as the dominant avant-garde tendency or the latest fashion. Indeed, the implication in his lecture 'Imaginación, inspiración, evasión', once more by association,

[14] Pierre Bourdieu, 'The Field of Cultural Production, or: The Economic World Reversed', in Pierre Bourdieu, *The Field of Cultural Production: Essays on Art and Literature*, ed. and introd. Randal Johnson (Cambridge: Polity Press, 1993), 29–73 (p. 30).

[15] Federico Bonaddio, 'Introduction: Biography and Interpretation', in Bonaddio 2007, 1–15 (p. 11).

is that he himself now belongs to that avant-garde line of poets who 'se preocupan de reducir la poesía a la creación del hecho poético y seguir las normas que este mismo impone, sin escuchar la voz del razonamiento lógico ni el equilibrio de la imaginación' (*OC*, III, p. 261). By the same token, his reservations in respect of the value of all forms of 'evasión' – in other words, of Surrealism proper – indicate a resistance to the latest fashion that could be seen as having its origin in the poet's concomitant desire to differentiate himself. Yet perhaps we should not discount, either, the possibility that this position-taking is actually quite fundamentally reactionary and defensive and that it owes itself as much to factors of temperament as it does to artistic conviction.

At stake were Lorca's claims to modernity, relevance and novelty, all of which had been jeopardized by the reception of *Romancero gitano*. For this reason it is not difficult to imagine that Lorca's ambivalent position in respect of contemporary trends reveals both the need for association in order to compensate for, or repair, the damage to his credibility and the need to stand his ground vis-à-vis his detractors.[16] He may have comprehended Dalí's criticism but, as he suggested to Gasch, he still felt that his work had been misunderstood: 'Claro que mi libro no lo han entendido los putrefactos, aunque ellos digan que sí' (*EC*, p. 585). It is precisely this ambivalence, I would suggest, which is carried over into the New York poems. The ambivalence is there from the start, in Lorca's seemingly glib comment that his stay in a city he thought of as horrible would be a good one. In fact, whether by sheer coincidence or not, the visit to New York presented Lorca with a unique opportunity not only to explore new artistic directions but also to defend his achievements to date. As will become evident, the incorporation into his New York poems of polar opposites such as nature and the city, order and chaos, freedom and oppression, spirit and matter, harmony and dissonance, where the poet is aligned firmly with the former, allows him to act upon the criticisms of *Romancero gitano* by attacking the very premise upon which that criticism rested. Since what had been put into question was the very idea that his ballads and their images were in fact modern at all, now he would produce a work that at once sprang from and (importantly) undermined an exemplar of modernity: New York City. In so doing, he would, of course, be

---

[16] Anderson (1991, p. 153) suggests that it might 'be plausible to think that one of Lorca's goals [in 'Imaginación, inspiración, evasión'] was to rehabilitate (salvage?) the *Romancero* by presenting the mode of operation of its metaphors from a particular perspective that would tend to situate the poetry as more in accord with Dalí's current aesthetic than Dalí himself had found the collection to be'.

engaging with the movement, characteristic of the late 1920s and the years leading up to the Spanish Civil War, away from art-for-art's sake and towards an art that was socially aware and politically committed.[17] Yet in the process he would engage with concerns that were also intensely personal and artistic. Lorca went to New York, it seems, determined to make a point about his own creativity. To understand this is to understand the poet's choice of destination and to put into perspective this outsider's often vehement attack on modern city life.[18]

In the introduction to a recital of his New York poems he gave in Madrid in 1932, Lorca suggested that the title of the event, 'Un poeta en Nueva York', was misleading: 'he debido decir,' he explained, "Nueva York en un poeta"' (*OC*, III, p. 347), thus shifting the emphasis away from the fact of his residence in the city onto its effect on him and his response to it. Importantly, however, an element common both to the title of the recital and to its recasting, as well as to the title given to the collection of New York poems published posthumously, is the self-reference embodied in the figure of the poet. Throughout the collection, the first-person singular voice is tied specifically to this figure which takes on a number of guises, including those of witness and visionary, victim and martyr. Because the self that is voiced is inseparable from the persona of the poet, what it has to say, and the way it says it, has resonances for the very art and practice of poetry. In 'Vuelta de paseo' (*OC*, III, p. 447), for example, alienation and disorientation in the city naturally have a human toll; but they have consequences also for poetic creation:

> Asesinado por el cielo,
> entre las formas que van hacia la sierpe
> y las formas que buscan el cristal,
> dejaré crecer mis cabellos.
>
> Con el árbol de muñones que no canta
> y el niño con el blanco rostro de huevo.

---

[17] For a discussion of Lorca's response to the politicization of the arts in Spain in the late 1920s and 1930s, see Nigel Dennis, 'Politics', in Bonaddio (2007), 170–93.

[18] Beverly J. Delong-Tonelli, in 'In the Beginning Was the End: Lorca's New York Poetry', *Anales de la Literatura Española Contemporánea*, 12 (1987), 243–57 (p. 244), also sees concerns about his work as being central to the collection, suggesting that 'the New production has as its beginning the yearning to undertake a journey, that the journey is metaphorically linked to Lorca's visceral relationship to his work, that the journey becomes a quest for the origin of his poetic voice, and that the quest is the dominant thread which weaves through all the New York poetry'.

> Con los animalitos de cabeza rota
> y el agua harapienta de los pies secos.
>
> Con todo lo que tiene cansancio sordomudo
> y mariposa ahogada en el tintero.
>
> Tropezando con mi rostro distinto de cada día.
> ¡Asesinado por el cielo!

The poem conveys a sense of the oppressive burden of the city skyline upon the eye and spirit, but also, necessarily, its effect on poetry itself. That oppression is articulated by the verb *asesinar*, the victim of which is the now dead poet who reacts by saying he will let his hair grow. This growth, a wisp of fertility in an otherwise sterile place, alludes to poetic creation perhaps via an allusion to the cliché of the long-haired poet or to the myth that our hair continues growing long after our death.[19] Either way, whether it is to be taken as a statement of defiance or of resignation, it represents the only direction for a poet who is so overwhelmed by the metropolis that he loses any sense of a fixed and stable identity ('mi rostro distinto de cada día') and thus comes to resemble the indistinct forms and broken life that surround him. By placing himself amidst ('entre') the figures of the poem's fragmented cityscape, the poet sets himself in an antagonistic relationship with his surroundings, where he embodies the principle of creativity, and the city, the principle of death. The implication is that his experience of the city is first-hand and this idea is reinforced by the visible traces of the city's ravages upon poetry itself. Indeed, as the three couplets each beginning with 'con' suggest, any response the poet does make can only occur because he aligns himself with, or is informed by, the mutilated elements of the city in which he resides.[20] Whereas in *Libro de poemas* and *Romancero gitano* we were presented with animate landscapes – the product of a Symbolist world view on the one hand and the poet's own creative ingenuity on the other – here the cityscape is synonymous with soullessness and the deadening of the senses ('el árbol de muñones que no canta',

---

[19] As Terence McMullan explains in his essay 'Federico García Lorca's *Poeta en Nueva York* and *The City of Tomorrow*', *Bulletin of Hispanic Studies*, 73 (1996), 65–79 (p. 71), 'The long-haired poet is, of course, a cliché and Lorca ruefully presses it into service as a device to reassert his artistic vocation in what is for him an inaesthetically intractable milieu.'

[20] Robert Havard, in his essay 'The Riddle Register in Lorca's *Poeta en Nueva York*', in David George and John London (eds), *Spanish Film, Theatre and Literature in the Twentieth Century. Essays in Honour of Derek Gagen* (Cardiff: University of Wales Press, 2007), 43–56 (pp. 45–6), argues that 'the key to the poem [...] is the implicit dimensional contrast between large and small, power and powerlessness, construction and destruction, as Lorca effectively rejects the unmentioned skyscrapers and instead identifies or aligns himself *with* weaker brethren'.

'el niño con el blanco rostro de huevo', 'cansancio sordomudo') as the poet is dispossessed of his abilities either as poet-seer or poet-creator, now a seemingly powerless witness to the obvious, but obliged nonetheless to render his testimony a poetic exploit. The connection between the poet and the outside world, problematic in the context of anti-discursive and dehumanized art, is now re-established as a result, ironically, of that world's debilitating effect on the poet's traditional creative powers. The meaning of dehumanization in Lorca's New York poems transcends artistic spaces to evoke the all too literal toll of city life on its inhabitants. The metaphorical construction of *Romancero gitano* gives way to the mere evocation of forms which, in the alienating context of the city, can mean no more than the evocation of fragments, formlessness, anonymity and absence. If ever we imagined that poetry could give meaning and shape to experience, the indiscernible character of the world conveyed in the lines of 'Vuelta de paseo' evokes the difficulty of such a task in the metropolis. Sense and signification have clearly not been done away with altogether, for amongst the poem's disparate elements we can see symbols of alienation, abjection and decline. Yet they arise out of a poetic logic from which the principles of control and, of course, the imagination have been banished, thus recalling the principles of Surrealism and giving rise to images whose jarring associations and strange juxtapositions are seemingly – but only seemingly – Surrealist in character.[21] The tension between what the poet wishes to create and what he is constrained to create is conjured up in the poem by the rather naive metaphor that evokes artistic difficulty by cancelling out the traditionally positive creative associations of butterflies and inkwells: 'mariposa ahogada en el tintero'. Here we have the paradox: the poet in New York produces art in a world which he tells us is not conducive to artistic processes. Significantly, the art he does produce not only bears the mark of the modern, artless world around him but also resembles the kind of modern art alongside which his *Romancero gitano* was once judged so unfavourably. Yet the fact that the poet should self-consciously

---

[21] On the tensions between traditional and Surrealist imagery in *Poeta en Nueva York*, as well as the specific mechanics of the latter, see Derek Harris's essays 'A la caza de la imagen surrealista en Lorca', *Insula*, 368–9 (1977), 19, and 'La elaboración textual de *Poeta en Nueva York*: el salto mortal', *Revista Canadiense de Estudios Hispánicos*, 18.2 (Invierno 1994), 309–15. Harris (1977, p. 19) points to condensation as a principal technique in Lorca's construction of his New York images which leads to Surrealist distortion, but always as a product of poetic control: 'La condensación es, en efecto, una manera de distorsionar que inhibe la comprensión racional y hace precisa una comprensión emocional. La razón se evade y ya vamos camino al surrealismo, pero no se pierde el control poético.'

voice his resistance to this art reveals the logical, conceptual control that distinguishes his New York poetry from the kind of art it appears on the surface to be becoming.

An even more striking testimony to the creative difficulties that the poet faces in his new environment is provided by 'Paisaje de la multitud que vomita' (*OC*, I, pp. 473–4), a poem which bears all the hallmarks of art cut loose from the principles of control. Inspired by scenes of merrymakers on their Sunday outing to Coney Island, the poem evokes through its form (or formlessness) what the poet sees as the sickening and overpowering excesses of the occasion; hence the series of almost endless lines, often connected by conjunctions or prepositions, that aptly convey the poetic equivalent of constant retching. Moreover, as nauseating as its form are the surfeit of surrealistic images that are hurled one upon the other.

The drum-playing fat woman with whom the poem opens has a precursor in the figure of the tambourine-playing gypsy girl in 'Preciosa y el aire'. Whereas Preciosa throws down her tambourine in what we have interpreted as a fearful flight from the spur of chaotic nature to the order represented by dispassionate art, here the fat woman, strident and destructive, holds on to her drums and displays neither fear nor respect for the natural world:

> La mujer gorda venía delante
> arrancando las raíces y mojando el pergamino de los tambores;
> la mujer gorda
> que vuelve del revés los pulpos agonizantes.
> La mujer gorda, enemiga de la luna,
> corría por las calles y los pisos deshabitados
> y dejaba por los rincones pequeñas calaveras de paloma
> y levantaba las furias de los banquetes de los siglos últimos
> y llamaba al demonio del pan por las colinas del cielo barrido
> y filtraba un ansia de luz en las circulaciones subterráneas.
> Son los cementerios, lo sé, son los cementerios
> y el dolor de las cocinas enterradas bajo la arena;
> son los muertos, los faisanes y las manzanas de otra hora
> los que nos empujan en la garganta.

The fat woman embodies the principle of excess; her recklessness and acts of mutilation have implications for art, representing as they do the product of a process that simply cannot digest the surfeit of chaotic images and sensations thrown up. Just as with Preciosa's instrument, the use of parchment ('pergamino') to refer to the skins of the fat woman's drums calls to mind the written word; the fact that their surfaces are wet with vomit connects the word to the nauseous production the fat woman induces, which is characterized in this stanza by the furies of centuries of banqueting she raises and is reproduced formally by the long phrases connected by 'and' ('y'). While the tambourine that Preciosa played had lunar associations, here the fat woman is cast as an enemy of that heavenly body, suggesting perhaps her dissociation from mythical, cyclical or celestial domains. Importantly, amongst the crowd in her sickly domain we find the poet too, not only in his first-person-singular acknowledgement of what is happening ('lo sé') but also in his first-person-plural self-inclusion in the widespread desire to retch ('que nos empujan en la garganta'). Indeed, as the poem continues on its nauseous path, the poet-witness inevitably becomes a participant too:

> Llegaban los rumores de la selva del vómito
> con las mujeres vacías, con niños de cera caliente,
> con árboles fermentados y camareros incansables
> que sirven platos de sal bajo las arpas de la saliva.
> Sin remedio, hijo mío, ¡vomita! No hay remedio.
> No es el vómito de los húsares sobre los pechos de la prostituta,
> ni el vómito del gato que se tragó una rana por descuido.
> Son los muertos que arañan con sus manos de tierra
> las puertas de pedernal donde se pudren nublos y postres.

As the poet exclaims, there is no option other than to vomit. The poetic product of this retching is literally to be found in the waves of images pushing reality to its sickly limits; to a place where trees ferment and waiters serve plates of salt amidst harp strings of saliva that conjure up the most nauseating of music. The following stanza confirms the irrepressible character of the fat woman's march and the helplessness of the poet not to succumb to the effect of this uncontrollable muse:

> La mujer gorda venía delante
> con las gentes de los barcos y de las tabernas y de los jardines.
> El vómito agitaba delicadamente sus tambores
> entre algunas niñas de sangre
> que pedían protección a la luna.
> ¡Ay de mí! ¡Ay de mí! ¡Ay de mí!
> Esta mirada mía fue mía, pero ya no es mía,
> esta mirada que tiembla desnuda por el alcohol
> y despide barcos increíbles
> por las anémonas de los muelles.
> Me defiendo con esta mirada
> que mana de las ondas por donde el alba no se atreve,
> yo, poeta sin brazos, perdido
> entre la multitud que vomita,

> sin caballo efusivo que corte
> los espesos musgos de mis sienes.

The poet's desperate cries ('¡Ay de mí!') are followed by the realization that he has become disconnected from his faculty of sight ('Esta mirada mía fue mía, pero ya no es mía'), his gaze inebriated by the scenes of revellers boarding boats at the pier. At least this loss of control over his vision permits him some defence against the images assailing him ('Me defiendo con esta mirada'), although it also renders him incapable of shaping his experience, as is suggested by the image of the armless poet whose mental incapacity is conveyed by the image of temples overgrown with moss. The poem is finally brought to an end with lines that convey something of the numb and hollow feeling we experience once our retching has stopped:

> Pero la mujer gorda seguía delante
> y la gente buscaba las farmacias
> donde el amargo trópico se fija.
> Sólo cuando izaron la bandera y llegaron los primeros canes
> la ciudad entera se agolpó en las barandillas del embarcadero.[22]

What is at stake in *Poeta en Nueva York*, amongst other things, is the integrity of the poet and his craft. In the final lines of 'Nocturno del hueco' (*OC*, III, pp. 504–6), the first-person subject is singled out from amongst a series of dislocated images, drawing us nonetheless to the nature of the relationship between it and its context:

> Yo.
> Con el hueco blanquísimo de un caballo,
> crines de ceniza. Plaza pura y doblada.
>
> Yo.
> Mi hueco traspasado con las axilas rotas.
> Piel seca de uva neutra y amianto de madrugada.
>
> *Toda la luz del mundo cabe dentro de un ojo.*
> *Canta el gallo y su canto dura más que sus alas.*
>
> Yo.
> Con el hueco blanquísimo de un caballo.
> Rodeado de espectadores que tienen hormigas en las palabras.

---

[22] In Arturo del Hoyo's edition of the *Obras completas*, 'Sólo' appears without an accent. I have followed here, and throughout, the accentuation for poems indicated in Miguel García-Posada's edition, *Obras II: Poesía 2* (Madrid: Akal, 1982).

En el circo del frío sin perfil mutilado.
Por los capiteles rotos de las mejillas desangradas.

Yo.
Mi hueco sin ti, ciudad, sin tus muertos que comen.
Ecuestre por mi vida definitivamente anclada.

Yo.
*No hay siglo nuevo ni luz reciente.*
*Sólo un caballo azul y una madrugada.*

Its solitary position rounded off by the delimiting full stop suggests the integrity and independence of the 'Yo' but also its isolation. On the other hand, its juxtapositional relationship to the elements conveyed in the couplets suggests that the 'Yo' may also be defined by them. Ultimately all these positions are not incompatible. The insistence implicit in the repetition of the first-person pronoun throughout this extract may evoke not integrity or independence itself but rather the desire for it in face of the experiences and images conveyed in the couplets, which are simultaneously the origin of the poet's concern and the subject of his poetic output, thereby defining his poetic identity at this moment in time. What characterizes these experiences and images is the void alluded to in the poem's title. It is there and not there (since presence and absence here are one and the same) in the ensemble of hollow and mutilated figures and places that are rendered surrealistically unfamiliar: 'el hueco blanquísimo de un caballo', 'crines de ceniza', 'Plaza pura y doblada', 'axilas rotas', 'uva neutra', 'amianto de madrugada', 'el circo del frío', 'capiteles rotos' and so forth. Made up almost entirely of prepositional phrases, the poem's prepositions connect disconnectedness, disfigurement and dislocation: 'Con el hueco', 'con las axilas rotas', 'sin perfil mutilado', 'Por los capiteles rotos', 'sin tus muertos que comen'. Speech becomes a similarly alienating and defamiliarizing experience ('espectadores que tienen hormigas en las palabras'), while movement is at once immobility ('Ecuestre por mi vida definitivamente anclada'). The poem therefore functions on the principle of cancelling out, a principle that impacts on the ability of readers to make sense of the images as well as, of course, on the poet's capacity to give sense in the first place. In this way the 'Yo' and the void, although at odds, are also one. There may be some redeeming aspect in the italicized couplets in which we both hear and see (by virtue of the italics) a voice rising above the hollow experience – both real and poetic – dominating the rest of the poem. The role of the poet as witness is possibly alluded to in the first of these ('*Toda la luz del mundo cabe dentro de un ojo*') as well as the capacity for his 'song' to transcend the material limits of his own mortality ('*Canta el gallo y su canto dura más que sus alas'*). However, despite its seemingly privileged position in the poem, suggesting a resistant intactness on the part of the speaker, this voice seems able to do little more for the time being than confirm the limitations, darkness and solitary nature of the poet's experience: '*No hay siglo nuevo ni luz reciente. / Sólo un caballo azul y una madrugada*'.

By his own account, Lorca had chosen to visit a city he already thought of as horrible; one which, as we have seen, he characterizes in his poems as being hostile to the creative spirit itself. For this reason we should not be surprised to see the figure of the poet-martyr emerge from amidst his New York pages. He is there in the shape of the armless poet of 'Paisaje de la multitud que vomita' or in the hollow form of the speaker 'traspasado con las axilas rotas' in 'Nocturno del hueco'. These mutilated figures are matched in the poem 'Navidad en el Hudson' (*OC*, I, pp. 478–9) by the poet whose throat is slit:

> ¡Esa esponja gris!
> Ese marinero recién degollado.
> Ese río grande.
> Esa brisa de límites oscuros.
> Ese filo, amor, ese filo.
> Estaban los cuatro marineros luchando con el mundo,
> con el mundo de aristas que ven todos los ojos,
> con el mundo que no se puede recorrer sin caballos.
> Estaban uno, cien, mil marineros,
> luchando con el mundo de las agudas velocidades,
> sin enterarse de que el mundo
> estaba solo por el cielo.
>
> El mundo solo por el cielo solo.
> Son las colinas de martillos y el triunfo de la hierba espesa.
> Son los vivísimos hormigueros y las monedas en el fango.
> El mundo solo por el cielo solo
> y el aire a la salida de todas las aldeas.
>
> Cantaba la lombriz el terror de la rueda
> y el marinero degollado
> cantaba al oso de agua que lo había de estrechar;
> y todos cantaban aleluya,
> aleluya. Cielo desierto.
> Es lo mismo, ¡lo mismo!, aleluya.
>
> He pasado toda la noche en los andamios de los arrabales
> dejándome la sangre por la escayola de los proyectos,
> ayudando a los marineros a recoger las velas desgarradas.
> Y estoy con las manos vacías en el rumor de la desembocadura.

No importa que cada minuto
un niño nuevo agite sus ramitos de venas,
ni que el parto de la víbora, desatado bajo las ramas,
calme la sed de sangre de los que miran el desnudo.
Lo que importa es esto: hueco. Mundo solo. Desembocadura.
Alba no. Fábula inerte.
Sólo esto: desembocadura.
¡Oh esponja mía gris!
¡Oh cuello mío recién degollado!
¡Oh río grande mío!
¡Oh brisa mía de límites que no son míos!
¡Oh filo de mi amor, oh hiriente filo!

Here the fatal wound provides an empathetic connection between the poet and New York's inhabitants. In the final exclamatory lines, echoing those with which the poem opened, the poet claims as his own the sailor's slit throat, along with the circumstances of this violent act. The connection is later reinforced in the first three lines of the final stanza, in the reference to nights spent on the outskirts of the city where the poet left trails of his own blood and helped sailors to take in their torn sails, yet another image denoting limitation and incapacity. McMullan (1996, p. 77) interprets the first two of these lines as an allusion to 'the duties of the quantity surveyor on the construction site [which] become associated with suffering' ('andamios', 'escayola', 'proyectos'). He also makes the important observation that here as elsewhere in the collection we can see the product of Lorca's disenchantment with 'the ordering principles of geometry' underlying modern town planning as epitomized, of course, by the architectural philosophy of Le Corbusier (McMullan 1996, pp. 76–7). The fact that these principles 'owed much to Cubism' brings us face to face once more with the aesthetic agenda of *Poeta en Nueva York*; for in the contrast between the hard, angular shapes of the city and the soft, organic forms of nature we can detect not only concerns of a social character but also the rejection on aesthetic grounds of the geometric fixations of Cubism.[23] McMullan (1996, p. 77) points in particular to the many references throughout the collection to street-corners ('esquinas') as well as to edges, intersections and angles ('aristas').

[23] In his excellent essay, McMullan notes Lorca's ambivalent attitude to Le Corbusier's *The City of Tomorrow*. Although the poet now rejected its Cubist precepts, he did accept 'the need for social reform [it] articulated' (McMullan, 1996, p. 76).

The concept of dehumanization, now and throughout *Poeta en Nueva York*, transcends aesthetic considerations to encompass social concerns, thus providing the common ground for criticisms of either society or art. Indeed, in 'Navidad en el Hudson', both the urban and the poetic are configured as spaces where humans struggle to remain human and where nature struggles to take root. Cubist angularity provides one obstacle, the four sailors of the first stanza having to struggle with 'el mundo de aristas que ven todos los ojos' – an appropriately visual onslaught. Another is provided by speed, whose measure is so intense that it requires even greater resistance: 'Estaban uno, cien, mil marineros / luchando con el mundo de las agudas velocidades'. Of course, speed is a virtue of modernity and as such was exalted by Futurism. The third cardinal point of F. T. Marinetti's Futurist Manifesto proclaimed that 'la magnificencia del mundo se ha enriquecido con una belleza nueva: la belleza de la velocidad. Un automóvil de carrera,' it continued, 'con su tosco adorno de gruesos tubos, semejantes a serpientes de hálito explosivo … un automóvil rugiente, que parece correr sobre metralla, es más bello que la *Victoria de Samotracia*.'[24] The sailors in Lorca's poem, however, are in a struggle with speed, an ironic inversion of the battles not against but with modernity exalted in the Futurist Manifesto: 'No hay belleza,' goes the seventh point, 'sino es en la lucha. Ninguna obra que no tenga un carácter agresivo pueda ser una obra maestra. La poesía debe ser concebida como un asalto contra las fuerzas ignotas, para reducirlas a postrarse delante del hombre' (Ilie, p. 85). In the case of Lorca's New York experience, there may well be a struggle but poetry is the victim, not the vanquisher, of unknowable forces just as mankind is forced to fight desperately hard in order not to succumb to the pace of modernity. When he describes a world 'que no se puede recorrer sin caballos', the sounds of Marinetti's galloping proclamations once again spring to mind, as when the Italian declared in his 1919 *Futurist Words in Freedom* that the poet endowed with lyricism (by which he meant 'the very *ability to be intoxicated with life and to intoxicate it with ourselves*') 'will bombard your nerves with all his visual, auditory, and olfactory sensations, as their mad gallop takes him' ('leur galop affolant' in the French original); or when in Gómez de la Serna's Spanish translation of Marinetti's 'Proclama futurista agli spagnoli' we read: '¡Gran *galop* sobre las viejas ciudades y sobre los hombres sesudos […]!' or '¿Qué hay allí aún? ¿Un nuevo obstáculo? ¡No es más que un cementerio! ¡Al galope!

---

[24]  From Andrés González Blanco's 1910 article 'El futurismo (una nueva escuela literaria)', reproduced in Paul Ilie (ed.), *Documents of the Spanish Vanguard* (Chapel Hill: University of North Carolina Press, 1969), 81–95 (pp. 84–5).

Al galope!25 A horse, it seems, is indispensable to keep apace of modernity, and we are reminded of the static connotations of the line 'Ecuestre por mi vida definitivamente anclada' in 'Nocturno del hueco', which alongside these exhortations acquires an ironic and resistant character in respect of the speed and pace which Futurism exalted.

In his 1928 lecture 'Sketch de la nueva pintura', in which there is yet another equine reference, Lorca's contempt for Futurism was plain for all to see. 'El futurismo', he explained, 'exalta el movimiento, quiere vibrar sus cuadros en el vértice de la más desenfrenada dinámica. Odia la estatua y ama el caballo desbocado. Junta, asimismo, las sensaciones exteriores con las interiores y, en suma, no es más que la exaltación del *gesto*' (*OC*, III, p. 276). In 'Navidad en el Hudson', contempt gives way to desperation as the poet is forced to respond to a world apparently so amenable to the precepts of Futurism. In this response, any positive associations attached to iconic objects of modern life – industrial machinery, skyscrapers, money and automobiles – are cancelled out in a visual tussle with nature, where hammers pound into hills ('Son las colinas de martillo'), buildings are as impersonal and chaotic as anthills ('vivísimos hormigueros'), coins are stuck in the mire ('las monedas en el fango') and earthworms shriek beneath the tyres of cars ('Cantaba la lombriz el terror de la rueda'). This response is all the poet can muster. If we take free-flowing water to epitomize life, the inert grey sponge that is the River Hudson ('¡Esa esponja gris!') tells a murky story of lifelessness in a poem where death usurps the place of birth at the time of the Nativity. How different it is, along with the dark, foreboding sunrise, as we shall see, of 'La aurora' (*OC*, I, p. 485), from the rivers and dawn put to figurative use in Futurism's revolutionary and anticlerical proclamations to the Spanish:

> ¡Ya al fin podéis desenfrenar vuestras miradas, en libertad bajo
> el recio flamear revolucionario de la gran bandera de la aurora!
> ¡Los ríos en libertad os indicarán el camino!
> ¡Los ríos que desdoblan sus verdes y sedeñas *echarpes* lozanas y
> frescas, sobre la tierra, de la que habéis barrido las inmundicias
> clericales! (Ilie, p. 77)

In 'Navidad en el Hudson', the estuary ('desembocadura') at night is overwhelming in its enormity, darkly emblematic of the spiritual and creative

---

25 See *Futurist Words in Freedom* (1919), in F. T. Marinetti, *Selected Poems and Related Prose*, trans, Elizabeth R. Napier and Barbara R. Studholme (New Haven and London: Yale University Press, 2002), 85–94 (p. 85); 'Proclama futurista a los españoles', reproduced in Ilie (ed.), 73–80 (pp. 74, 77).

void the poet faces in a place deprived of the dawn and of the promise of fables ('Alba no. Fábula inerte'). If, as indicated in Derek Harris's edition of the collection, the four sailors in the first stanza are none other than the four Evangelists, the implication may be that in such a godless world ('el mundo / estaba solo por el cielo', 'El mundo solo por el cielo solo', 'Cielo desierto') their messages of spirituality, justice and redemption will inevitably fall on deaf ears ('Es lo mismo, ¡lo mismo!, aleluya'), a failure paralleled by the poet's difficulties in voicing and practising his own creative beliefs.[26] In this sense too, the sailor's death is also his own; they are companions together in a futile yet necessary engagement – a martyr's engagement – with their surroundings.

Similar tensions and sentiments are to be found in 'La aurora', which is precisely the evocation of the hopeless tomorrow conveyed throughout 'Navidad en el Hudson' and in particular in the line 'Alba no. Fábula inerte':

> La aurora de Nueva York tiene
> cuatro columnas de cieno
> y un huracán de negras palomas
> que chapotean las aguas podridas.
>
> La aurora de Nueva York gime
> por las inmensas escaleras
> buscando entre las aristas
> nardos de angustia dibujada.
>
> La aurora llega y nadie la recibe en su boca
> porque allí no hay mañana ni esperanza posible.
> A veces las monedas en enjambres furiosos
> taladran y devoran abandonados niños.
>
> Los primeros que salen comprenden con sus huesos
> que no habrá paraíso ni amores deshojados;
> saben que van al cieno de números y leyes,
> a los juegos sin arte, a sudores sin frutos.
>
> La luz es sepultada por cadenas y ruidos
> en impúdico reto de ciencia sin raíces.
> Por los barrios hay gentes que vacilan insomnes
> como recién salidas de un naufragio de sangre.

Here the morning that comes with daybreak is one in which the traditionally positive associations of natural phenomena so frequently put at the service of art ('aurora', 'palomas', 'aguas', 'frutos', 'raíces') are negated by, or

---

[26] See Federico García Lorca, *Romancero gitano. Poeta en Nueva York. El público*, ed. Derek Harris (Madrid: Taurus, 1993), p. 163, n.

buried under, the principles ('números y leyes', 'juegos', 'ciencia'), forms ('inmensas escaleras', 'aristas', 'cadenas y ruidos') and effects ('angustia dibujada', 'naufragio') of an uncompassionate modernity that has gained the upper hand even where it is itself conveyed in terms of natural imagery ('columnas de cieno', 'monedas en enjambres furiosos'). The absence of the first-person subject locates the poet's own perspective as that of witness rather than participant, his own suffering and resistance detectable only in the outrage implicit in the poem's negative imagery.

The figure of the poet is not, however, limited in *Poeta en Nueva York* to either martyr or witness. On more than one occasion it is the foreboding voice of the poet-prophet that is most audible. This voice is noted by Robert Havard (2007), for whom the emergence of the prophetic voice is the result of a gradual process that permits the poet to overcome his initial bewilderment and helplessness in face of an alien and hostile environment. If, as Havard (2007, p. 48) suggests, 'it is fair to say that Lorca, in New York, loses the identity we had come to associate with him,' he does nonetheless manage to gain 'another that is altogether more powerful.' We hear it emerging in, amongst others, the poem 'El rey de Harlem' (*OC*, I, pp. 459–63) in which the poet warns New York's population that Harlem will one day rise up against its white oppressors:

> Es la sangre que viene, que vendrá
> por los tejados y azoteas, por todas partes,
> para quemar la clorofila de las mujeres rubias,
> para gemir al pie de las camas ante el insomnio de los lavabos
> y estrellarse en una aurora de tabaco y bajo amarillo.
>
> Hay que huir,
> huir por las esquinas y encerrarse en los últimos pisos,
> porque el tuétano del bosque penetrará por las rendijas
> para dejar en vuestra carne una leve huella de eclipse
> y una falsa tristeza de guante desteñido y rosa química.

Just as he aligns himself with mutilated nature in 'Vuelta de paseo' or with the wounded sailor in 'Navidad en el Hudson', here the poet is firmly on the side of the black population whom he sets, albeit from a naively primitivist perspective, in a paradigm where they evoke the nostalgia of pristine nature and are totally out of place in an urban environment. 'Otra vez,' he explained in his 1932 recital of his New York poems, 'vi a una niña negrita montada en bicicleta. Nada más enternecedor. [...] Miré fijamente y ella me miró. Pero mi mirada decía: «Niña, ¿por qué vas en bicicleta? ¿Puede una negrita montar en ese aparato? ¿Es tuyo? ¿Dónde lo has robado? ¿Crees que sabes guiarlo?» Y efectivamente,' he added, 'dio una voltereta y se cayó con piernas y ruedas por una suave pendiente' (*OC*, III, p. 351). This anecdote dates Lorca, of course, but needs to be understood in the context of his own disagreements with modernity. His interest lay not so much in claiming for the black population the right to have an equal share of the benefits of modern living as it did in undermining modern values and pointing to the dissonance of modern life. On the one hand, we hear, in 'El rey de Harlem', his clear protestations at the injustices which befall Harlem's inhabitants:

> ¡Ay Harlem! ¡Ay Harlem! ¡Ay Harlem!
> ¡No hay angustia comparable a tus rojos oprimidos,
> a tu sangre estremecida dentro del eclipse oscuro,
> a tu violencia granate sordomuda en la penumbra,
> a tu gran rey prisionero con un traje de conserje!

On the other hand, what the poet himself hears connects the blacks firmly to nature, rendering them emblematic of the alienating consequences of modernity in general and for the poet in particular:

> ¡Ay, Harlem disfrazada!
> ¡Ay, Harlem, amenazada por un gentío de trajes sin cabeza!
> Me llega tu rumor,
> me llega tu rumor atravesando troncos y ascensores,
> a través de láminas grises,
> donde flotan tus automóviles cubiertos de dientes,
> a través de los caballos muertos y los crímenes diminutos,
> a través de tu gran rey desesperado,
> cuyas barbas llegan al mar.

The prophetic voice, therefore, speaks out against the alienating and oppressive consequences of modernity and in support of its victims, amongst whom we can count not only sections of New York's population but also poetry itself. In 'Ciudad sin sueño' (*OC*, I, pp. 480–1), the promise seems to be that if ever there is to be a new day, it will also involve the rise and return of creativity, which is alluded to in the images of resurrected butterflies and roses blooming on the tongue:

> Otro día
> veremos la resurrección de las mariposas disecadas
> y aun andando por un paisaje de esponjas grises y barcos mudos
> veremos brillar nuestro anillo y manar rosas de nuestra lengua.

And while 'New York. Oficina y denuncia' (*OC*, I, pp. 517–9) clearly has its

sights on condemning the excesses and cold indifference of society as epitomized by its mechanical slaughter of millions of animals each day ('Todos
los días se matan en New York / cuatro millones de patos, / cinco millones
de cerdos'), it also raises questions of a self-consciously artistic nature.
McMullan (1996, p. 76) has noted the possible reference to Cubism in the
following line which he sees as a 'scathingly sarcastic dismissal of [its] principles': '¿Qué voy a hacer, ordenar los paisajes?' This dismissal is followed,
I would suggest, by the insistence that the only possible route is protest art:

> ¿Ordenar los amores que luego son fotografías,
> que luego son pedazos de madera y bocanadas de sangre?
> No, no; yo denuncio.
> Yo denuncio la conjura
> de estas desiertas oficinas
> que no radian agonías,
> que borran los programas de la selva,
> y me ofrezco a ser comido por las vacas estrujadas
> cuando sus gritos llenan el valle
> donde el Hudson se emborracha con aceite.

In the poems of New York, it is to this principle of protest ('yo denuncio') that
both prophesy and martyrdom belong, each an aspect of the social dimension
central to the new art of choice, which is also, no doubt, an art born of necessity (whether this be personal, social, aesthetic or, as in the case of *Poeta en
Nueva York*, a combination of all three).

That protest is heard loud and clear in 'Grito hacia Roma (desde la torre
del Chrysler Building)' (*OC*, I, pp. 525–7), one of two odes in the collection.
This poem is Lorca's response to the signing of the Lateran Treaty between
Mussolini and the Vatican in 1929 ('la gran cúpula / que untan de aceite las
lenguas militares'), which established the independence of the Holy See,
although one wonders whether even here there is not a surreptitious dig at
Futurism given this movement's own relationship with Italy's Fascist state.[27]
'Marinetti,' Lorca sarcastically explained in his lecture 'Sketch de la Nueva
Pintura', 'ha llevado el futurismo a una consagración oficial, en el cual el otro
gran futurista, Mussolini, le dio un abrazo bajo la bandera de sesenta metros
que regaló el pueblo de Milán' (*OC*, III, p. 277); while earlier the poet had
also suggested that '[e]ntre un futurista y un orador de mitin no hay gran

---

[27] As Derek Harris explains in *Federico García Lorca. Poeta en Nueva York* (London:
Grant & Cutler / Tamesis, 1979), p. 57), the poem was 'written not long after the signing of
the Papal Concordat with Mussolini in February 1929'.

diferencia. Marinetti, su fundador, es eso, un delicioso orador que ha tenido la valentía de decir palabras malsonantes en ocasiones solemnes' (*OC*, III, p. 276).[28] What is interesting, therefore, is that 'Grito hacia Roma' should have something of the oratorical protestation of Futurist manifestos about it:

> la muchedumbre de martillo, de violín o de nube,
> ha de gritar aunque le estrellen los sesos en el muro,
> ha de gritar frente a las cúpulas,
> ha de gritar loca de fuego,
> ha de gritar loca de nieve,
> ha de gritar con la cabeza llena de excremento,
> ha de gritar como todas las noches juntas,
> ha de gritar con voz tan desgarrada
> hasta que las ciudades tiemblen como niñas
> y rompan las prisiones del aceite y la música,
> porque queremos el pan nuestro de cada día,
> flor de aliso y perenne ternura desgranada,
> porque queremos que se cumpla la voluntad de la Tierra
> que da sus frutos para todos.

The calls for people to shout their anger in cathedral squares, alluded to metonymically in the reference to domes ('las cúpulas'), do not, however, reveal a simple relationship between the antipapal sentiment of this poem and the anticlericalism of Marinetti's proclamations to Spaniards in which there is an intensely violent assault on hallowed ground: '¡Que la vieja Catedral, toda negra, se siga desplomando lienzo a lienzo, con sus vitrales místicos y sus claraboyas en la bóveda adornadas del manchón fétido de la clericalla de sus cráneos mondos!' (Ilie, p. 78). Here the attack on the Church is founded on a rejection of Catholic morality and of pacifism in particular. In Marinetti's view, it is a cowardly mistake for the people of Europe to adhere to pacifism, 'preparándose así un lecho en que morir' (Ilie, p. 79). Clearly, therefore, the outrage expressed in 'Grito hacia Roma' cannot be equated with the militarist

---

[28] Manfred Lentzen, in 'Marinetti y el futurismo en España', *Actas del IX Congreso de la Asociación Internacional de Hispanistas* (1986), ed. Sebastian Neumeister (Frankfurt: Vervuert, 1989), 309–18, notes two specific periods of interest in Marinetti in Spain. The first of these follows immediately after the publication of the first Futurist Manifesto in 1909; the second comes in the late 1920s and has as its impetus a visit by the Italian to Spain early in 1928. 'Considerando', writes Lentzen (p. 35), 'las dos fases de la incidencia de Marinetti en España, podremos resumir que la primera se sitúa sobre todo en el marco del debate en torno a las ideas vanguardistas [...]; la segunda, por el contrario, tiene marcado carácter político'. Indeed, Lorca's irreverent references to Marinetti in his lecture were no doubt made in full knowledge of the enthusiasm the Italian had inspired in Fascist sympathizers, amongst whom we find, as Lentzen (p. 313) notes, Ernesto Giménez Caballero, editor of *La Gaceta Literaria*.

and anticlerical stance of Futurism. Instead it parodies the form and content of Futurism's repetitive exclamations that call for 'los hombres politicos, los literatos y los artistas' to '[d]iferenciar resueltamente la idea del militarismo de la idea de otros poderes y de la reacción clerical' and to 'fundir la idea del ejército poderoso y de la guerra posible con la idea del proletariado libre industrial y comerciante' (Ilie, pp. 78, 79). By contrast Lorca's text, in similarly prophetic terms, urges the proletariat, artists and idealists ('la muchedumbre de martillo, de violín o de nube') to rail against Pius XI and his pact of convenience with the 'gran futurista'; and it does so precisely because it is, by default, a pact with militarism and thus can only undermine the messages of love, peace and justice the old Pope now hypocritically proclaims:

> [...] el Viejo de las manos traslúcidas
> dirá: amor, amor, amor,
> aclamado por millones de moribundos;
> dirá: amor, amor, amor,
> entre el tisú estremecido de ternura;
> dirá: paz, paz, paz,
> entre el tirite de cuchillos y melones de dinamita;
> dirá: amor, amor, amor,
> hasta que se le pongan de plata los labios.

In the other of the two odes of the collection, 'Oda a Walt Whitman' (*OC*, I, pp. 528–32), the final prophetic lines are, as Havard (2007, p. 53) suggests, 'voiced in the spirit of Whitman himself, another prophet-poet':

> Quiero que el aire fuerte de la noche más honda
> quite flores y letras del arco donde duermes
> y un niño negro anuncie a los blancos del oro
> la llegada del reino de la espiga.

This ode, of course, is well known for being Lorca's most frank and open treatment of homosexuality to date. Indeed, it is difficult not to concur with Richard Saez's view that to read the poem solely as 'an evocation of the glorious virility of figures like Walt Whitman and their dream of a democratic Utopia and a lamentation of the perversion to which this dream has been subjected', is to underestimate it.[29] For 'it is the silent agony, the other side of the virile figure of Walt Whitman, that gives the poem its depth and

---

[29] Richard Saez, 'The Ritual Sacrifice in Lorca's *Poeta en Nueva York*', in Manuel Duran (ed.), *Lorca. A Collection of Critical Essays* (Englewood Cliffs, N.J.: Prentice Hall, 1962), 108–29 (p. 125).

meaning' (Saez, p. 125). Yet the idea that 'North America, tragically, has betrayed Whitman's dream for his nation', as Havard (2007, p. 53) so puts it, is present nonetheless:

> Y tú, bello Walt Whitman, duerme a orillas del Hudson
> con la barba hacia el polo y las manos abiertas.
> Arcilla blanda o nieve, tu lengua está llamando
> camaradas que velen tu gacela sin cuerpo.
> Duerme, no queda nada.
> Una danza de muros agita las praderas
> y América se anega en máquinas y llanto.

In a by now familiar paradigm, the poet aligns Whitman with nature against industry and the machine. What is more, as Saez (p. 126) suggests, he mythologizes this literary giant 'into a fertility god', rendering him 'the American counterpart to the divine kings, Attis, Osiris, and Adonis':

> Ni un solo momento, viejo hermoso Walt Whitman,
> he dejado de ver tu barba llena de mariposas,
> ni tus hombros de pana gastados por la luna,
> ni tus muslos de Apolo virginal,
> ni tu voz como una columna de ceniza;
> anciano hermoso como la niebla
> que gemías igual que un pájaro
> con el sexo atravesado por una aguja,
> enemigo del sátiro,
> enemigo de la vid
> y amante de los cuerpos bajo la burda tela.
> Ni un solo momento, hermosura viril,
> que en montes de carbón, anuncios y ferrocarriles,
> soñabas ser un río y dormir como un río
> con aquel camarada que pondría en tu pecho
> un pequeño dolor de ignorante leopardo.

Amongst the qualities Lorca extols is Apollonian beauty in contrast to the chaos of Dionysus or Bacchus to whom the satyr and the vine allude. The bird's mutilated sex recalls, as Saez (p. 125) rightly observes, 'the eunuch priests of Attis'; the castration with which Whitman is figuratively associated thus serves as an emblem of his purity, self-sacrifice and restraint.[30] The

---

[30] According to James George Frazer, *The Golden Bough. A Study in Magic and Religion*, Abridged Edition (London: Papermac, 1987), p. 347, the priests of Attis 'regularly castrated themselves on entering the service of the goddess [Cybele]'.

context for these virtues is, at one level, Lorca's criticism of the superficiality of other homosexuals ('Contra vosotros siempre, / *Faeries* de Norteamérica, / *Pájaros* de la Habana'); but it is surely also poetry itself, Whitman serving as a role model for the poet, who has had to stand firm against the excesses and depravity of a city that has threatened to overwhelm him. It is for this reason that he says 'Ni un solo momento [...] / he dejado de ver', Whitman representing the ideal standards by which he has measured himself and to which he has clung. And if he can say it so confidently and is able to prophesy the arrival of a 'kingdom of wheat', it is because 'Oda a Walt Whitman' testifies, amongst other things, to his emergence from the poetic crisis into which he was plunged.

In this respect, 'Oda a Walt Whitman' resolves issues that are raised in perhaps the most self-reflective poem of the whole collection: 'Poema doble del lago Edén' (*OC*, I, pp. 489–90). Presumably written away from the city, during a visit to Vermont in late August 1929 where Lorca stayed with his friend Philip Cummings at a cabin the young American was renting on the shores of Lake Eden (see Gibson 1989, pp. 251, 259–64), the poem is preceded by an epigraph: a line of verse from Garcilaso's Second Eclogue which, as Andrew Anderson points out, 'is the opening line of the description of a *locus amoenus*'.[31] The implication is that the place alluded to by the poem is a pastoral refuge from hectic city life. 'Eden Mills, Vermont,' writes Anderson (1997, p. 417), '[...] in its literary transposition, becomes simultaneously a New England Arcadia and, by dint of its name, the biblical Garden'; and in this place the poet is visited by his former voice, 'where his voice,' according to Anderson (1997, p. 412) once more, 'stands simultaneously for self and self-expression and for poetry and poetic expression':

> Era mi voz antigua
> ignorante de los densos jugos amargos.
> La adivino lamiendo mis pies
> bajo los frágiles helechos mojados.
>
>  ¡Ay voz antigua de mi amor,
> ay voz de mi verdad,
> ay voz de mi abierto costado,
> cuando todas las rosas manaban de mi lengua
> y el césped no conocía la impasible dentadura del caballo!

---

[31] Andrew A. Anderson, '*Et in Arcadia Ego*: Thematic Divergence and Convergence in Lorca's "Poema doble del lago Edén", *Bulletin of Hispanic Studies*, 74 (1997), 409–29 (p. 417).

Estás aquí bebiendo mi sangre,
bebiendo mi humor de niño pesado,
mientras mis ojos se quiebran en el viento
con el aluminio y las voces de los borrachos.

Déjame pasar la puerta
donde Eva come hormigas
y Adán fecunda peces deslumbrados.
Déjame pasar, hombrecillo de los cuernos,
al bosque de los desperezos
y los alegrísimos saltos.

The tranquillity of Lake Eden, it seems, has at once provided the space for and been disturbed by thoughts that have turned to familiar creative dilemmas: the attachment to self-expression in art ('ay voz de mi verdad, / ay voz de mi abierto costado'), to a time when creativity was freer – the line 'cuando todas las rosas manaban de mi lengua' reprises the image we find in 'Ciudad sin sueño' – and the contrast with a more difficult moment for the creative task, with the reference to the 'impasible dentadura del caballo' – that horse once more! – suggesting modes which are not concerned to reveal sentiment or emotion. The vampiric images of the third stanza convey the debilitating effect of his former voice on a poet who suffers as a result of the comparison with yesteryear; while the biblical and classical allusions in the fourth, with the references to Adam and Eve and then to Pan ('hombrecillo de los cuernos'), evoke a desire to return to a carefree, childlike and innocent way of being, in contrast to the experience of a world tainted by the science of industrial materials or the immoral indulgence denoted by drunken voices ('mis ojos se quiebran en el viento / con el aluminio y las voces de los borrachos').

The following stanzas continue to emphasize the obstacles to creative fulfilment:

Yo sé el uso más secreto
que tiene un viejo alfiler oxidado
y sé del horror de unos ojos despiertos
sobre la superficie concreta del plato.

Pero no quiero mundo ni sueño, voz divina,
quiero mi libertad, mi amor humano
en el rincón más oscuro de la brisa que nadie quiera.
¡Mi amor humano!

Esos perros marinos se persiguen
y el viento acecha troncos descuidados.
¡Oh voz antigua, quema con tu lengua
esta voz de hojalata y de talco!

If there is a connection between the rusty pin in the second line and the
instrument of mutilation in 'Oda a Walt Whitman', its secret use might relate
to the sacrifice implicit in the poet's service and allegiance to the truth and
dignity of art. The image of open eyes served on a plate might convey the
mutilation resulting from overpowering images, an inevitable consequence of
the poet's duty to bear testimony regardless. Similarly, in 'Ciudad sin sueño',
we are reminded of that duty and its implications:

> Pero si alguien cierra los ojos,
> ¡azotadlo, hijos míos, azotadlo!
> Haya un panorama de ojos abiertos
> y amargas llagas encendidas.

If on the shores of Lake Eden the speaker now demands his freedom, equated
here with love and humanity, it is because the burden of the poetic duty
has taken its toll – emotionally, spiritually, but also at the level of verse.
Indeed, the reason why the writing and images in the poem, as Anderson
(1997, pp. 414–15) rightly notes, waver between moments of transparency
and complexity is because there is a tension between what the speaker once
was and what he has become, each embodied in the lucidity and obscurity
of the text respectively. It is in this sense, amongst others, that the poem
is 'double', because it pits a former, integral voice recuperated in and by
nostalgic yearnings ('Era mi voz', 'La adivino', 'ay voz de mi verdad') with
a voice that is tainted and fractured by recent experience and, post-lapsarian,
can only speak in the very terms of that experience: 'voz de hojalata y talco'.

Nowhere in *Poeta en Nueva York* is the desire for self-affirmation greater
than in this poem, as the speaker insists in stanza after stanza on his need for
free and authentic self-expression:

> Quiero llorar porque me da la gana
> como lloran los niños del último banco,
> porque yo no soy un hombre, ni un poeta, ni una hoja,
> pero sí un pulso herido que sonda las cosas del otro lado.
>
> Quiero llorar diciendo mi nombre,
> rosa, niño y abeto a la orilla de este lago,
> para decir mi verdad de hombre de sangre
> matando en mí la burla y la sugestión del vocablo.
>
> No, no, yo no pregunto, yo deseo,
> voz mía libertada que me lames las manos.
> En el laberinto de biombos es mi desnudo el que recibe
> la luna de castigo y el reloj encenizado.

His claim in the first of these stanzas that he is a wounded pulse ('pulso herido'), rather than a man, poet or leaf (or even page), strips him down to the barest of elements in an effort to rid himself of the expectations which come with socially-constructed roles. Language too ('la burla y la sugestión del vocablo') is seen as an obstacle to the articulation of true essence, an idea that is a given in the context of Modernism but which here may relate specifically to the fractured expression that has been the unavoidable consequence of the poet's New York experience. In each of these stanzas, the strength of feeling is augmented by the use of the present tense, as it has been till now throughout the whole poem, with the exception of the opening two lines that are cast in the imperfect and thus convey the passage of time between the voice which was once had and that which is then sought. Yet in the final stanza there is a change of tense once again which, as Anderson (1997, p. 414) explains, 'acts as a retroactive framing device, putting the preceding stanzas into a different perspective' altogether:

> Así hablaba yo.
> Así hablaba yo cuando Saturno detuvo los trenes
> y la bruma y el Sueño y la Muerte me estaban buscando.
> Me estaban buscando
> allí donde mugen las vacas que tienen patitas de paje
> y allí donde flota mi cuerpo entre los equilibrios contrarios.

'Así hablaba yo.' This statement not only sets all that precedes it in the past but simultaneously brings into play a different voice; one that has gained distance and perspective on the desiring and desired voices that have been the subject of the poem so far. Whatever meaning we might seek to ascribe to the image of Saturn holding back the trains (for Anderson [1997, p. 420], the Roman god's identification with the Greek god Cronus holds the key), the suggestion in Lorca's 1932 public recital was that it signalled the summer's end: 'Se termina el veraneo porque Saturno detiene los trenes y he de volver a New York' (*OC*, III, p. 356). Returning to New York necessarily meant returning to the domain of Dream (with all its implications of verse distorted by oneiric forces) and of Death, both of whom have been seeking the poet out in his pastoral location. Yet rather than panic in the speaker's voice, there is at worst a sense of resignation and at best an air of self-assurance. Reminiscent of the phrase 'Ecuador entre la naranja y el limón', which he employed to describe himself in his letter to Fernández Almagro, dated 17 February 1922, and of the lines 'Ecuador entre el jazmín / y el nardo', which he used to characterize Amparo in the poem from *Poema del cante jondo* that goes by her name, the final image of the speaker's body floating 'entre los equilibrios contrarios' evokes the virtues of composure and balance. This is the quiet before the storm, before the prophetic voice takes hold, 'Poema doble del lago Eden' representing nothing other than the moment of self-reflection, away from the city, that is necessary for the emergence of that 'altogether more powerful' voice referred to by Havard (2007). 'Después ...,' explained Lorca in his recital, referring to his return to the city, 'otra vez el ritmo frenético de Nueva York. Pero ya no me sorprende, conozco el mecanismo de las calles, hablo con la gente, penetro un poco más en la vida social y la denuncio' (*OC*, III, p. 356).

If 'Poema doble' is double it is because of the tension between two voices; but it manages to resolve this tension with the addition of the third and final, prophetic voice. Like so many of the poems of *Poeta en Nueva York*, 'Poema doble' touches on questions relating to the need to express the self, to affirm the first person (with all that this implies at the level of personal identity and the poetic voice). Yet whereas it begins by equating self-expression and self-affirmation with the desire for self-revelation that has its roots in the sincere expression of a youthful lyric, it ends by allying this desire to a higher principle, one where the poet protests not only about himself but also on behalf of others in a voice that we might call 'authentic' where authenticity implies, vis-à-vis sincerity, that 'more moral experience', that 'more exigent conception of the self and of what being true to it consists in', that 'wider reference to the universe and man's place in it', and that 'less acceptant and genial view of the social circumstances of life' of which Trilling (p. 11) writes. In other words, the poet does indeed find his voice, and times oblige that it be the voice of a prophet. Social, personal and artistic aims are not mutually exclusive. Instead they converge in the realization, evident in 'Poema doble', that the poet can speak not only agonizingly but also prophetically in the language of modernity in order to contest and undermine modernity's reality and aesthetic. This said, once the New York experience is behind him, it is perhaps not surprising that the poet, in 'Son de negros en Cuba' (*OC*, III, pp. 541–2), should present us with a first-person subject that, now free of the burden of responsibility, affirms itself rhythmically through joyful repetition, cast in the optimism and openness of the liberating first-person future form:

> Iré a Santiago.
> Brisa y alcohol en las ruedas.
> Iré a Santiago.
> Mi coral en la tiniebla.
> Iré a Santiago.
> El mar ahogado en la arena.
> Iré a Santiago.

Calor blanco, fruta muerta.
Iré a Santiago.
¡Oh bovino frescor de cañavera!
¡Oh Cuba! ¡Oh curva de suspiro y barro!
Iré a Santiago.

# 6

# The Late Poetry: The Poet Recognized

Così adocchiato da cotal famiglia,
fui conosciuto da un, che mi prese
per lo lembo e gridò: «Qual maraviglia!»
(Dante, *Inferno* XV, 22–4)

'I've become a fashionable little boy,' Lorca told his parents, 'after my useful and advantageous trip to America' (Stainton, p. 268). Indeed, our poet was much sought after upon his return to Spain. 'Ahora,' he wrote to his family from Madrid in October 1930, 'todos los editores me acosan de tal manera que tengo que ir a Granada para recoger todas mis cosas, absolutamente todas, y publicarlas' (*EC*, p. 695). 'Aquí soy el de siempre,' he added, 'cada vez más temido, pero con una enorme influencia y un número fuerte de amigos, mucho más de lo que yo creía.' His celebrity would be boosted also by a musical collaboration with Encarnación López Júlvez, 'La Argentinita', the poet accompanying the singer on the piano on five records of Spanish folk songs released by His Master's Voice (see Gibson 1989, pp. 309–10, and Stainton, p. 284). There would be lectures, readings and, eventually, another trip across the Atlantic, this time to Buenos Aires where he stayed from October 1933 till March 1934 (see Gibson 1989, pp. 362–83, and Stainton, pp. 339–69). Above all, he would focus his attention on the theatre, writing and staging some of his best known plays, as well as involving himself with La Barraca, the touring student theatre group charged with the mission of taking the classics to the provinces (see Dennis, pp. 183–5; Gibson, pp. 320–4; and Stainton, pp. 294–8). Notwithstanding the protestations which had found their way into his New York poems only a short while before, in the turbulent years of the Second Republic, proclaimed in April 1931, it was the theatre and not poetry which provided the platform for Lorca to engage with social concerns. 'As we move from 1931 to 1936,' explains Andrew A. Anderson, 'he tended to channel the more immediate, public and social themes into his drama, the genre which he likewise came to conceive of increasingly as one appropriate to those particular demands.'[1]

By contrast, the poems Lorca wrote – relatively few compared with his production up to and including *Poeta en Nueva York* – 'were very much personal expressions of mostly individual sentiments' (Anderson 1990, p. 13). Morris (p. 400) notes also how, '[a]fter his stay in New York, Andalusia would be restored to its role as the frame and setting of situations, with the essential difference that places are now inseparable from personal problems and that emotional dilemmas affect the depiction of places', a legacy, Morris implies, of the poet's New York experience. The work Morris particularly has in mind is *Diván del Tamarit* (composed for the most part between 1931 and 1935), the title of which refers specifically to the Huerta del Tamarit, a country house owned by Lorca's uncle, Francisco García Rodríguez, situated just outside Granada and not far from his own family's Huerta de San Vicente, 'Lorca was not only enchanted with the name and address but was much taken by the actual house and gardens' (Anderson 1990, p. 17; see also Gibson 1989, p. 386, and Stainton, pp. 374–5). Its name is Arabic in origin and combines here with the Spanish word *diván* (a derivation from the Persian *diwan* meaning, amongst other things, 'a collection or anthology of poetry, particularly Arabic, Persian or Turkish' [Anderson 1990, p. 17]), to provide a suitably evocative title for a collection of poems composed 'in honour of the old Arab poets of Granada' (Gibson 1989, p. 386).

Despite its title and the fact that its two sections comprise *gacelas* and *casidas* respectively, there does not seem to be, as Anderson (1990, pp. 20–1) points out, any close formal or thematic relationship between the poems of *Diván del Tamarit* and the *ghazals* or *kasidas* of classical Arabic verse, even though we might find some 'occasional lexical similarities in images and situations' (Anderson 1990, p. 21).[2] Even the use of the terms *gacela* and *casida* appears arbitrary given that 'one of the two poems which most nearly approaches the form of a *casida* fragment is actually entitled "*Gacela del recuerdo del amor*"' (Anderson 1990, p. 24; see *OC*, I, pp. 579–80).[3] Although Emilio Barón Palma has attempted to draw thematic links between

---

[1]   Andrew A. Anderson, *Lorca's Late Poetry: A Critical Study*, Liverpool Monographs in Hispanic Studies 10 (Leeds: Francis Cairns, 1990), p. 13.

[2]   For a summary of the formal and thematic characteristics of the *ghazal* and *kasid*, see Daniel Devoto, *Introducción a 'Diván del Tamarit' de Federico García Lorca* (Paris: Ediciones Hispanoamericanas, 1976), 85–6.

[3]   Anderson (1990, p. 25) does accept that there might be some correlation between the form announced by the title of poems and their content, the *gacelas* dealing predominantly with love while the *casidas* focus on metaphysical issues and death, although he stresses that 'the

the poems and Arab-Andalusian verse, Anderson's claim that it is not possible to 'isolate any proper examples of conscious imitation' (Anderson 1990, p. 21) in the work is rather convincing.[4] 'The love theme', writes Anderson (1990, p. 21), 'is a primary one of Arabic poetry, as it is of almost every other kind of poetry, while other common topics, such as wine, elegy, panegyric and natural description, are touched on scarcely or only in passing. Conversely,' he adds, 'death, which appears as a major preoccupation in the *Diván*, is a rare subject for Arabic poetry. In fact,' Anderson concludes, 'Lorca's themes and motifs respond in very large part to much more personal concerns and exigencies.' The significance, therefore, of the collection's Arabic reference must lie elsewhere. Indeed, it has been suggested that the *Diván*'s reference to Arabic civilization may have stemmed from its author's attraction to that civilization's 'greater sexual tolerance and openness which resulted, among other things, in the atmosphere of indulgent, carnal sensuality often to be found in Arabic verse, wherein hetero- and homosexual love are viewed and treated on entirely the same footing' (Anderson 1990, p. 28).[5]

Equally, however, in a collection that contains little of the frankness or openness about homosexuality found in 'Oda a Walt Whitman' (even if it might be considered as 'both more personal and more erotic' [Stainton, p. 376] than anything which the poet had written before), it might be possible to detect a need on the part of Lorca, after the deracinating experience of New York, to root himself once more – with all the confidence of a poet recognized – in the rich poetic heritage of his native Andalusia. What is more, for someone whose familiarity with Arab-Andalusian verse stretched back to at least before his 1922 lecture on *cante jondo*, in which he cites and quotes from Gaspar María de Nava's anthology, *Poesías asiáticas* (see Anderson 1990, p. 18), this was a most propitious time at which to renew his interest in the form. For it coincided with the 'widespread revival of interest in Arab culture in the early 1930s in Spain' (Stainton, p. 375), which saw the inauguration of a School of Arab Studies at the University of Granada in 1932,

---

division is far from perfect'. For, as Stainton (p. 375) explains, 'throughout the collection love and death intermingle'.

    [4] See Emilio Barón Palma, *Agua oculta que llora. El 'Diván del Tamarit' de García Lorca* (Granada: Editorial Don Quijote, 1990), 36–7.

    [5] This possibility is cited by Maurer (2007, p. 36), who notes Alberto Mira's suggestion that in some authors 'the association of Arab culture and southern Spain had been "tinged" with homoerotic elements after the publication of García Gómez's 1931 [sic] anthology, *Poemas arábigoanadaluces*'. See Alberto Mira, 'Modernistas, dandies y pederastas: articulaciones de la homosexualidad en la "edad de plata"', *Journal of Iberian and Latin American Studies*, 7.1 (2001), 63–75 (p. 72).

headed by Emilio García Gómez, scholar of Arab literature and editor of the influential anthology *Poemas arábigoandaluces*, published in 1930 (see Gibson 1989, p. 393, Mira, p. 72, and Stainton, p. 375). 'In the summer of 1934,' writes Stainton (p. 375), 'García Gómez told Lorca that he intended to devote his next book to Ibn Zamrak, the poet whose work adorned the walls of the Alhambra.' Not uncharacteristically, our poet, as Stainton (p. 375) adds, 'countered by announcing that he intended to publish his own homage to the poets who once inhabited Arab Granada', namely his *Diván*.

Whatever the motivations behind its conception might be, what soon becomes clear is that there is little about *Diván del Tamarit* that is overtly self-conscious in the manner of previous or indeed subsequent works. At a formal level, the *Diván* for the most part represents a return to conventional metre after the predominance of free verse in the New York poems (see Anderson 1990, pp. 20–1, and Stainton, pp. 375–6), even though, as Morris (pp. 400, 405–7) argues, at the level of imagery and motifs it is still indebted to the poetic logic of its predecessor. Thematically, love and death provide yet another point of continuity with the New York poems and previous works, and yet the pain and emotions associated with these are no longer entwined, and are thus not to be confused, with the aesthetic doubts and concerns troubling the voices we hear in *Libro de poemas*, *Romancero gitano* or *Poeta en Nueva York*. In general terms, this lack of self-consciousness might be explained by the newfound confidence and status of a poet who had completed a successful period abroad and was now enjoying an equally, if not more, successful return. More specifically, it appears to signal the end of a process of poetic distillation which began with the effusions of *Libro de poemas* and led eventually to the reaffirmation of the relevance of the first-person voice in *Poeta en Nueva York*, though in the context of an aesthetic far removed from that which manifests itself in the earlier work. This process is marked by necessary stages – the focus on art in *Poema del cante jondo*, the ludic aspect of the Suites, the transcendence of emotion in *Canciones* and the flight from nature in *Romancero gitano* – although the novelty of the impersonal along with Lorca's mistrust of it meant that the process would inevitably be a self-conscious one. By the time Lorca set about writing *Diván del Tamarit*, he had, in effect, served his apprenticeship: the lyrical tree of Romanticism and Post-Romanticism had been well and truly cut back, and the human had begun to regain its legitimacy in face of the dehumanizing effects of modernity. The tensions at the root of his self-consciousness thus far seem no longer to be there, replaced instead by coherence between the poetic possibilities of a text and its engagement with the world (both physical and emotional) in which human beings move; a coherence which is evoked by the relationship between the words *diván* and *Tamarit* in the title, in terms of both their Arabic provenance and the way they connect poetry with a real place.

The opening poem of the collection, 'Gacela del amor imprevisto' (*OC*, I, p. 573), is a good example of the personal yet tightly controlled nature of much of the collection. Passions and emotions are articulated in the intimate context afforded by a first-person addresser and second-person addressee, but the poetic discourse never yields to the temptation of unbridled or effusive self-expression. It remains instead, as Maurer (2007, p. 35) notes in respect of the collection as a whole, even 'more sparse, intense and difficult [...] than in previous works', *Poeta en Nueva York* included:

> Nadie comprendía el perfume
> de la oscura magnolia de tu vientre.
> Nadie sabía que martirizabas
> un colibrí de amor entre los dientes.
>
> Mil caballitos persas se dormían
> en la plaza con luna de tu frente,
> mientras que yo enlazaba cuatro noches
> tu cintura, enemiga de la nieve.
>
> Entre yeso y jazmines, tu mirada
> era un pálido ramo de simientes.
> Yo busqué, para darte, por mi pecho
> las letras de marfil que dicen *siempre*,
>
> *siempre, siempre:* jardín de mi agonía,
> tu cuerpo fugitivo para siempre,
> la sangre de tus venas en mi boca,
> tu boca ya sin luz para mi muerte.

A self-conscious reading of the opening stanza permits us to understand intimate knowledge as belonging to the domain of the poet ('Nadie sabía'). The secrets shared between lovers are equivalent to the poem's veiling metaphors and strikingly uncommon combinations which only the poet can intuit and craft, and which present a screen between the reader and the things for which they stand: 'la oscura magnolia de tu vientre'; 'un colibrí de amor'; 'luna de tu frente'; 'tu cintura, enemiga de la nieve'; 'tu mirada / era un pálido ramo de simientes'; 'la sangre de tus venas en mi boca'. The imperative of poetic invention, therefore, still defines, as it has since the young Lorca's exposure to the avant-garde, not only the parameters of self-expression but of communication too. It is also possible to detect in this poem a remnant of the awareness of the dislocation between art and reality; it is one that is forced on the poet not by aesthetic precepts, but by recognition of the unpredictability and mutability of life. In the second couplet of the third stanza, the immutable implications and character of the word 'forever' (*siempre*) are unable to forestall the relationship's end, just as the poem itself can do little more than convey a moment, an emotion. The enjambment between the third and fourth stanzas transforms the potentially emphatic repetition of '*siempre*' into a sad reflection on the limitations of this word. The word 'siempre' only rings true when, no longer italicized, it describes the absence of the addressee's body ('fugitivo para siempre'), another admission of poetry's inability to preserve the physicality of a moment or provide a satisfactory alternative to lived experience. Ultimately, it is on the impossibility of 'forever' that agony's garden lies, the poet cast as a 'martyr of unrequited love', as Maurer (2007, p. 35) puts it, who 'declares from his own garden of Gethsemane [...] the universal presence of death': 'tu boca ya sin luz para mi muerte'.

In 'Casida del llanto' (*OC*, I, p. 590) we find the familiar subject of the lament, which Anderson (1990, p. 102) interprets as 'the human expression' of 'the anguish of existence, its ubiquitousness and inescapability'; in it 'one person's distress is projected out on to the outside world and assumes universal proportions'. Importantly, however, the poem's treatment of the subject is one that seeks, and at one level manages, to close the door on uncontainable grief and uncontrollable tears:

> He cerrado mi balcón
> porque no quiero oír el llanto,
> pero por detrás de los grises muros
> no se oye otra cosa que el llanto.
>
> Hay muy pocos ángeles que canten,
> hay muy pocos perros que ladren,
> mil violines caben en la palma de mi mano.
>
> Pero el llanto es un perro inmenso,
> el llanto es un ángel inmenso,
> el llanto es un violín inmenso,
> las lágrimas amordazan al viento,
> y no se oye otra cosa que el llanto.

There is clearly a tension here between the processes of containment and the irresistible force of that which is being contained. The poem oscillates between the possibility of shutting out the lament ('He cerrado mi balcón', 'no quiero oír el llanto', 'Hay muy pocos ángeles que canten' etc.) and the impossibility of such a task ('no se oye otra cosa', 'el llanto es un ángel inmenso' etc.).

The logic of the poem's progression from reduction ('pocos ángeles', 'pocos perros' etc.) to augmentation ('perro inmenso', ángel inmenso' etc.) would suggest that containment has failed, as would the introduction of additional elements in the final two lines ('las lágrimas amordazan al viento' etc.) which makes for a longer final stanza culminating in the seemingly unambiguous 'no se oye otra cosa que el llanto'. Yet in this poem, which is fundamentally a self-conscious articulation of the tension between the chaos of human emotion and the formal constraints of poetic achievement, one self-reflexive moment provides the context for the truth of the final line. It appears in the second stanza, with the line 'mil violines caben en la palma de mi mano'. The paradox lies herein: the poem may serve as testimony to the unbearable pressure exerted by personal anguish, but it does so by containing the uncontainable, the poet's hand applying artistic form, control and significance to the brute force of grief, equivalent to the sound and effect of a thousand violins.

The role of art in expressing, containing and shaping grief is central to Lorca's last major book of poetry, *Llanto por Ignacio Sánchez Mejías* (*OC*, I, pp. 549–58), which provides a very specific and personal context for the return of the self-conscious perspective. Published in 1935, the book was an elegy to the death of a close friend, the Sevillian bullfighter who died on Monday, 13 August 1934, as a result of wounds received in the bullring at Manzanares two days before.[6] Given the circumstances, it is not unreasonable to suppose that the decorum expected of a genre with a distinctly panegyric aspect would, in the production of this elegy, have had to vie with the personal exigencies of feelings of bereavement. Here the tension between form and emotion is of primary importance and is complicated further by the issue of prestige, in terms both of the status that is a pre-requisite for writing elegies in the first place – particularly one in honour of a figure as public as Sánchez Mejías – and of the 'cultural respectability' which, as Xon de Ros has noted, is conferred on the author as a result of the undertaking.[7] The risk is always that either or both of these might have a detrimental

---

[6]   For an account of the circumstances surrounding Sánchez Mejías's death, see Gibson 1989, pp. 387–91, and Anderson 1990, pp. 153–8.

[7]   See Xon de Ros, 'Ignacio Sánchez Mejías Blues', in Bonaddio and De Ros (eds) (2003), 81–91 (p. 88). De Ros (2003, p. 88) links this 'cultural respectability' to the complicity of Lorca's poem with 'the androcentric ideology of traditional elegies'. For an account of the debt Lorca's poem owes to the elegiac tradition, see Calvin Cannon, 'Lorca's *Llanto por Ignacio Sánchez Mejías* and the Elegiac Tradition', *Hispanic Review*, 31 (1963), 229–38. Cannon (pp. 229–30) lists ten devices in *Llanto* which relate to it: 'announcement of the death of the person to be mourned, expression of grief and bitter resentment against the cruelty of death, exaltation and apotheosis of the dead man, eulogy of the life of the dead man, account of how and when

influence on the emotional aspect of the work, not only at the level of public perceptions about the poet's motivation but also with regard to the extent to which aesthetic considerations (as these relate to fashion, invention or accomplishment) displace core sentiments. The risk of the latter was arguably limited in the case of Lorca's elegy, since any aesthetic self-awareness might well have been deemed appropriate to honour a man who himself had artistic interests. Indeed, Sánchez Mejías had written three plays and could be considered to have been a member (albeit a minor one) of the 1920s and 1930s Spanish literary avant-garde (see Anderson 1990, p. 154). Above all, however, what saves Lorca's *Llanto* from such judgements is precisely its self-conscious treatment of the tension between form and emotion in which, as De Ros has observed with reference to the last of the poem's four sections, the 'lyrical voice prefigures the principles propounded by Pablo Neruda in his piece "Sobre una poesía sin pureza", published exactly one year later, where he advocates a rehumanization of the poetic voice against the excesses of formalism'.[8] While, as I have suggested above, this rehumanized voice cohabits uncontroversially (and consequently, for the most part, unselfconsciously) with aesthetic enterprise in *Diván del Tamarit*, in *Llanto* the poet feels the need nonetheless to reiterate the human perspective once again with all that it implies, including 'sentiment and melancholy' (see De Ros 2000, p. 125).

In his famous lecture 'Juego y teoría del duende' (*OC*, III, pp. 306–18), which he first gave in Buenos Aires in 1933, Lorca had offered *duende* as an alternative to the inspiration of angels and muses. De Ros (2003, p. 82) reminds us that the Spanish dictionary definition of 'to possess *duende*' is 'to be inspired with disquiet'. Yet in his lecture Lorca casts the experience in more extreme terms, as an encounter with death, as an opening and healing of wounds:

> el duende no llega si no ve posibilidad de muerte, si no sabe que ha de rondar su casa, si no tiene seguridad de que ha de mecer esas ramas que todos llevamos y que no tienen, que no tendrán consuelo.
> Con idea, con sonido o gesto, el duende gusta de los bordes del pozo en franca lucha con el creador. Ángel y musa se escapan con violín o compás, y el duende hiere, y en la curación de esta herida, que no se cierra nunca, está lo insólito, lo inventado de la obra de un hombre. (*OC*, III, pp. 314–15)

---

he died, the funeral with other mourners, use of flowers, use of a refrain, use of a dramatic frame, and the conclusion of the poem on a note of consolation, tranquillity, or even rejoicing'.

[8]   Xon de Ros, 'Science and Myth in *Llanto por Ignacio Sánchez Mejías*', *The Modern Language Review*, 95.1 (2000), 114–26 (p. 125).

The healing process referred to might well be equivalent to the controlling and shaping abilities of the artist, the wounding and, more drastically, the encounter – indeed, the struggle – with death, an allegory of the artist's engagement with difficult, dark, painful material. As a version of the creative process, it unsettles Eliot's view of the perfect artist, since it is not clear just how separate, in the throes of the *duende*-inspired act, are 'the man who suffers and the mind which creates'. In any event, it is only an allegory, even though Lorca might want to give *duende* a physical presence by associating it in particular, though not exclusively, with live performance, be it song, dance or spoken poetry, 'formas que nacen y mueren de modo perpetuo y alzan sus contornos sobre un presente exacto' (*OC*, III, p. 311). Where the dividing line between the figurative and the real does become dangerously blurred is in the introduction of *duende* into the bullring, where 'en el momento de matar, se necesita la ayuda del duende para dar en el clavo de la verdad artística' (*OC*, III, p. 316). 'El torero', continues Lorca, 'que asusta al público en la plaza con su temeridad no torea, sino que está en ese plano ridículo, al alcance de cualquier hombre, de *jugarse la vida*; en cambio, el torero mordido por el duende da una lección de música pitagórica y hace olvidar que tira constantemente el corazón sobre los cuernos' (*OC*, III, pp. 316–17). 'España', he later adds, 'es el único país donde la muerte es el espectáculo nacional, donde la muerte toca largos clarines a la llegada de las primaveras, y su arte está siempre regido por un duende agudo que le ha dado su diferencia y su calidad de invención' (*OC*, III, p. 317). The view, no doubt, is much safer from the stands. The depiction of a bullfighter summoning *duende* in his encounter with an uncomfortably real and possible death brings into sharp focus the degree of poetic licence used in the deathly accounts of other artistic struggles. In *Llanto*, by contrast, Lorca finds himself having to deal with the stark reality of death. It is in the context of this encounter that human sentiment works its way into the text, its expression eventually displacing any idea of solace, reward, satisfaction or compensation which might be afforded by art. In her socio-political reading of the poem, De Ros (2000, p. 118) draws our attention to a fundamental dynamic of *Llanto*; that is, its organization around the principle of conflict.[9] If, as De Ros (2000, p. 118) explains, '[t]he pattern of conflict is a necessary part of bereavement and grief', in *Llanto* this sign of bereavement manifests itself in the range of competing poetic strategies and

---

[9]    Arguing against the view that in the 1930s Lorca used theatre to explore social issues whilst his poems become the site for personal expression, De Ros sees *Llanto* as being immersed in the conflicts of the period and reads the poem as an articulation of 'the tensions of a nation torn between faith and reason, tradition and modernity' (De Ros 2000, p. 118).

modes within each of the poem's four sections as well as between them. 'La verdadera lucha,' claimed Lorca (*OC*, III, p. 309), 'es con el duende', and in *Llanto* what the poet must struggle with is *duende* in the form of the disquieting inspiration of grief. In the opening section, 'La cogida y la muerte', the controlling principles of art seem to stake their claim in the references to Ignacio's wounding and death; yet the accumulative effect of this section's refrain, with its obsessive indication of time – five o'clock, the traditional hour at which bullfights begin –is to undermine containment, moving the stanzas instead towards an emotional breaking point.[10] In the first stanza, the initial temporal reference appears to be matter-of-fact, even though its increasing intensity is prefigured in the switch to italics:

> A las cinco de la tarde.
> Eran las cinco en punto de la tarde.
> Un niño trajo la blanca sábana
> *a las cinco de la tarde.*
> Una espuerta de cal ya prevenida
> *a las cinco de la tarde.*
> Lo demás era muerte y sólo muerte
> *a las cinco de la tarde.*

At this early stage, the refrain has yet to unsettle the controlled solemnity of the contextual detail (the boy and the linen sheet, the ready basket of lime, or even the overwhelming presence of death). In the second also, at least to begin with, there is still something scientific and orderly about lines which gather to them instances of factual detail and metaphor:

> El viento se llevó los algodones
> *a las cinco de la tarde.*
> Y el óxido sembró cristal y níquel
> *a las cinco de la tarde.*
> Ya luchan la paloma y el leopardo
> *a las cinco de la tarde.*
> Y un muslo con un asta desolada
> *a las cinco de la tarde.*
> Comenzaron los sones de bordón
> *a las cinco de la tarde.*
> Las campanas de arsénico y el humo
> *a las cinco de la tarde.*

---

[10] Anderson (1990, p. 173) points out that, although Sánchez Mejías's funeral procession in Madrid did begin at 5 o'clock exactly, his bullfight on that fateful day in Manzanares did not, nor did he suffer his wounds or die at that time.

> En las esquinas grupos de silencio
> *a las cinco de la tarde.*

Yet such is the accumulative pressure exerted by the refrain that it then begins to spill between and over lines, giving rise to a rare exclamation in the reference to the bull's elation before breaking up a complete sentence situating death's fatal involvement:

> ¡Y el toro solo corazón arriba!
> *a las cinco de la tarde.*
> Cuando el sudor de nieve fue llegando
> *a las cinco de la tarde,*
> cuando la plaza se cubrió de yodo
> *a las cinco de la tarde,*
> la muerte puso huevos en la herida
> *a las cinco de la tarde.*
> *A las cinco de la tarde.*
> *A las cinco en punto de la tarde.*

A similar pattern emerges in the final stanza. Here the depiction of the bull-fighter's lifeless body and wounds still belongs to the domain of poetic control and achievement – a mixture, once more, of prosaic detail and metaphorical sublimation. But the refrain persists, working its way between a compound sentence and then emerging from its italicization:

> Un ataúd con ruedas es la cama
> *a las cinco de la tarde.*
> Huesos y flautas suenan en su oído
> *a las cinco de la tarde.*
> El toro ya mugía por su frente
> *a las cinco de la tarde.*
> El cuarto se irisaba de agonía
> *a las cinco de la tarde.*
> A lo lejos ya viene la gangrena
> *a las cinco de la tarde.*
> Trompa de lirio por las verdes ingles
> *a las cinco de la tarde.*
> Las heridas quemaban como soles
> *a las cinco de la tarde,*
> y el gentío rompía las ventanas
> *a las cinco de la tarde.*
> A las cinco de la tarde.
> ¡Ay qué terribles cinco de la tarde!
> ¡Eran las cinco en todos los relojes!
> ¡Eran las cinco en sombra de la tarde!

The exclamatory nature of the final utterances means that they are far more than statements of fact. The grief which, in the rhetorical guise of a refrain, has shadowed and inevitably interfered with the poetic constructions of adjacent lines throughout the section, has now slipped through the cracks of poetic control to appear on the page in its own right, unashamedly prosaic and uncontained.

In the second section, 'La sangre derramada', the persistent phrase is now '¡Que no quiero verla!', the object pronoun here referring to the bullfighter's spilt blood:

> ¡Que no quiero verla!
>
> Dile a la luna que venga,
> que no quiero ver la sangre
> de Ignacio sobre la arena.
>
> ¡Que no quiero verla!

The exclamation is at once a sign of uncontained grief and, paradoxically, an attempt to contain that grief; it is both recognition and refusal, implicit in which are the expression and denial of feeling respectively. This double aspect is reproduced also in the section's movement between considered fragments which seek to mythologize the bullfighter, his art and death, sometimes by recourse to established mythology, and what seem to be, on the other hand, spontaneous and reactive lyrical outbursts, like the one we have just cited.[11] In the following extract, for example, a narrative sequence representing Ignacio's encounter with death in mythical terms is halted by a shout which is triggered by the account itself and is seemingly raised by the poet in spite of himself:

> Por las gradas sube Ignacio
> con toda su muerte a cuestas.
> Buscaba el amanecer,
> y el amanecer no era.
> Busca su perfil seguro,
> y el sueño lo desorienta.
> Buscaba su hermoso cuerpo
> y encontró su sangre abierta.
> ¡No me digáis que la vea!

---

[11] For an account of the mythology and folklore informing Lorca's elegy, particularly surrounding the bullfight and its prehistory, see Anderson 1990, pp. 158–71. For a treatment which emphasizes the Orphic references in the poem, see De Ros (2000 and 2003).

It is as if the mention of blood here is a slip on the part of the poet who immediately retreats to his position of containment and denial, substituting the pronoun for the dreaded noun, just as he does elsewhere. Another substitution then comes in the form of a metonymical reference, where 'chorro' appears for 'sangre'; in these lines poetry seeks again to gain the upper hand, instilling Ignacio's blood with magical properties, only to be halted by shouts once more:

> No quiero sentir el chorro
> cada vez con menos fuerza;
> ese chorro que ilumina
> los tendidos y se vuelca
> sobre la pana y el cuero
> de muchedumbre sedienta.
> ¡Quién me grita que me asome!
> ¡No me digáis que la vea!

The same principles weave their way through the final part of the section, in which the by now familiar outbursts punctuate, but also puncture, the mythical constructions intended to manage grief. In these lines, perhaps the most overtly self-conscious of the section, Ignacio's blood sings, just as the poem itself sings his blood:[12]

> Pero ya duerme sin fin.
> Ya los musgos y la hierba
> abren con dedos seguros
> la flor de su calavera.
> Y su sangre ya viene cantando:
> cantando por marismas y praderas,
> resbalando por cuernos ateridos,
> vacilando sin alma por la niebla,
> tropezando con miles de pezuñas
> como una larga, oscura, triste lengua,
> para formar un charco de agonía
> junto al Guadalquivir de las estrellas.

There is an implicit tension here between life and death, between the decay of a corpse at the mercy of natural elements ('los musgos y la hierba') and its revivification by poetry and myth. Whatever it signals in reality, a skull in this context can be a flower just as blood can sing and extend beyond both

---

[12] For De Ros (2003, p. 87), '[t]he singling blood [...] recalls images of the aftermath of Orpheus's decapitation, when his head, still singing, floats down the river Hebrus'.

anatomical and earthly limits to form a pool amongst the stars. But there is little as yet that is consolatory about the new life which death breathes, the song unable to transcend the moment of the goring ('resbalando por cuernos ateridos'; 'tropezando con miles de pezuñas') and characterized by soullessness ('sin alma'), sadness ('como una […] triste lengua') and agony ('charco de agonía').[13] In this respect the imagery, in all its ambivalence, coheres with the ambiguity of a poem in which the achievements of poetic control fail to repress the lyrical outbursts of real grief. Little wonder, then, that the attempt to draw life from death is succeeded by another series of exclamations and protestations:

> ¡Oh blanco muro de España!
> ¡Oh negro toro de pena!
> ¡Oh sangre dura de Ignacio!
> ¡Oh ruiseñor de sus venas!
> No.
> ¡Que no quiero verla!

The first four exclamations combine eulogy and grief, but the 'No' of the fifth line is unambiguously prosaic and, as Anderson (1990, p. 205) has noted, 'halts the movement of the verse' – 'breaks the scansion', as De Ros (2000, p. 119) puts it. It returns us abruptly to the domain of denial and containment although, as is implied by the ambivalent character of the first four exclamations, it is becoming increasingly difficult to control raw emotion. The next lines articulate the impossibility of containment via metaphors whose function, paradoxically, is precisely to perform that task, a contradiction of which the final negation – now a double exclamation – remains, as ever, both a symptom and an emblem:

> Que no hay cáliz que la contenga,
> que no hay golondrinas que se la beban,
> no hay escarcha de luz que la enfríe,
> no hay canto ni diluvio de azucenas,
> no hay cristal que la cubra de plata.
> No.
> ¡¡Yo no quiero verla!!

---

[13] In Arturo del Hoyo's edition of the *Obras completas*, instead of 'vacilando sin alma' we find 'vacilando su alma'. The version for which we have opted is given by García-Posada in his edition, *Obras II: Poesía 2*, p. 387.

In the third section of the poem, 'Cuerpo presente', the subject and spur of the poet's lament is the lifeless body of the bullfighter laid out on a stone slab:

> Ya está sobre la piedra Ignacio el bien nacido.
> Ya se acabó; ¿qué pasa? Contemplad su figura:
> la muerte le ha cubierto de pálidos azufres
> y le ha puesto cabeza de oscuro minotauro.

Francisco García Lorca has observed a tension between the principles of creative freedom and formal control in a section which is more restrained throughout than either 'La cogida y la muerte' or 'La sangre derramada'.[14] This section, unlike the others, is composed entirely of alexandrines which are organized mostly into quatrains, with the exception of the seventh stanza which is comprised of five lines. What is more, there is no metrical variation, no assonance or rhyme, and the thematic movement is for the most part uniform (see Anderson 1990, p. 207). The general sense of restraint created by these formal properties coheres with the nature of the section's subject matter, the silent reality of death – the bullfighter's body lying in state – having an understandably sobering effect on poetic discourse. It has indeed all come to an end ('Ya se acabó'), a realization that has also silenced the outbursts which characterized the previous section. Now there is a sense of having and wanting to bear witness to the intimate fact of one man's passing:

> ¿Quién arruga el sudario? ¡No es verdad lo que dice!
> Aquí no canta nadie, ni llora en el rincón,
> ni pica las espuelas, ni espanta la serpiente:
> aquí no quiero más que los ojos redondos
> para ver ese cuerpo sin posible descanso.

There are still expressions of a desire to free Ignacio from death ('Yo quiero que me enseñen dónde está la salida / para este capitán atado a la muerte'), but these relate rather more to the human inability to conceive of the corpse as the person now departed than they do to the mythologizing principle, evident particularly in the previous section, which seeks to give the dead new life. Instead, the predominant feeling is that Ignacio's body should be delivered once and for all from the reminder of the physical catastrophe – the goring – which sealed its fate:

---

[14] See Francisco García Lorca, *Federico y su mundo*, 2nd edn (Madrid: Alianza, 1981), 226.

> Yo quiero que me enseñen un llanto como un río
> que tenga dulces nieblas y profundas orillas,
> para llevar el cuerpo de Ignacio y que se pierda
> sin escuchar el doble resuello de los toros.
>
> [...]
>
> No quiero que le tapen la cara con pañuelos
> para que se acostumbre con la muerte que lleva.
> Vete, Ignacio: No sientas el caliente bramido.
> Duerme, vuela, reposa: ¡También se muere el mar!

Even if the final exclamation might render the bullfighter larger than life by virtue of the implicit association between him and the sea, it does so in a voice which does not so much seek to aggrandize as it does to accept the world's natural cycles.

In the final section, 'Alma ausente', the fact of Ignacio's death is emphasized by the enumeration of things that will not know or see him. This play of absence and presence is what also characterizes the use of the object pronoun *te* which at one level 'is', inasmuch as it signifies the addressee, but at another 'is not', since the addressee is no longer of this world:

> No te conoce el toro ni la higuera,
> ni caballos ni hormigas de tu casa.
> No te conoce el niño ni la tarde
> porque te has muerto para siempre.
>
> No te conoce el lomo de la piedra,
> ni el raso negro donde te destrozas.
> No te conoce tu recuerdo mudo
> porque te has muerto para siempre.
>
> El otoño vendrá con caracolas,
> uva de niebla y montes agrupados,
> pero nadie querrá mirar tus ojos
> porque te has muerto para siempre.

The recourse to myth-creation as a means of managing grief, already waning in 'Cuerpo presente', seems to have been abandoned altogether now, as the bullfighter's death is set brutally in context:

> Porque te has muerto para siempre,
> como todos los muertos de la Tierra,
> como todos los muertos que se olvidan
> en un montón de perros apagados.[15]

---

[15] De Ros (2000, p. 122) sees in the final line of this stanza a possible allusion to 'Andalusian dogs', the nickname given jokingly to southern poets in the Residencia de Estudiantes. If so,

In the following stanza, the poet finally offers something more positive. Whatever tensions might arise in an elegy between poetic achievement and grief, the poet does manage to preserve his faith in the ability of poetry at least to keep the memory of the dead alive:[16]

> No te conoce nadie. No. Pero yo te canto.
> Yo canto para luego tu perfil y tu gracia.
> La madurez insigne de tu conocimiento.
> Tu apetencia de muerte y el gusto de su boca.
> La tristeza que tuvo tu valiente alegría.

Francisco García Lorca (p. 254) interprets the temporal qualification 'para luego' as a cautious, even modest appraisal of the durability of the poem, also detecting in it something of 'la tonalidad real de la voz de Federico'. 'Hay,' he adds, 'hasta una leve tensión estilística, de tono arcaizante, en este cauteloso «para luego», en el que el poeta proyecta su propio futuro y también su propia muerte como cantor.'[17] Here and throughout the section a voice emerges which is sensibly more personal than what we have encountered so far in the work, both because the poet touches on his own mortality and because, as De Ros (2000, p. 124) has noted, he employs a 'direct mode of addressing Ignacio [which] signals a more [...] intimate relationship with the subject, at variance with the indirect, more guarded tone of the previous sections'. The final stanza loses nothing of this intimacy, even though, as Anderson (1990, p. 230) points out, Ignacio is now referred to in the third person:

> Tardará mucho tiempo en nacer, si es que nace,
> un andaluz tan claro, tan rico de aventura.
> Yo canto su elegancia con palabras que gimen
> y recuerdo una brisa triste por los olivos.

then the reference, as De Ros puts it, 'brings the identity of the deceased closer to that of the poet himself'.

16 De Ros (2000, p. 122) argues that the indifference towards Ignacio conveyed in the first four stanzas of the section undermines the assumption that the phrase beginning 'Yo canto para luego' is equivalent to 'I sing in order to perpetuate the memory of the bullfighter'. The interpretation provided by Anderson (1990, p. 228) is in line with that of Roy O. Jones and Geraldine M. Scanlon in their essay 'Ignacio Sánchez Mejías: the "Mythic Hero"', in Nigel Glendinning (ed.), *Studies in Modern Spanish Literature and Art Presented to Helen F. Grant* (London: Tamesis, 1972), 97–108 (p. 108). Jones and Scanlon accept that although '[m]en will forget, and for Ignacio there may [...] be no commemorative rite [...] he shall live again for a time in the poet's liturgy, the song of a friend'.

17 De Ros (2000, p. 122) also understands the time-span suggested here as pointing to the death of the poet, although she sees the use of the adverb 'luego' as undercutting the poet's appeal to the immortality of poetry.

How different the calm honesty of these lines from the exclamations and outbursts of other sections which served to disrupt all semblance of order and control. Here, by contrast, emotion and control are reconciled, bound by the simplicity and directness of the phrases. The reference to 'palabras que gimen', whether these be understood as pointing self-consciously to the elegy being written or as a comment on the strain which the lament places on words (see Anderson 1990, pp. 230–1), is no less an acknowledgement of strength and depth of emotion for not resorting to a more effusive tone. If set in opposition to the memory of a sad breeze in the final line, the 'elegant song' may represent, as De Ros (2003, p. 88) suggests, poetic achievement which has been arrived at throughout the elegy 'at the cost of dehumanizing nature'. However, elegance and nature are not incompatible, twinned as they are in the final line, which brings metre and measure to feeling and situates that feeling poignantly in an individual's subjective experience of the world.

Whether or not the eleven sonnets known as the 'Sonetos del amor oscuro', which Lorca composed towards the end of 1935, were inspired by real-life relationships, so general are the terms in which they are cast that it is difficult to argue with Anderson's conviction that they 'are above all about the tormented *experience* of love, passion and suffering, and only secondarily about the dynamics of being in a love affair' (Anderson 1990, p. 307).[18] Even where there is a second person addressee, there is little benefit to be had from knowing on whom the *tú* might be based, the sonnets appealing instead to broader discourses on love, including those established by the Petrarchan

---

[18]  Gibson (1989, p. 419), for example, links two sonnets – 'Soneto de la carta' (*OC*, I, p. 942) and 'El poeta dice la verdad' (*OC*, I, p. 943) – to Lorca's anxieties about his relationship with his friend Rafael Rodríguez Rapún. This is also the line taken by Maurer 2007, p. 37. Paul Binding, for his part, in *Lorca: The Gay Imagination* (London: GMP, 1985), 206, sees the sonnets as Lorca's 'fullest excursion into his *propia persona*' and claims that 'he stands for us [...] in all his nakedness as sexually-driven man, as a homosexual man desirous of speaking out about all that he has felt during a relationship which took him [...] to hell and heaven'. As regards the name of this collection of sonnets, Arturo del Hoyo refers to them in his edition of *Obras completas* only as 'Sonetos de amor', the title under which they first appeared together in the Madrid newspaper *ABC* in 1984. As García-Posada notes in his edition, *Obras II: Poesía 2*, p. 758, the version 'Sonetos del amor oscuro' 'sólo ha llegado hasta nosotros transmitido por los amigos del poeta.' For a discussion of the title, see Francisco Javier Díez de Revenga, 'Federico García Lorca: de los "poemas neoyorquinos" a los "sonetos oscuros"', *Revista Hispánica Moderna*, 41 (1988), 105–14 (pp. 105–6), and Anderson (1990, pp. 305–7), who also lists the many connotations of 'amor oscuro', including a love that is secret, or which relates to the Dionysian side of the passions, or to obsession, frustration, anguish and even death (p. 306).

sonnet.[19] Indeed, as critics have pointed out, the sonnets are clearly aware of the tradition to which they belong. 'Los *Sonetos*', writes Candela Newton, 'se escriben sobre el trasfondo de toda una tradición de autores como Quevedo, Góngora y, especialmente, San Juan de la Cruz, cuyos temas y motivos poéticos hallan eco constante en las composiciones de Lorca.'[20] Newton connects the sonnets to the mysticism of San Juan, amongst others, finding a modern twist in the opposite conclusions at which our poet arrives; namely, that 'la trascendencia es imposible, y el dolor y la muerte son la realidad inescapable que acompaña la vida' (Newton, p. 156). Yet it is equally possible to judge the sentiments of these poems, with their references to love suffered, disdained or misunderstood, to be somewhat clichéd, an evaluation which Francisco Javier Díez de Revenga (p. 107) seems to support in an essay questioning the sonnets' novelty and literary achievement.[21] What should not be forgotten, of course, as Anderson (1990, p. 308), Maurer (2007, p. 37) and indeed Díez de Revenga (p. 114) remind us, is that the eleven sonnets, which were only first published together as a set in 1984, are no more than first drafts. This and the fact that they may actually have been part of a much larger project may well account for any perceived lack of accomplishment or unevenness.

At all events, what is more important to us here than either the source or literary worth of these poems is the very fact of Lorca's attraction and strict adherence to the sonnet form.[22] To begin with, it is quite possible that the poet's attraction related to his desire, as ever, to keep abreast of the latest trends. The sonnet was, as Newton (p. 143), Díez de Revenga (p. 108) and Anderson (1990, pp. 309–10) have noted, the preferred mode for a number of young poets publishing in and around 1936, the year which marked the four-hundredth anniversary of the death of Garcilaso, 'the poet singly most responsible for establishing the Italianate Petrarchist mode in Spain'

[19] For an account of the connections and dissimilarities between Lorca's work and the Petrarchan sonnet, see Andrew A. Anderson, 'García Lorca como poeta petrarquista', *Cuadernos Hispanoamericanos*, 453–6 (September–October, 1986), 495–518.

[20] Candelas Newton, 'Los paisajes del amor: iconos centrales en los *Sonetos* de Lorca', *Anales de la Literatura Española Contemporánea*, 11 (1986), 143–59 (p. 143). See also Anderson 1990, pp. 305–99.

[21] Díez de Revenga (p. 106) characterizes the poems as 'inseguros, experimentales, vacilantes en cuanto a su construcción e inconexos entre sí'.

[22] Lorca's sonnets adhere to the classic Petrarchan model of fourteen lines in hendecasyllabic verse, with a rhyme scheme of abba/abba/cdc/dcd (the one variation coming in the sestet of 'El poeta habla por teléfono con el amor' [*OC*, I, p. 944], which reads cdc/cdc).

(Anderson 1990, p. 309).[23] Lorca acknowledged the trend when talking about his own sonnets in a much quoted interview with Felipe Morales in 1936. 'El libro de *Sonetos*', he explained, 'significa la vuelta a las formas de la preceptiva después del amplio y soleado paseo por la libertad de metro y rima. En España, el grupo de poetas jóvenes emprende hoy esta cruzada' (*OC*, III, p. 676). We should not discount either the possibility that Lorca may also have turned his attention to the sonnet because of the formal challenges it presented. Indeed, implicit in his words to Morales is an acknowledgement of the fact that adopting the sonnet meant having to work within the rules of its form. If there is something at all self-conscious about his approach (which to an extent I believe there is), then this may well have been a consequence of his coming to the sonnet aware not only of its currency but also of its aesthetic demands, in addition, of course, to the tradition to which it belonged.

Leaving to one side their debt to the Petrarchist mode or to the mystics, Díez de Revenga (p. 110) questions the novelty of the sonnets on the basis of their having barely gained ground on the images and themes of *Poeta en Nueva York*. A poem like 'Soneto de la dulce queja' (*OC*, I, p. 940), I would suggest, shows also that there are connections even with the tropes of *Canciones* or *Libro de poemas*, in particular via the recourse to the tree-metaphor:

> Tengo miedo a perder la maravilla
> de tus ojos de estatua, y el acento
> que de noche me pone en la mejilla
> la solitaria rosa de tu aliento.
>
> Tengo pena de ser en esta orilla
> tronco sin ramas; y lo que más siento
> es no tener la flor, pulpa o arcilla,
> para el gusano de mi sufrimiento.
>
> Si tú eres el tesoro oculto mío,
> si eres mi cruz y mi dolor mojado,
> si soy el perro de tu señorío,
>
> no me dejes perder lo que he ganado
> y decora las aguas de tu río
> con hojas de mi otoño enajenado.

If this return to old tropes can be taken as a sign of the poet's hesitancy or uncertainty – the very characteristics which Díez de Revenga (p. 106)

---

[23] For an introduction to the development of the sonnet form and its variations in Spain, see Antonio Quilis, *Métrica española* (Barcelona: Ariel, 1984), 132–42.

attributes to Lorca's sonnets – a similar effect is created by the poem's 'sweet complaint', which seems to have implications not only for the subject of love but for the very character of the creative task too. The fear of loss conveyed in the first quatrain might equally convey anxieties about the inability to capture the true effect of the loved one's features and presence in verse. The regret conveyed in the subsequent quatrain employs what are by now familiar tropes evoking incapacity and the inability to deal with suffering, all of which has the potential to extend beyond the sphere of love into the domain of art. Although the speaker's intention in the final sestet may be to reaffirm his bonds with his lover, the use of the verb *decorar* for the action that might possibly signal their reconnection ('decora las agua de tu río') brings aesthetic considerations into play once again. Ultimately, whether we consider the poem to be reminiscent of previous works by the author or even, as Anderson (1990, p. 321) suggests, 'of the Petrarchist's equivocal "sweet sorrow"', the fear of loss appears to translate into reticence and conformity, the sonnet's conceits speaking of convention and artifice before they do of love or sorrow.

In 'Llagas de amor' (*OC*, I, p. 941), although passions seem to be on display, the lyric subject itself, at least to begin with, is less prominent than in 'Soneto de la dulce queja', the elements which constitute love's wounds now taking its place:

> Esta luz, este fuego que devora.
> Este paisaje gris que me rodea.
> Este dolor por una sola idea.
> Esta angustia de cielo, mundo y hora.
>
> Este llanto de sangre que decora
> lira sin pulso ya, lúbrica tea.
> Este peso del mar que me golpea.
> Este alacrán que por mi pecho mora.
>
> Son guirnalda de amor, cama de herido,
> donde sin sueño, sueño tu presencia
> entre las ruinas de mi pecho hundido.
>
> Y aunque busco la cumbre de prudencia,
> me da tu corazón valle tendido
> con cicuta y pasión de amarga ciencia.

The effect is that these elements ('luz', 'fuego', 'paisaje gris', 'dolor por una sola idea', 'angustia de cielo, mundo y hora', 'llanto de sangre', 'peso del mar', 'alacrán') are rendered external to the poet who, in naming them, asserts his rational, if poetic, control over the suffering for which they stand.

Subjects in a grammatical sense, they are emotion objectified, suffering reduced to fragments which may then be reconstructed as a wounded man's bed or woven into a garland of love, at once painful and decorative. The result can only be a sonnet in which decorum comes before passion. As in 'Soneto de la dulce queja', the poet has recourse here to the verb *decorar*, the 'lament of blood' becoming, in lines 5 and 6, a decorative element adorning the lyre – an age-old symbol of poetry – which is in turn rendered impassive by the lack of a pulse. To decorum we can also add prudence, which the speaker identifies as his goal in line 12. The loved one, it seems, stands between him and this goal, but what the speaker attains instead is hardly more passionate, tempered as it is by being cast as knowledge ('ciencia'), however bitter that knowledge may be.

In 'El poeta dice la verdad' (*OC*, I, p. 943), one of five sonnets that include a reference to the poet in the title, truth is a complex affair.[24] We could understand it in terms of the earnest self-revelation which Newton (p. 145) sees as being characteristic of sonnets whose sole protagonist is 'el corazón del poeta, expuesto en toda su verdad y en diálogo constante con su pasión'. Alternatively, it could be understood as being a reference to the acute sensibilities which poets supposedly possess and with them the magical capacity to reveal hidden truths. Whichever it is, truth is immediately called into question as the sonnet opens by conveying an ulterior motive for drawing attention to its expression of sorrow:

> Quiero llorar mi pena y te lo digo
> para que tú me quieras y me llores
> en un anochecer de ruiseñores,
> con un puñal, con besos y contigo.
>
> Quiero matar al único testigo
> para el asesinato de mis flores
> y convertir mi llanto y mis sudores
> en eterno montón de duro trigo.
>
> Que no se acabe nunca la madeja
> del te quiero me quieres, siempre ardida
> con decrépito sol y luna vieja.

---

[24] The other four poems are 'El poeta habla por teléfono con el amor' (*OC*, I, p. 944), 'El poeta pregunta a su amor por la «Ciudad Encantada» de Cuenca' (*OC*, I, p. 945), 'Soneto gongorino en el que el poeta manda a su amor una paloma' (*OC*, I, p. 946), and 'El amor duerme en el pecho del poeta' (*OC*, I, p. 948).

> Que lo que no me des y no te pida
> será para la muerte, que no deja
> ni sombra por la carne estremecida.

If the poet is speaking at all of his desire to cry his pain, it is so that he will receive love and compassion in return, an admission which could itself be seen as an example of the poet's truthfulness, as truthful as the very sorrow of which he sings, but equally beguiling given its allusion to artifice. In the second quatrain, the poet's admission of a murderous desire is similarly ambiguous. Although it may suggest the extent of the poet's anguish, 'in light of the title,' as Anderson (1990, p. 343) contends, 'it is difficult to decide [...] whether this extreme vocabulary is "genuinely" melodramatic or an example of ironic overstatement'. Along with the ulterior motive, this lack of proportion throws into doubt exactly what is meant by the truth; it also sits uneasily in the quatrain alongside the image of wheat, which offers a more fruitful and sustainable possibility for those able to face and overcome their suffering. If lines 9 to 11 express the desire for eternal reciprocity, the final tercet deals with the brutal reality of its failure. To be in a situation where nothing is given nor sought is neither to live nor to leave any trace. Of all the truths and untruths conveyed in the poem, this may be the one to which the title particularly refers. For it points to the essential yet truthful paradox of a sonnet that only exists because the poet's requests for reciprocity have not been met.

What is apparent in all three sonnets discussed so far is that a combination of reticence, reason and artifice is keeping emotion at bay. In other words, an inordinate emphasis on device appears to be getting in the way of feeling, a literary complication which Anderson (1990, p. 398) attributes to Lorca's somewhat arch redevelopment of the works of the mystics. An invasive literariness, for example, arguably shares the phone booth with the poet in 'El poeta habla por teléfono con el amor', in which a charmingly modern setting for the exploration of the emotional proximity and physical distance between lovers is poorly served by an archaic discourse that seems contrived and implausible by comparison:

> Tu voz regó la duna de mi pecho
> en la dulce cabina de madera.
> Por el sur de mis pies fue primavera
> y al norte de mi frente flor de helecho.
>
> Pino de luz por el espacio estrecho
> cantó sin alborada y sementera

y mi llanto prendió por vez primera
coronas de esperanzas por el techo.

Dulce y lejana voz por mí vertida.
Dulce y lejana voz por mí gustada.
Lejana y dulce voz amortecida.

Lejana como oscura corza herida.
Dulce como un sollozo en la nevada.
¡Lejana y dulce en tuétano metida!

In 'El poeta pregunta a su amor por la «Ciudad Encantada» de Cuenca', the
emotional subject appears once more to be kept at arm's length, even though
Newton (p. 145) judges it to be a poem in which 'Lorca presenta los compo-
nentes centrales del icono /yo/.' Yet the two are perhaps not incompatible.
Indeed, the defensive mechanism of maintaining distance, achieved in this
poem by posing question after question – each laced with tones of bitterness
and irony – may actually speak volumes about the suffering within:

¿Te gustó la ciudad que gota a gota
labró el agua en el centro de los pinos?
¿Viste sueños y rostros y caminos
y muros de dolor que el aire azota?

¿Viste la grieta azul de luna rota
que el Júcar moja de cristal y trinos?
¿Han besado tus dedos los espinos
que coronan de amor piedra remota?

¿Te acordaste de mí cuando subías
al silencio que sufre la serpiente,
prisionera de grillos y de umbrías?

¿No viste por el aire transparente
una dalia de penas y alegrías
que te mandó mi corazón caliente?[25]

---

[25] This device of structuring an entire poem as a series of unanswered questions invites
comparisons with its use in two of Quevedo's love sonnets: poems 352 and 368. See Francisco
de Quevedo, *Obras completas I. Poesía original*, ed. José Manuel Blecua, 2nd. ed (Barcelona:
Planeta, 1968), 375–6 and 385–6 respectively. In his book *Contradictory Subjects. Quevedo,
Cervantes, and Seventeenth-Century Spanish Culture* (Ithaca and London: Cornell University
Press, 1991), what George Mariscal has to say regarding the second of these poems, which
begins '¿Qué imagen de la muerte rigurosa / qué sombra del infierno me maltrata?', has
a particular resonance for our discussion of Lorca's sonnets; both in terms of the tensions
between lyric and form we have been describing and in respect of the perceived currency of
the sonnet form amongst writers in 1930s Spain. 'Few subjects produced by the Petrarchan
tradition', suggests Mariscal (p. 111), 'have been more estranged from the lyric situation that

The same may be said of those other sonnets which we characterized before as being overly concerned with device. Whether it be the uncertainty implicit in the recourse to familiar tropes, the dominance of reason, the artifice of truth and lies, or even the cover provided by archaic discourses, each creates a distance (perhaps even ironic or parodic) by which to measure the depth of the feeling suppressed. The 'yo' is present yet elusive amidst it all, as we would expect it to be in the work of a poet who has tussled with personality from the start and has come with time to know its virtues and its vices. What complicates matters now is the question of the sonnet form, where device is doubly important given that expression must fit both metre and rhyme, and where nature – in terms of its representation by natural expression – is consequently always at risk. How much, for example, in 'Soneto de la dulce queja', was the choice of the adjective 'enajenado' governed by its usefulness in completing the rhyme scheme cdc/dcd and providing sufficient syllables (elision included) to complete the obligatory eleven in the final line? After all, it sits rather awkwardly alongside the poet's figurative autumn, qualifying a condition in which the estrangement or alienation to which it refers was arguably already implicit in the specified season. We might make a similar observation about 'transparente' in 'El poeta pregunta a su amor por la «Ciudad Ecantada» de Cuenca', somewhat redundant in its qualification of 'aire' but a rhyming companion for 'serpiente' in the previous tercet. Then what of 'contigo' in the final line of the first quatrain of 'El poeta dice de la verdad'? Were it not for the fact that it rhymes with 'digo' in the first line, could it really be considered the most fitting end to a list in which 'con un puñal' and 'con besos' precede it? And we might wonder also whether, in the following quatrain, the recourse to natural imagery with the reference to wheat ('trigo') – possibly redeeming after the initial thoughts of murder and yet seemingly inconsistent with the violent character of these previous sentiments – was not in fact triggered solely by the rhyming demands of 'testigo' itself.

Formal demands have no doubt played their part too in the creation of caesuras in the only untitled sonnet of the collection, which begins '¡Ay voz secreta del amor oscuro!' (*OC*, I, p. 947). Yet these pauses, above all, have the effect of conveying and emphasizing emotion, as exclamation follows

---

surrounds them and from which they attempt to speak [...]. The key to this particular poem', he later adds, 'should not be sought in a theory of expression or in the poet's biography but in his implication in specific aesthetic and social practices: aesthetic because Quevedo's "serious" lyric voices often seem constrained by the sonnet form and social because aristocratic tradition demanded that the successful man of letters exercise his hand at the sonnet form within the economy of courtly literary production.'

exclamation, separated only by the briefest of moments in which to catch a breath or muster the energy for the next outburst:

> ¡Ay voz secreta del amor oscuro!
> ¡ay balido sin lanas!¡ay herida!
> ¡ay aguja de hiel, camelia hundida!
> ¡ay corriente sin mar, ciudad sin muro!
>
> ¡Ay noche inmensa de perfil seguro,
> montaña celestial de angustia erguida!
> ¡Ay perro en corazón, voz perseguida,
> silencio sin confín, lirio maduro!
>
> Huye de mí, caliente voz de hielo,
> no me quieras perder en la maleza
> donde sin fruto gimen carne y cielo.
>
> Deja el duro marfil de mi cabeza,
> apiádate de mí, ¡rompe mi duelo!,
> ¡que soy amor, que soy naturaleza!

Emotion dominates here, albeit within the parameters set by the sonnet form. Both at a thematic level and in terms of its first-person exclamatory character, this sonnet affirms the need of the subject to speak his suffering, which is associated here with the secret of his dark love. If the unspoken is to be spoken, then the voice will have to emerge from the limbo that is conveyed by its qualification in the first tercet as both hot and icy. This paradox in effect cancels out the possibility of self-expression and points instead to its containment, leaving the speaker in the unproductive place designated by 'la maleza / donde sin fruto gimen carne y cielo'. The imperatives in both tercets appeal to other modes, seeking to banish that unproductive voice so that sorrow ('duelo') may finally be expressed. Of course, the sonnet itself owes something to either voice, being both an impassioned plea and a controlled reflection on the difficulties of expressing passion. This ambivalence is conveyed also by the movement from metaphorical expression (albeit in the context of exclamations) to a less convoluted style, particularly in the second tercet and above all in the final line: '¡que soy amor, que soy naturaleza!'

'For I am love, for I am nature!' There could be no more appropriate finale for this sonnet or, indeed, for my treatment of Lorca's poetry in this book. So frank and direct is this exclamation that it seems to detach itself from the page, as if to affirm its existence not only in poetry but outside the text as well. It is a moment also when the poet declares himself for emotion and the things of the world. This was most likely always his position, one that was as much at the root of his self-consciousness as was his search amidst dehumanization and the various '-isms' for both acceptance and a voice. Thus the world and all that it implies – emotion, personality, nature, life – throbs in the melancholy tones of *Libro de poemas* ('Esta tristeza juvenil se pasa, / ¡ya lo sé!') and peers out from behind the riddles of the Suites ('Me siento atravesado / por la grave *Y* griega'); is embedded in the artistic subjects of *Poema del cante jondo* ('Empieza el llanto / de la guitarra') and unsettles the control of emotionalism in *Canciones* ('¡Alma, / ponte color de amor!'); contests impersonal culture in *Romancero gitano* ('Sobre la tela pajiza, / ella quisiera bordar / flores de su fantasía') and emerges violently in *Poeta en Nueva York* ('queremos que se cumpla la voluntad de la Tierra / que da sus frutos para todos'); is irrepressible in *Diván del Tamarit* ('por detrás de los grises muros / no se oye otra cosa que el llanto') and becomes a human necessity in *Llanto por Ignacio Sánchez Mejías* ('No te conoce nadie. No. Pero yo te canto').

We should not, however, confuse this world with the biography of Lorca the man. Just as there is little to be had from applying the facts of his personal life to the sonnets, his poetry in general also resists such an approach. In his introductory words to *Libro de poemas* Lorca did, of course, once claim that that book was intimately related to his life – that it was an exact image of his adolescence and youth. Yet the claim is somewhat overstated, and it soon becomes apparent that what he called a faithful reflection of his heart or spirit was not at all equivalent to a kind of poetry from which we might glean, for example, precise details of movements, names, places, relations and dates. In the sonnets, with the exception of one or two place names, the references remain general – in accordance with what Anderson (1990, p. 306) calls 'Lorca's abiding concern to generalize' – the only nominal self-reference coming in the form of the archetypal *poeta*. Here, as in the rest of his work, it is as a poet that Lorca engages with and enters his texts. He may recognize the man, but he does so as a poet, and if we are to recognize anyone, then it must surely be – as he wished of his peers also – the poet deep within the man.

# BIBLIOGRAPHY

Aguirre, J. M., 'El sonambulismo de García Lorca', *Bulletin of Hispanic Studies*, 44 (1967), 271–4

Álvarez de Miranda, Ángel, *La metáfora y el mito* (Madrid: Taurus, 1963)

Anderson, Andrew A., 'García Lorca como poeta petrarquista', *Cuadernos Hispanoamericanos*, 453–6 (September–October 1986), 495–518

——, *Lorca's Late Poetry: A Critical Study*, Liverpool Monographs in Hispanic Studies 10 (Leeds: Francis Cairns, 1990)

——, 'Lorca at the Crossroads: "Imaginación, inspiración, evasion" and the "novísimas estéticas"', *Anales de la Literatura Española Contemporánea*, 16 (1991), 149–73

——, 'Ramón Gómez de la Serna and F. T. Marinetti: Epistolary Contacts and the Genesis of a Manifesto', in Derek Harris (ed.), *Changing Times in Hispanic Culture* (Aberdeen: Centre for the Study of the Hispanic Avant-Garde, 1996), 19–31

——, '*Et in Arcadia Ego*: Thematic Divergence and Convergence in Lorca's 'Poema doble del lago Edén', *Bulletin of Hispanic Studies*, 74 (1997), 409–29

András, Lázló, 'El caso de la gitana sonámbula', in Mátyás Horányi (ed.), *Actas del Simposio Internacional de Estudios Hispánicos* (Budapest: Akadémiai Kiadó, 1978), 181–94

Aranda, J. Francisco, *Luis Buñuel: biografía crítica* (Barcelona: Lumen, 1969)

Barón Palma, Emilio, *Agua oculta que llora. El 'Diván del Tamarit' de García Lorca* (Granada: Editorial Don Quijote, 1990)

Belamich, André, 'Presentación de las *Suites*', in Federico García Lorca, *Suites*. Edición crítica de André Belamich (Barcelona: Ariel, 1983), 9–26

Binding, Paul, *Lorca: The Gay Imagination* (London: GMP, 1985)

Bonaddio, Federico, 'Lorca's *Poeta en Nueva York*: Creativity and the City', in 'The Image of the City', *Romance Studies*, No. 22 (Autumn 1993), 41–51

——, 'Lorca and the Spanish Avant-Garde: Autonomous and Elitist Art', in Derek Harris (ed.), *Changing Times in Hispanic Culture* (Aberdeen: Centre for the Study of the Hispanic Avant-Garde, 1996), 97–109

——, 'Lorca's "Romance sonámbulo": the Desirability of Non-Disclosure', *Bulletin of Hispanic Studies*, 72 (1995), 385–401

——, and Xon de Ros (eds), *Crossing Fields in Modern Spanish Literature* (Oxford: Legenda [European Humanities Research Centre], 2003)

——, What's in the Joke?: Buñuel, Dalí, Lorca and the title *Un Chien andalou*', in Isabel Sataolalla *et al.* (eds), *Buñuel, Siglo XXI* (Zaragoza: Prensas Universitarias de Zaragoza, 2004), 53–8

——, 'Grammar and Poetic Form: Limits and Transcendence in Juan Ramón Jiménez's "Una a una, las hojas secas van cayendo"', *Words in Action: Essays in Honour of John Butt*, ed. Xon de Ros and Federico Bonaddio, *Bulletin of Spanish Studies*, 83.1 (January 2006), 149–60

——, 'Lorca, Self-Consciousness (and Myself)', in Catherine Boyle (ed.), *Exploración y proceso: investigando la cultura hispánica* (Valencia: Biblioteca Valenciana, 2007), 277–91

—— (ed.), *A Companion to Federico García Lorca* (Woodbridge: Tamesis, 2007)

——, 'Introduction: Biography and Interpretation', in Federico Bonaddio (ed.), *A Companion to Federico García Lorca* (Woodbridge: Tamesis, 2007), 1–15

Bourdieu, Pierre, *The Field of Cultural Production: Essays on Art and Literature*, ed. and introd. Randal Johnson (Cambridge: Polity Press, 1993)

Cannon, Calvin, 'Lorca's *Llanto por Ignacio Sánchez Mejías* and the Elegiac Tradition', *Hispanic Review*, 31 (1963), 229–38

Cardwell, Richard A., *Juan Ramón Jiménez: The Modernist Apprenticeship 1895–1900* (Berlin: Colloquium Verlag, 1977)

Castro Lee, Cecilia, 'La "Oda a Salvador Dalí": significación y trascendencia en la vida y creación de Lorca y Dalí', *Anales de la Literatura Española Contemporánea*, 11 (1986), 61–78

Chevalier, Jean and Alain Gheerbrant, *Dictionary of Symbols*, trans. John Buchanan-Brown (London: Penguin, 1996)

Cockburn, Jacqueline, 'Gifts from the Poet to the Art Critic', in Federico Bonaddio and Xon de Ros (eds), *Crossing Fields in Modern Spanish Literature* (Oxford: Legenda [European Humanities Research Centre], 2003), 67–80

——, and Federico Bonaddio, 'Drawing', in Federico Bonaddio (ed.), *A Companion to Federico García Lorca* (Woodbridge: Tamesis, 2007), ch. 4, 84–100

De Ory, Carlos Edmundo, 'Salvador Rueda y García Lorca', *Cuadernos Hispanoamericanos*, 255 (March 1971), 417–44

Delgado Morales, Manuel, 'Embroiderers of Freedom and Desire in Lorca's Poetry and Theater', in Manuel Delgado Morales and Alice J. Poust (eds), *Lorca, Buñuel, Dalí: Art and Theory* (London and Toronto: Associated University Presses, 2001), 37–51

Delgado Morales, Manuel and Alice J. Poust (eds), *Lorca, Buñuel, Dalí: Art and Theory*) (London and Toronto: Associated University Presses, 2001)

DeLong-Tonelli, Beverly J., 'The Lyric Dimension in Lorca's "Romance sonámbulo"', *Romance Notes* 12 (1971), 289–95

——, 'In the Beginning Was the End: Lorca's New York Poetry', *Anales de la Literatura Española Contemporánea*, 12 (1987), 243–57

Dennis, Nigel, 'Politics', in Federico Bonaddio (ed.), *A Companion to Federico García Lorca* (Woodbridge: Tamesis, 2007), ch. 8, 170–93

Devoto, Daniel, *Introducción a 'Diván del Tamarit' de Federico García Lorca* (Paris: Ediciones Hispanoamericanas, 1976)

Díez de Revenga, Francisco Javier, 'Federico García Lorca: de los "poemas neoyorquinos" a los "sonetos oscuros"', *Revista Hispánica Moderna*, 41 (1988), 105–14

Drummond, Phillip, 'Surrealism and *Un Chien andalou*', in Luis Buñuel and Salvador Dalí, *Un Chien andalou* (London: Faber & Faber, 1994), v–xxiii

Durán, Manuel, 'Lorca y las vanguardias', *Hispania*, 69.4 (December 1986), 764–70

*El Romancero Viejo*, ed. by Mercedes Díaz Roig (Madrid: Cátedra, 1992)

Eliot, T. S., *The Waste Land and Other Poems* (London: Faber & Faber, 1985)

——, 'Tradition and the Individual Talent', *The Sacred Wood. Essays on Poetry and Criticism* (London and New York: Methuen, 1986), 47–59

English, Alan, 'Paul Verlaine', *The Literary Encyclopedia*, 21 July 2004 [http://www.litencyc.com/php/speople.php?rec=true&UID=4536, accessed 5 October 2009]

Fernández Cifuentes, Luis, '1918: García Lorca at the Crossroads', in *Lorca, Buñuel, Dalí: Art and Theory*, ed. Manuel Delgado Morales and Alice J. Poust (London and Toronto: Associated University Presses, 2001), 66–85

Frazer, James George, *The Golden Bough. A Study in Magic and Religion*, abridged edition (London: Papermac, 1987)

Gallego Morell, Antonio, 'El primer poema publicado por Federico García Lorca', *Bulletin Hispanique*, 69 (1967), nos 3–4, 487–92

García Lorca, Federico, *Obras I: Poesía 1*, ed. Miguel García-Posada (Madrid: Akal, 1982)

——, *Obras II: Poesía 2*, ed. Miguel García-Posada (Madrid: Akal, 1982)

——, *Suites*. Edición crítica de André Belamich (Barcelona: Ariel, 1983)

——, *Poema del Cante Jondo* and *Romancero gitano*, ed. Allen Josephs and Juan Caballero, 7th edn (Madrid: Cátedra, 1984)

——, *Obras completas*, ed. Arturo del Hoyo, 3 vols, 22nd edn (Madrid: Aguilar, 1986)

——, *Romancero gitano*, ed. Derek Harris, Grant & Cutler Spanish Texts (London: Grant & Cutler, 1991)

——, *Romancero gitano. Poeta en Nueva York. El público*, ed. Derek Harris (Madrid: Taurus, 1993)

——, *Poesía inédita de juventud*, ed. Christian de Paepe, Letras Hispánicas 374, 2nd edn (Madrid: Cátedra, 1996)

——, *Epistolario Completo*, ed. Andrew A. Anderson and Christopher Maurer (Madrid: Cátedra, 1997)

——, *Poemas en prosa*, ed. Andrew A. Anderson (Granada: Comares / La Veleta, 2000)

——, *Collected Poems*, revised bilingual edition, ed. Christopher Maurer (New York: Farrar, Straus & Giroux, 2002)

García Lorca, Francisco, *Federico y su mundo*, 2nd edn (Madrid: Alianza, 1981)

García-Posada, Miguel, *Lorca: interpretación de 'Poeta en Nueva York'* (Madrid: Akal, 1981)

Geist, Anthony Leo, *La poética de la generación del 27 y las revistas literarias: de la vanguardia al compromiso (1918–1936)* (Barcelona: Labor, 1980)

Gibson, Ian, *Federico García Lorca: A Life* (London: Faber & Faber, 1989)

——, *Lorca-Dalí. El amor que no pudo ser* (Barcelona: Plaza & Janés, 1999)

Harris, Derek, 'A la caza de la imagen surrealista en Lorca', *Insula*, 368–9 (1977), 19

——, *Federico García Lorca. Poeta en Nueva York* (London: Grant & Cutler / Tamesis, 1979)

——, 'Green Death: An Analysis of the Symbolism of the Colour Green in Lorca's poetry', in Nicholas G. Round and D. Gareth Walters (eds), *Readings in Spanish and Portuguese for Geoffrey Connell* (Glasgow: Glasgow University, 1985), 89–91

——, 'Introduction', in Federico García Lorca, *Romancero gitano*, ed. Derek Harris, Grant & Cutler Spanish Texts (London: Grant & Cutler, 1991), 7–87

——, 'La elaboración textual de *Poeta en Nueva York*: el salto mortal', *Revista Canadiense de Estudios Hispánicos*, 18.2 (Invierno 1994), 309–15

—— (ed.), *The Spanish Avant-Garde* (Manchester: Manchester University Press, 1995)

—— (ed.), *Changing Times in Hispanic Culture* (Aberdeen: Centre for the Study of the Hispanic Avant-Garde, 1996)

Havard, Robert G., 'The Symbolic Ambivalence of "Green" in García Lorca and Dylan Thomas', *Modern Language Review*, 67 (1972), 810–19

——, *From Romanticism to Surrealism: Seven Spanish Poets* (Cardiff: University of Wales Press, 1988)

——, 'The Riddle Register in Lorca's *Poeta en Nueva York*', in David George and John London (eds), *Spanish Film, Theatre and Literature in the*

*Twentieth Century. Essays in Honour of Derek Gagen* (Cardiff: University of Wales Press, 2007), 43–56

Herrero, Javier, 'Los Lorca y Juan Ramón. Una Amistad poética', in Francisco Javier Díez de Revenga and Mariano Paco (eds), *Pasión de mi vida. Estudios sobre Juan Ramón Jiménez* (Murcia: Fundación Cajamurcia, 2007), 91–11

Hierro, José, 'El primer Lorca', *Cuadernos Hispanoamericanos*, 224–5 (August–September 1968), 437–62

Hoyle, Alan, 'Ramón Gómez de la Serna and the Avant-Garde', in Derek Harris (ed.), *Changing Times in Hispanic Culture* (Aberdeen: Centre for the Study of the Hispanic Avant-Garde, 1996), 7–16

Huidobro, Vicente, *Obras completas*, I (Santiago de Chile: Zig-Zag, 1964)

Hussein, Abdirahman A., *Edward Said. Criticism and Society* (London and New York: Verso, 2002)

Iarocci, Michael, 'Romanticism, Transcendence, and Modernity in Lorca's *Libro de poemas*, or the Adventures of a Snail', in *Lorca, Buñuel, Dalí: Art and Theory*, ed. Manuel Delgado Morales and Alice J. Poust (London and Toronto: Associated University Presses, 2001), 120–35

Ilie, Paul (ed.), *Documents of the Spanish Vanguard* (Chapel Hill: University of North Carolina Press, 1969)

Jiménez, Juan Ramón, *Segunda antolojía poética (1898–1918)* (Madrid: Espasa Calpe, 1976 [1st edn 1975])

Jobes, Gertrude, *Dictionary of Mythology, Folklore and Symbol*, 3 vols (New York: The Scarewood Press, 1961)

Jones, Roy O. and Scanlon, Geraldine M., 'Ignacio Sánchez Mejías: the "Mythic Hero"', in Nigel Glendinning (ed.), *Studies in Modern Spanish Literature and Art Presented to Helen F. Grant* (London: Tamesis, 1972), 97–108

Kristeva, Julia, *Revolution in Poetic Language* (New York: Columbia University Press, 1984)

Lentzen, Manfred, 'Marinetti y el futurismo en España', *Actas del IX Congreso de la Asociación Internacional de Hispanistas* (1986), ed. Sebastian Neumeister (Frankfurt: Vervuert, 1989), 309–18

Leopardi, Giacomo, *Canti*, ed. Giorgio Ficara (Milan: Mondadori, 1987)

McKinlay, Neil C., 'Clues that Confuse: Lorca's *Canciones*', *Romance Studies*, 17.1 (June 1999), 75–88

McMullan, Terence, 'Federico García Lorca's *Santa Lucía y San Lázaro* and the Aesthetics of Transition', *Bulletin of Hispanic Studies*, 67.1 (1990), 1–20

——, 'Federico García Lorca's *Poeta en Nueva York* and *The City of Tomorrow*', *Bulletin of Hispanic Studies*, 73 (1996), 65–79

Machado y Álvarez (Demófilo), Antonio, *Poesía popular* (Seville: Francisco Álvarez, 1883)

Marinetti, F. T., *Selected Poems and Related Prose*, trans. Elizabeth R. Napier and Barbara R. Studholme (New Haven and London: Yale University Press, 2002)

Mariscal, George, *Contradictory Subjects: Quevedo, Cervantes, and Seventeenth-Century Spanish Culture* (Ithaca and London: Cornell University Press, 1991)

Maurer Christopher (ed.), *Sebastian's Arrows: Letters and Mementos of Salvador Dalí and Federico García Lorca* (Chicago: Swan Isle Press, 2004)

——, 'Poetry', in Federico Bonaddio (ed.), *A Companion to Federico García Lorca* (Woodbridge: Tamesis, 2007), 16–38

Miller, Norman C., *García Lorca's 'Poema del cante jondo'* (London: Tamesis Books, 1978)

Mira, Alberto, 'Modernistas, dandies y pederastas: articulaciones de la homosexualidad en la "edad de plata"', *Journal of Iberian and Latin American Studies*, 7.1 (2001), 63–75

Mitchell, Timothy, *Flamenco Deep Song* (New Haven and London: Yale University Press, 1994)

Morris, C. Brian, *Son of Andalusia: The Lyrical Landscapes of Federico García Lorca* (Liverpool: Liverpool University Press, 1997)

Newton, Candelas, 'Los paisajes del amor: iconos centrales en los *Sonetos de Lorca*', *Anales de la Literatura Española Contemporánea*, 11 (1986), 143–59

Orledge, Robert, 'Debussy the Man', in Simon Trezise (ed.), *The Cambridge Companion to Debussy* (Cambridge: Cambridge University Press, 2003), 9–24

Ortega y Gasset, José, 'La deshumanización del arte', *Obras completas, III (1917–1928)*, 5th edn (Madrid: Revista de Occidente, 1962), 353–86

Perri, Dennis, 'Fulfillment and Loss: Lorca's View of Communication in the Twenties', *Hispania* 75.3 (September 1992), 484–91

——, 'Lorca's *Canciones*: Speaker and Reader', *Anales de la Literatura Española Contemporánea*, 20 (1995), 173–98

Poust, Alice J., 'Federico García Lorca's Andalusia in Light of Oswald Spengler's Theory of Magian Cultures', in *Lorca, Buñuel, Dalí: Art and Theory*, ed. Manuel Delgado Morales and Alice J. Poust (London and Toronto: Associated University Presses, 2001), 175–90

Quevedo, Francisco de, *Obras completas I. Poesía original*, ed. José Manuel Blecua, 2nd edn (Barcelona: Planeta, 1968)

Quilis, Antonio, *Métrica española* (Barcelona: Ariel, 1984)

Ramsden, Herbert, *Lorca's 'Romancero gitano'. Eighteen Commentaries* (Manchester: Manchester University Press, 1988)

Rodrigo, Antonina, *Lorca-Dalí. Una Amistad traicionada* (Barcelona: Planeta, 1981)

Ros, Xon de, 'Science and Myth in *Llanto por Ignacio Sánchez Mejías*', *Modern Language Review*, 95.1 (2000), 114–26

——, 'Ignacio Sánchez Mejías Blues', in Federico Bonaddio and Xon de Ros (eds), *Crossing Fields in Modern Spanish Literature* (Oxford: Legenda [European Humanities Research Centre], 2003), 81–91

Saez, Richard, 'The Ritual Sacrifice in Lorca's *Poeta en Nueva York*', in Manuel Duran (ed.), *Lorca. A Collection of Critical Essays* (Prentice Hall: Englewood Cliffs, N.J., 1962), 108–29

Said, Edward W., *The World, the Text, and the Critic* (Cambridge, Mass.: Harvard University Press, 1983)

——, *Orientalism* (London: Penguin Books, 2003)

Salazar Rincón, Javier, *'Rosas y mirtos de luna ...' Naturaleza y símbolo en la obra de Federico García Lorca* (Madrid: Universidad Nacional de Educación a Distancia, 1999)

Sánchez Vidal, Agustín, *Buñuel, Lorca, Dalí: El enigma sin fin* (Barcelona: Planeta, 1988)

——, 'Góngora, Buñuel, the Spanish Avant-garde and the Centenary of Goya's Death', in Derek Harris (ed.), *The Spanish Avant-Garde* (Manchester: Manchester University Press, 1995), 110–22

Schopenhauer, Arthur, *The World as Will and Idea*, 3 vols (London: Kegan Paul, Trench, Trübner, 1981)

Southworth, Eric, 'Religion', in Federico Bonaddio (ed.), *A Companion to Federico García Lorca* (Woodbridge: Tamesis, 2007), ch. 6, 129–48

Stainton, Leslie, *Lorca: A Dream of Life* (London: Bloomsbury, 1998)

Stanton, Edward F., *The Tragic Myth: Lorca and 'Cante Jondo'* (Lexington: University of Kentucky, 1978)

Stone, Rob, *The Flamenco Tradition in the Works of Federico García Lorca and Carlos Saura. The Wounded Throat* (Lewiston, Queenston and Lampeter: The Edwin Meller Press, 2004)

Talens, Jenaro, *The Branded Eye: Buñuel's 'Un Chien andalou'*, trans. Giulia Colaizzi (Minneapolis and London: University of Minnesota Press, 1993)

Trilling, Lionel, *Sincerity and Authenticity* (London: Oxford University Press, 1972)

Vilaseca, David, *The Apocryphal Subject: Masochism, Identification, and Paranoia in Salvador Dalí's Autobiographical Writings* (New York: Peter Lang, 1995)

Walters, D. Gareth, '"Comprendí. Pero no explico": Revelation and Concealment in Lorca's *Canciones*', *Bulletin of Hispanic Studies*, 68 (1991), 265–79

——, *'Canciones' and the Early Poetry of Lorca* (Cardiff: University of Wales Press, 2002)

——, 'Parallel Trajectories in the Careers of Falla and Lorca', in Federico

Bonaddio and Xon de Ros (eds), *Crossing Fields in Modern Spanish* (Oxford: Legenda [European Humanities Research Centre], 2003), 92–102

——, 'Music', in Federico Bonaddio (ed.), *A Companion to Federico García Lorca* (Woodbridge: Tamesis, 2007), ch. 3, 63–83

Washabaugh, William, *Flamenco: Passion, Politics and Popular Culture* (Oxford: Berg, 1996)

# INDEX OF POEMS

# GENERAL INDEX